IRISH FEMINIST REVIEW

Volume One
2005

General Editor: Rebecca Pelan

© Individual contributors, 2005
© Collection copyright Women's Studies Centre, National University of Ireland, Galway, 2005

The views expressed in this publication are not necessarily those of the editors or the publisher

First published September 2005 by
Women's Studies Centre
National University of Ireland
Galway
Republic of Ireland

ISBN 0-9549924-1-5
ISSN 1649-6825

Cover Design: A & D, Envision House, Flood Street, Galway
Cover Image: Martina Hynan, 15 The Green, Lifford, Ennis, Co. Clare

Typesetting and Design: Women's Studies Centre
Printed by Cahill Printers, East Wall Road, Dublin 3

Acknowledgements:
To Vivienne Batt, Alan Hayes and Kieran Hoare (NUI, Galway) for their help in putting the journal together; to Barry Castle and Martina Hynan for the wonderful images; to all academic referees for giving so generously of their time and expertise.

IRISH FEMINIST REVIEW
Volume 1, 2005

Contents

Acknowledgements 2

Introduction 5

Cauldron

Christine St Peter	Women's Studies in Canada	11
Carole Ferrier	Women's and Gender Studies in Australia Today	15
Gabriele Griffin	Subject in Process: Women's Studies in Europe	20
Catherine M Orr	Women's Studies Reflects on its Prime of Life: A View from the United States	25
Rebecca Pelan	Women's Studies in Ireland	30
Niamh Hehir	'The Perfect Narrative Nature of Blue': Memory and the Chora in Medbh McGuckian's *Marconi's Cottage*	37
Hanna Herzog and Agate Krauss	Women's Knowledge: A Resource and Policy Research Centre as a Lever for Discursive Change	53
Yvonne McKenna	A Gendered Revolution: Vatican II and Irish Women Religious	75

Colour Section

Barry Laverty Castle	Retrospective	97
Alan Hayes	Origins: Feminist Publishing in Ireland, 1984	105
Martina Hynan	'Stitch-up.' An Exhibition of Contemporary Paintings	113

Women United for an End to Violence	Living to Tell the Tale … As Told by Survivors of Domestic Violence	128
Toni Johnson-Woods	Lurid Lasses of Australian Pulp Fiction 1950-1960	143
Sonja Tiernan	Tipping the Balance with Historical Fiction: *Tipping the Velvet* as a Lesbian Feminist Device	161
Eva Rus	From *New York Radical Feminists* to *Rivolta Femminile:* Italian Feminists Rethink The Practice of Consciousness Raising, 1970-1974	185

Creative Pieces	*Georgia Rhoades, Philomena van Rijswijk, Sheila Phelan, Adrienne Anifant, Kathleen O'Driscoll, Kathleen Vejvoda Chaplin, Lorna Shaughnessy, Martina Boyle, Nuala Ní Chonchúir*

Reviews:	*Myrtle Hill; Anna-Katharina Pelkner; Constantina Katsari*	196
Notes on Contributors		206

INTRODUCTION

Welcome to volume one of the **Irish Feminist Review**. The *Review* continues the tradition set by the *Women's Studies Review*, also published out of the Women's Studies Centre at NUI, Galway, between 1989 and 2004, in its commitment to women's scholarly and creative publishing, and to the publication of work by new researchers alongside established, international scholars. **Irish Feminist Review** is now the only remaining feminist journal published in Ireland, and its existence marks our continued commitment to the fields of Women's Studies, feminist scholarship, and women's creative practices, as different strands of a lively and politicised feminist agenda in Ireland and beyond. In my role as general editor, I have been humbled by the level of goodwill from those experts who anonymously read and reported on the academic essays included here. The giving of their time and expertise so willingly has been greatly appreciated, but so, too, has their enthusiasm for the project. I would like to extend a very sincere thanks to them all.

Our change of name reflects a desire to reinstate an explicit feminist politics into our work in the face of ever-increasing, conservative forces that continue to deplete the connection between Women's Studies as an emerging academic discipline and its feminist origins. Equally, the 'Irish' in our title is not meant to signal Irish feminist research alone but, rather, reflects an Irish interest in feminist scholarship in its broadest possible configurations.

The creation of a new section – Cauldron – is designed to function as a forum for the discussion of different topics from a variety of perspectives. In this, our first volume, the topic of Women's Studies is addressed from a number of different geographical locations: Canada, Australia, UK/Europe, America and Ireland. The result is a fascinating mixture of unevenly distributed development in the field of Women's Studies in industrialised countries, yet one that shares an extraordinary level of similarities in terms of origins and current challenges. Our hope is that Cauldron will function as a source of debate as well as for the purpose of disseminating information concerning specific topics and, in this regard, we would be happy to hear your suggestions for future Cauldron topics. I sincerely hope you enjoy reading **Irish Feminist Review** as much as I have enjoyed editing it.

Rebecca Pelan

The Forbidden Planet

I could not live beside your violent withdrawals;
I could not sleep for the whitewater roar
of your arid silences;
your undead ghost was a sock-footed stalker
that watched my sleeping,
sniffed and unwound the cloyed hairs from my brush,
pocketed moon-shaped clippings from my bedroom floor.

You left the marks of an intruder:
the gouges of a chipped chisel
around the lock of my battered door, and
the drawers of my night-secrets rummaged.
With a greasy lipstick, you scrawled on the mildewy mirror
of my identity, my I.D., that easily-mistaken entity,
smearing terrible words
invisible to the innocent corpse-green light of day.
Your control was a clench-jawed rapist, dryly
penetrating the most unawake places with its horrible patience.

Like the Sixties' black-and-white monster from the id
that haunted my flannelette-pyjama'd dreams –
the only things that gave you away were those hollow footfalls
encroaching,
coming closer,
even closer,
out-sucking the floor to the shape
of an unseeable beast-like tread.

Philomena van Rijswijk

Divorcing George

For Sister Frances

I met a nun in Derry who said,
"I don't like your president."
And I said, "No, neither do I."
And she said, "Well, what are you going to do about it?"
And then she fixed me with her evil eye.

Well, this is just too familiar:
Sitting out here on the front porch waiting for the sun to come up,
Some man on my mind.
I am so tired of trying to change him.
My friend Kim told me that in the Cherokee way
A woman gathers up all the man's possessions
And puts them out on the front porch,
And when he gets home he knows
That it's really over this time, and he gets everything together
   and goes on home to his mama.

I've tried logic: I used the words of Gertrude Stein.
I said, "There is no there there, George."
He didn't get it.
I gave him a copy of *Three Guineas* by Miss Virginia Woolf for the Solstice, but
   I don't think he ever read it.
I rented *The Atomic Cafe* twice, but he fell asleep both times.

And I've even tried leaving copies of *The Onion* in the bathroom.
And when he said, "Well, it's been a year now; what do you want to do for our
   anniversary?"
I said, "Well, Voltaire said that hot places make you feel and cold places make
   you think,

And Josephine Humphreys says that travel is the enemy of war,
So I thought first we could go to a hot place and visit the bazaar and haggle,
  bring back armfuls of gold and scarlet cloth, and eat melons
  and let the juices trickle down our dusty throats.
And after a while maybe we could sit in the shade of a wall and listen to a
  language we don't understand,
And maybe we could learn something.
And he said, "No, can't do that; it'd take too long; I don't need to learn
  anything, and it's going to get hot soon."
And I said, "You live in Texas, George: when did you get afraid of the
  summertime?"

I thought maybe I'd appeal to his love of the land.
He does love wide, open spaces and fields of tough scrub grass,
  big rolls of barbed wire,
Kind and wandering cows who used to have horns.
But love of the land always seems to get these guys in trouble.
It must be all that rhetoric they swallowed with their Post Toasties
  back in the 1950s: I think it's curdled love of the land into patriotism.
Now Kurt Vonnegut, he's a citizen of the planet, but George isn't;
He's a citizen of some time and galaxy far, far away that most of us thought we'd
  left way behind us a long time ago.

But those coffins have opened up and the men in the grey suits are loose again.
Makes me think of what Wanda used to say about where we used to work;
She said, "You know, this place wouldn't be half bad
  if the dead guys would just lie down."

Now I know what Starhawk would say, she'd say, "Feed that boy at your table."

And I did; for a long time there I was always cooking pinto beans and cornbread,
   pies and cakes and casseroles.
And I'd put the leftovers in Tupperware for him to take to the office,
Meat and two veg in those plastic triangular sections that he could heat up later
   in the microwave.
And I even had potlucks for his people.

And I admit it: I tried the honeypot.
I said, "Come to bed, George.
Come woo me like you used to before the election."
And I tried flattery (well, you do, don't you?),
I said, "George, you know that brief concern you showed for the women
   under the Taliban for a short time there after you finally discovered that they existed,
Well, that really excited me, George."
I pretended to be Elizabeth Taylor in that scene where she says,
"My hips are wide and welcoming."
I even bought a Cleopatra wig.

I was hoping he'd do a Richard Burton/Marc Antony kind of move and leave the
   warships behind and follow me back to Alexandria
Even if it was Alexandria, Virginia, honey; I didn't care.
But he couldn't focus.
He just kept talking about drawing lines in the sand.

And I thought now I have tried love and novelty, logic and beauty,
And I have watched him, greedy and oblivious.
I think he's forgotten everything he ever learned in Sunday school
   about getting along with other people.
And we don't have any friends any more.
No, he's threatened all of them and people have just stopped asking us over.
He thinks it's okay to bribe people that you don't even know.
He embarrasses me every time we go out together, especially in Europe.

So finally I said, "Right! We are going to a counsellor!"
And he said, "No, can't talk, already talked, time for talking's over."
And I said, "That's funny; I don't ever remember you talking."
And then I got really huffy and said, "And I sure don't ever remember you
  listening."
So I went to the counsellor's by myself, and there in the waiting room was that
  sweet Cherie Blair.
She took hold of my hand and said, "Honey, I know it's got to be hard for you,
  but at least you knew you were marrying a Tory."
And then she said something else just to make me feel better, something I'll never
  forget; she said, "Remember, Winston Churchill once said,
  'Americans always do the right thing, after they have tried
  everything else'."

After Florida there was no way I was going to go the judicial route,
And I am ashamed to show my face at the World Court.
So I called the Vatican, but all they cared about was whether the union had been
  consummated.
And then they took offence when I said,
"Hell, yes: he's fucked the whole country!
He's even made Bill look like an amateur."

I waited as long as I could about telling the girls,
But when I did, they just said,
"Well, mom, it's like really, really time."
So finally I called his momma, and she said,
"I'm tired of covering for those boys.
Pick me up on your way out of town."

                                                  Georgia Rhoades

CAULDRON

Christine St. Peter
Department of Women's Studies
University of Victoria, British Columbia

Women's Studies in Canada

It is dangerous to generalise about Women's Studies programmes in a country which is so huge geographically, with its multicultural population of 32,000,000 distributed among three major cities along the Canada/USA border (Montreal, Toronto, Vancouver), or in scattered towns or rural locations spread across vastly diverse, often balkanised, regions. But with that serious *caveat*, a few generalisations might still be ventured. The first, and perhaps most significant, is that all the state-supported universities in the country – in other words, virtually all Canadian universities – have some form of undergraduate Women's Studies. Unlike the pattern in European universities, which often started at the graduate level, the Canadian programmes all began on the undergraduate level and this emphasis continues. Several, however, now have postgraduate programmes as well, fifteen with Master's degree programmes, several others with cross-departmental, interdisciplinary MA programmes, and four with free-standing PhD[1] programmes. Very few private universities exist in Canada, and those that do tend to be denominational and conservative, and are, therefore, less likely to give a formal, institutional welcome to a discipline created to question orthodoxies of all sorts. To state the obvious, then, this discipline – however contested that word is in this interdisciplinary context – is established and successful, to varying degrees across the country. From there, the picture gets more complicated.

The first point of divergence can be found in the diversity of academic structures and of funding formulae, two places that reveal significant differences in possibilities and institutional stability. At my own university, the westernmost in Canada, we have an established department with seven tenure-track positions and the possibility of hiring part-time faculty; we have permanent 'base budget' funding for faculty salaries, administrative services and library purchases, a large corridor of our own, complete with splendid Reading Room and other amenities. We have some nine hundred student undergraduate enrolments per year (the university has 18,000 students) doing minor, major or Honours Bachelor of Arts degrees in the department. This situation, especially the number of tenure-track departmental appointments, is unusually good for the Canadian context. But, to date, we still do not have a free-standing postgraduate programme, mainly because we have refused to mount this until we have funding and support adequate to the extra demands – additional faculty appointments and secure financial support for the graduate students. Strong situations resembling the University of Victoria model exist in several other universities and certainly in all the largest institutions (albeit often with fewer tenure-track positions and fewer students). But dozens of other Canadian post-secondary institutions are less generous to Women's Studies, supporting only small programmes with three typical models, none adequate to the task of providing the necessary stability, depth and diversity for a healthy program: 1) the WS faculty may be 'borrowed' from other departments to mount a course(s) under the rubric of Women's Studies; 2) the WS programme may have only one academic position and that person acts as instructor AND coordinator for the program; 3) the WS programme relies entirely on cross-appointments with other departments, a situation that makes for difficulty in career advancement, as the person has to participate in two programmes, with the traditional department, what Canadian feminist scholar Ursula Franklin wryly calls the "academic chaperone"[2] in charge of the faculty position. These under-funded, under-staffed programmes are, in my estimation, quite vulnerable. The feminist faculty who created these programmes as early as 1970, maintaining them for a generation, sometimes in hostile or indifferent environments, are beginning to retire. When these committed feminist scholars leave, their programmes may disappear if the larger 'host' departments replace them with faculty who have no interest in serving Women's Studies programmes. Yet that Cassandra-like observation probably underestimates the solidity of the ongoing existence of Women's Studies in Canada. At institutional and ideological levels, this country has a predominantly liberal culture with a strong human rights orientation, something made clear again this summer when same-sex marriage became the law of the land. Within such a culture, Women's Studies is a good fit with other politicised educational agendas – as long as we do not demand too many of the always-scarce and fiercely contested resources. But, if Women's Studies is likely to survive into another generation, the regional and ideological differences make for problematic relations within Women's Studies more generally.

We have, for example, hundreds of members in the Canadian Women's Studies Association/*Association canadienne des études sur les femmes*, the official 'society' of our discipline in this country. And, yet, despite the bilingual title of the association, there is little presence in or from Quebec, a province with 7,400,000 inhabitants, many of whom – particularly academics and artists – are likely to think of themselves, not as citizens of Canada, but of (the 'nation' of) Quebec. Even the four major Women's Studies journals in Canada divide linguistically; the readers of the anglophone journals (do not be fooled by their bilingual titles), *Atlantis: A Women's Studies Journal, RFR/dfr,* and *Canadian Woman Studies/les cahiers de la femme* are as unlikely to read the francophone journal *Études feministes* as the Quebec scholars are to read the English. While the French culture of Quebec has official recognition of its 'distinctness' and of its language, Quebec now has a huge immigrant population, as do most of the other regions of Canada. This multicultural diversity (with its cultural differences and the 100 different languages still actively spoken across the country) makes federalism and Women's Studies organisation difficult.

These regional differences were neatly illustrated in the 1980s when our federal government gave several million dollars to the creation of five Federal Chairs of Women's Studies in what were considered the five distinct regions of Canada: 1) Atlantic Canada; 2) Quebec; 3) Ontario; 4) the Prairie provinces; 5) British Columbia/Yukon Territory. The absurdity of these groupings figures in every region. For example, the 'Prairie' chair is located across two different universities in the multicultural city of Winnipeg, Manitoba and has as its vast service territory, not just the three prairie provinces (Saskatchewan, Manitoba and Alberta), but also the Northwest Territories and the new Aboriginal territory of Nunavut. Everywhere in Canada there is under-representation of, and continuing discrimination against, the Indigenous peoples[3] even as we also find very uneven distribution of power and resources among the 'settler' peoples who have come to Canada from all the nations of the earth.[4] All of these problems create fault lines within our programmes as we struggle to theorise – and live – the differences among us. A growing (and to do the Cassandra act again), perhaps terminal, difference has to do with definitions and naming: how can we continue with the term 'women' in 'women's studies' without succumbing to an unsophisticated kind of identity politics with its humanistic assumptions about that 'subject category.'[5] But these debates are the healthy ones that challenge us to refine or recreate our understandings. They are also the ones we ourselves can control as we work to reshape our programmes.

Another threat, and a more difficult one, comes from outside academia and afflicts all the academic units of every university in the country. This is the increasing pressure to acquire corporate funding to support academic work, with a consequent reduction of public funding for universities and their research.[6] In its least problematic, but still distressing, manifestation, we find that every university in Canada is either is a 'Pepsi' or a 'Coca-cola' site, with every vending machine on the campus belonging to, and furnishing profits to, a particular business monopoly in exchange for minimal financial support. But research endeavours increasingly are being forced to seek corporate funding in partnership with federal or provincial funding. In such a climate, much more than Women's Studies is threatened.

Notes

1. Visit the website of the Canadian Women Association/*Association canadienne des études sur les femmes* at cwsaacef@yorku.ca for the names and locations of the programmes. See also the website of *Réseau d'études féministes universitaires* (de Québec) at http://www.scom.ulaval.ca/ Note that while many institutions have the possibility of inter-disciplinary post-graduate degrees, those having free-standing postgraduate programs are relatively few.
2. Conversation with the author.
3. For a recent discussion by Indigenous women of this situation, see 'Indigenous Women: The State of Our Nations.' Special issue. *Atlantis: A Women's Studies Journal*, 29.2 (Fall, 2004).
4. These divisions in difference are discussed in many Canadian feminist publications. Recent examples include Bannerji, Himani. *The Dark Side of the Nation: Essays on Multiculturalism, Nationalism and Gender* (Toronto: Canadian Scholars' Press, 2000); Razack, Sherene H., *Looking White People in the Eye: Gender, Race and Culture in Courtrooms and Classrooms* (Toronto: University of Toronto Press, 2000); *Canadian Woman Studies/Les cahiers de la femme*, Special Issue: 'National Identity and Gender Politics.' 20:2 (Summer, 2000).
5. The most recent discussion of this debate in the Canadian context can be found in Ann Braithwaite, Susan Heald, Susanne Luhmann and Sharon Rosenberg, eds. *Troubling Women's Studies: Pasts, Presents and Possibilities* (Toronto: Sumach Press, 2004).
6. See James L. Turk, ed. *The Corporate Campus: Commercialization and the Dangers to Canada's Colleges and Universities* (Toronto: J. Lorimer, 2000); Reimer, Marilee, ed. *Inside Corporate U: Women in the Academy Speak Out* (Toronto: Sumach Press, 2004).

Carole Ferrier

Centre for Research on Women, Gender, Culture and Social Change, School of English, Media Studies and Art History,
The University of Queensland

Women's and Gender Studies in Australia Today

Women's Studies began in Australia in the early 1970s with the first cross-disciplinary subjects at Queensland and Flinders (Adelaide). Through the 1970s and early '80s they spread to almost every campus, associated (sometimes uneasily) with an activist and socialist-inflected second wave Women's Liberation movement. They articulated new perspectives that came into the universities from the end of the 1960s that addressed – and sought to bring centrally into play in critical reading – along with issues of gender, those of class, race and ethnicity, and sexuality.

In 1996 a conference at the University of Sydney entitled 'The Return of the Repressed', revisited the successful 1973 strike over the introduction of 'Philosophical Aspects of Feminist Thought.' Typical feminist sentiments of the 1970s were recalled by Susan Magarey – for whose courses "the goal was to foster the revolution that I thought the Women's Movement was bringing about and, while I knew that I could not spell out such a goal to curriculum-approving bodies within the university, I was sure that it would gain recognition among students and among a broader feminist community outside the university."[1] Some, such as Jean Curthoys, now critique these ideas as "a negative morality of the assertion of difference",[2] others would still like to retain some of the commitment and fire of association with a feminism whose demise has been repeatedly announced throughout the twentieth century.[3] From the 1990s, we saw widespread university restructuring and an increasing dominance of economic rationalism. Along with this, as Maryanne Dever points out, there was a "fragmentation of feminist movements locally and internationally, on-going public and media 'debate' about political correctness and the death of feminism, and the emergence of intergenerational conflict as a popular leitmotif for 'post-feminism.'"[4]

These factors have produced a very different context for the continuing evolution of Women's Studies, ranging from Sydney University's Gender Studies, closely meshed with Cultural Studies, to the ANU's major in Gender, Sexuality and Culture, to Monash's major in Feminist Cultural Studies, to what appear to be five different majors available at Macquarie in various permutations of women, gender, culture, media, history and sexuality.

The long-running debate about the directions of Women's Studies has sometimes involved a standoff over names. Gender Studies has been seen, in some instances, as almost synonymous with Women's Studies, in others as facilitating a displacement of feminist analyses by, for example, the concerns of Critical Men's Studies or Masculinity Studies[5] or, even, as reinscribing the demise, yet again, of a *passe* political practice. Heather Brook suggests:

> women's studies could offer a potential 'home' for gender studies just as comfortably as the more frequently posited reverse case. However, perhaps gender studies offers a future for feminist and other critically progressive scholarship which avoids the perennial pejoratives dogging women's studies .... Ironically the success of women's studies – the transformations in thinking that have been wrought across so many bodies of knowledge - seems almost to require 're-branding' in order to occupy its rightful place in the academy. [6]

This reflects a desire to retain the 'old' approach for Women's Studies of 'doing feminism' and engaging with the power relations between women and men that many have felt was in decline after the 1980s. Women's Studies paradoxical position as an interdisciplinary discipline means that it has both had great influence for decades as a model of interdisciplinarity, and is also vulnerable to recuperation by other disciplines or interdisciplines (of which cultural studies and postcolonialism spring to mind).

Some idea of the current state of Women's and Gender Studies teaching in Australia can be gleaned from the list of the offerings from the 40-odd universities (and about 55 campuses).[7] In terms of undergraduate courses, in all but a few places, one can do substantial study – a double major (at about ten universities), a major (at a further fifteen) and/or a minor (at a further six or so) in Women's/Gender Studies and, at the majority, Honours at fourth year in Women's Studies, assessed generally half by coursework and half by thesis. In some places, one can do postgraduate coursework, or an MA or PhD in Women's or Gender Studies, but this output of named degrees does not reflect the very large amount of postgraduate research degrees in the area since, historically, many have also been done in departments such as English, History or Sociology, where many of the leading Women's Studies scholars are based. The first professor of Women's Studies was at Griffith in 1990 (Judith Allen), and the first full Department of Women's Studies at Adelaide in 1992. I think Chilla Bulbeck at Adelaide is now the only remaining professor of Women's Studies – but, again, many of the main practitioners of Women's Studies in the area of research as well as teaching have always had a variety of roles and expertise in connected areas and disciplines – and some may have operated in terms of the logic of the position Gretchen Poiner describes – "if we had no place how could we be kept in it?"[8] Accordingly, the actual strength of Women's Studies cannot be measured simply by counting up the appearances (or indeed disappearances) of its particular name. This is not to say, however, that there are not strong institutional pressures towards incorporation, since (they tell us) 'everybody does gender now': they are aware, as Terry Threadgold has put it, that "simply adding women to existing knowledge structures had and would have little effect", and there may now be less purchase for the earlier approach that involved challenges to "the academic knowledges and organisational structures that had proved so intractable to feminist interventions."[9]

In 2003, women were 54.4% of the university student population in Australia. They are still concentrated in Humanities and Social Sciences and this is where most Women's Studies teaching (and a lot of the research) done by women academics (38% of academic staff in 2003) also remains. And, as Louise Morley points out, despite more women students coming into the university, "the academy is slow to change in terms of equity whereas it has been rapidly transformed in relation to new managerialism and neo-liberalism."[10] Everyday practices of gendered hegemony are still taken for granted. Poiner recalls when she was investigating the barriers to women's advancement at Sydney in the early 1980s: "Within the university, conservative anti-feminist voices were beginning to sound either decidedly cracked or destructively self-serving."[11] But these voices have spoken with a new force again from the 1990s, with the offensive espousal by the Federal government of new conservative 'family ideologies', and the assertion of men's – and boys' – rights, designed to correct the supposed enormous ideological influence of a 'feminism gone too far.' Institutions have also learnt how to use our own arguments against us. Fifteen years ago, on The University of Queensland's Academic Board, the socialists and feminists would be a minority alliance with the conservatives against the policy that said all University committees should have at least one-third women members. These days, lone voices that complain that promotions committees have fewer and fewer women members are dismissed with assertions that everybody knows that women do not want to be tokens and 'senior women' should not be 'overloaded' with committee work, while most of the room nods sagely.

Vocational pathways were much talked of in the 1990s, but Dever makes the point that what has emerged is a much less neat fit between qualifications and careers. In this context, the useful question is not necessarily, as it might have been in the past, 'What is Women's Studies?' but, rather, 'What do you think you can do, or what do you want to do with Women's Studies?' She suggests that a key feature of Women's Studies has been that "beyond knowledge of feminism and gender issues, it offered important ways to read or negotiate systems, ideologies and power structures. As one student so aptly phrased it, Women's Studies gave her the 'ability to see through bullshit.'"[12]

Feminists in universities today can still demonstrate, through a variety of disciplinary and multidisciplinary approaches, the usefulness of their deconstructive (and bullshit-detecting) critique and its applicability beyond the area of gender relations. Of course, Women's (or Gender) Studies subjects, majors and research degrees will only continue and survive if students want to do them. Reported in my first year interdisciplinary course in recent years has been what seems to be an increased hostility to feminism and Women's Studies on the part of the students' friends and acquaintances, and sometimes families. But this might be interpreted as a good thing, in that whatever it is we do, or what they think we do, continues to make many people uncomfortable.

Notes

1. Magarey 83.
2. Curthoys 61.
3. Ferrier 2003.
4. Dever (2001) 5.
5. Allen 2000.
6. Brook 258.
7. These can be found in more detail on my Australian Women's Studies Resources website, at www.emsah.uq.edu.au/awsr
8. Poiner 95.
9. Threadgold 40.
10. Morley 116.
11. Poiner 94.
12. Dever (2003) 42.

References

Allen, Margaret. 'Women's Studies Into Gender Studies – Will it Go?' *Australian Feminist Studies* 15, no. 31 (March 2000): 103-4.

Brook, Heather. 'Gender Studies Casts Off.' *Australian Feminist Studies*, 20, No. 47 (July 2005): 255-59.

Curthoys, Jean. 'Memoirs of a Feminist Dinosaur.' *Australian Feminist Studies* 13, No. 27 (1998): 55-62.

Dever, Maryanne. 'How Students Characterise the Vocational Gains from Women's Studies (Or, Why We Need Not Be Anxious).' *Hecate* 29.2 (2003): 34-49.

Dever, Maryanne. 'Futures for Women's Studies: A Discussion Paper.' Working Papers in Women's Studies, Centre for Women's Studies and Gender Research, School of PSI, Monash University, Feb. 2001.

Ferrier, Carole. 'Is Feminism Finished?' *Hecate* 29.2 (2003): 6-22.

Magarey, Susan. 'Setting Up the First Research Centre for Women's Studies in Australia, 1983-1986.' *Australian Feminist Studies* 13, No. 27 (April 1998): 81-90.

Morley, Louise. 'Sounds, Silences and Contradictions: Gender Equity in British Commonwealth Higher Education.' *Australian Feminist Studies* 20, no. 46 (March 2005): 109-119.

Poiner, Gretchen. 'The Women's Research Unit: Being There.' *Australian Feminist Studies* 13, no. 27 (April 1998): 91-98.

Threadgold, Terry. 'Gender Studies and Women's Studies.' *Australian Feminist Studies* 13, no. 31 (March 2000), 39-48.

Gabriele Griffin

Gender Studies
University of Hull, UK

Subject in Process: Women's Studies in Europe

Women's Studies as a discipline, and I make no apologies for using that term – discipline – has certain traits that, from its inception, have established it as a challenging innovator in academe, for Women's Studies as it is configured in Europe today remains:

- a single-sex subject which promotes women in predominantly secular, co-educational cultures that do not practise very overt forms of gender segregation[1];
- an overtly political discipline with a transformative agenda focused on gender relations in cultures and institutions dominated at the managerial and decision-making levels by men,[2] and – despite best theoretical efforts – by the notion of objective, un-invested knowledge[3];
- an interdisciplinary subject in educational structures that are still, for the most part, mono-disciplinary.

These disciplinary specificities have made it difficult for Women's Studies to become integrated into European academe. In an EU-funded project involving eleven partners from nine European countries conducted between 2001-2003,[4] we found that the following additional factors either impeded or fostered the integration of Women's Studies in academe:[5]

Factors *fostering* Women's Studies institutionalisation	Factors *impeding* Women's Studies institutionalisation
High degree of university autonomy in developing curricula	Little autonomy of university in developing curricula
Modularity	Rigid disciplinary structures
Support or neutrality of the women's movement toward institutionalisation	Anti-institutional attitudes of the women's movement
State support for Women's Studies	Absence of state support for Women's Studies

Source: Silius (2002)

Although these factors impact differentially on the institutionalisation of Women's Studies in the diverse European countries, it is nonetheless possible to suggest that, in 2005, generally speaking, Women's Studies as a discipline is more clearly established as a subject in its own right, with named degree routes and staff dedicated to the discipline (as opposed to conducting double shifts in some 'home', 'traditional' discipline *as well as* in Women's Studies), in north-western European countries, such as Finland, the Netherlands, Ireland and the UK, than it is in the southern and eastern European countries, such as France, Spain, Hungary, or Slovenia, for example. This does not mean that there is not a thriving feminist academic and research community in these countries. Indeed, across Europe in disciplines such as literature, history and sociology, Women's Studies academics and researchers have done much to innovate the curricula, gaining a significant hold in those disciplines. But the numbers of staff whose professional appellation and teaching focus centres exclusively on Women's Studies remains small, and courses struggle to establish and maintain themselves, though for different reasons in different European countries.[6]

The institutionalisation of Women's Studies across the European countries was initially – no matter when and where the discipline began to emerge – fuelled by the actions of individual women academics or groups of such academics, often with one foot in an activist and the other in a campaigning camp. More recently, much of this momentum has been sustained by international gender agendas and, indeed, one of the changes that has occurred across Europe since the mid-1990s has been the increasing use of the phrase 'Gender Studies' instead of 'Women's Studies', not least in recognition of the fact that international agendas by transnational bodies, such as the European Union, UNESCO, the World Bank etc., regarding the mobilisation of women, recognised as an under-utilised resource[7] by these bodies, take the word 'gender' rather than 'women' as their key term. Despite this seemingly more neutral and inclusive word, men's participation in 'Gender Studies' across Europe remains low and Critical Men's Studies,[8] which has emerged as one way of seeking to interrogate the need for change regarding men and masculinities, remains very much marginalised and under-developed.

One of the benefits, however, of these inter-/transnational gender agendas has been the extensive opportunity for conducting funded research on Women's Studies-related topics. Women remain an under-utilised resource, and the investigation of why this is the case and how it can be changed continues to exercise feminists and inter-/transnational organisations as well as governments. The resultant opportunities for Women's Studies research funding have led to a significant rise in the number of research centres across Europe, both inside and outside academe, dedicated to such research and, indeed, such research and related postgraduate work, constitutes the most vibrant aspect of Women's Studies across Europe today.[9] Since that research is frequently internationally, rather than nationally, funded, it has also resulted in significant international networking among feminist researchers in Europe and beyond.

The expansion of Women's Studies-related research in Europe has not been accompanied by a similar or uniform expansion of Women's Studies degrees, especially at undergraduate level. From the mid-1990s there has been a decline of such courses in European countries, such as the UK and the Netherlands, which had early and rapid expansions of the discipline during the 1980s and early '90s. By contrast, European countries where the discipline was established only slowly or not at all (as in many of the post-communist countries), are now seeing an expansion of that provision, so that across Europe the state of Women's Studies undergraduate provision must be regarded as unevenly developed, and facing an uncertain future.

For, in 2005, Europe is in the grip of the so-called Bologna process,[10] designed to streamline higher education across Europe with comparable degrees, degree contents, qualifications, timeframes, etc. This process will impact significantly on how Women's Studies fares in the future, not least in those eastern and southern European countries where the discipline is still very much in development. One issue with that process (and this is visible in the various reports on the website mentioned above), is that whilst the European Union has established targets for 2010, it has not produced an implementation plan regarding how these will be reached and, in consequence, the various European countries are using the Bologna process to differing ends, with some, such as Spain, for example, reinforcing disciplinisation (which hinders Women's Studies as an interdisciplinary subject) and others, such as Norway, loosening the hold of the disciplines. It, thus, becomes very difficult to anticipate how the Bologna process will impact on Women's Studies in the academy across Europe over the next ten years.[11] Without doubt, though, that process will have a significant impact on the development of the discipline.

Women's Studies across Europe remains a subject in process.[12] In 2005, most European countries have it in some form, ranging from the embryonic integration of Women's Studies topics into 'traditional' disciplines to the fully-fledged degree course at all higher educational levels. Its curricula have increasingly branched out from the social sciences, literature and history bases it originally had to areas such as feminist legal, science, and technology studies. Its research base across the spectrum is its greatest strength; its institutionalisation its most precarious aspect. One might argue that this is as it should be since over-identification with institutions can lead to fossilisation and detract from the critical political impetus that the discipline continues to claim as its own.

Notes

1 I write 'not very overt' because even a superficial social analysis of European countries will reveal deeply entrenched forms of gender segregation, from gender-segregated social clubs, to sex-segregated sports, to gendered media domains, etc.
2 See Colosimo *et al* (2000) and Braithwaite (2001) for relevant figures.
3 The emergence of standpoint theory, postcolonial theory and other elaborated theoretical frameworks that interrogate such notions has, interestingly, gone hand-in-hand with a re-scientisation of academe in the sense of a re-investment in 'objective' knowledge, underpinned by advances in biotechnology.
4 www.hull.ac.uk/ewsi
5 For a discussion of the differential impact of these factors see Griffin (2005a).
6 Griffin (2005b).
7 This terminology may seem harsh to some, but it reflects the realities under which we operate – international organisations by and large do not have feminist agendas and their support for women is driven by the sense of women as a resource. This can be utilised by feminists to support their own agendas, which, in any event, may well sometimes coincide with those of these organisations.
8 Hearn 2004.
9 This is evident in countries such as Germany, the Nordic countries and Switzerland which have recently developed graduate schools in the discipline (largely post-2000), complete with funded PhD studentships and dedicated staff; and in the formation of entities such as 'Gendergraduates', a Marie Curie Early Researcher Training Network funded by the European Commission and coordinated by the University of Utrecht.
10 www.bologna-bergen2005.no
11 Isable Carrera Suarez and Vinuela Suarez (2005).

12   Griffin and Braidotti (2002).

References

Braithwaite, Mary. *Gender in Research: Improving Human Research Potential and the Socio-Economic Knowledge Base*. Brussels: European Commission, 2001.

Carrera Suarez, Isabel and Laura Vinuela Suarez. *The Impact of the Bologna Process on Disciplinization: A Comparative Report on Eight European Countries* at http://www.hull.ac.uk/researchintegration (2005).

Griffin, Gabriele. 'The Institutionalization of Women's Studies in Europe: Findings from an EU-funded Research Project on Women's Studies and Women's Employment.' E Blimlinger and T. Garstenauer, eds. *Women's/Gender Studies: Against All Odds*. Vienna: Studienverlag, 2005a. 43-55.

Griffin, Gabriele and Rosi Braidotti, eds. *Thinking Differently: A Reader in European Women's Studies*. London: Zed Books, 2002.

Hearn, Jeff. 'From Hegemonic Masculinity to the Hegemony of Men.' *Feminist Theory* 5/1 (2004): 49-72.

Silius, Harriet. *Summary Report – Background Data on Women's Employment, Equal Opportunities and Women's Studies in Nine European Countries* at http://www.hull.ac.uk/ewsi (2002).

CAULDRON

Catherine M. Orr

Women's and Gender Studies
Beloit College Wisconsin

Women's Studies Reflects on its Prime of Life: A View from the United States

Officially launched with a handful of undergraduate courses in the fall of 1970 at San Diego State College (California), Women's Studies in the United States has expanded in the last 35 years, now claiming hundreds of outposts throughout the nation's community colleges, regional state universities, liberal arts colleges, religious schools, historically black colleges and universities, PhD-granting institutions, and the private universities of the 'Ivy League' (Harvard, Yale, Princeton, etc.). Born of the culture wars of the late 1960s, in which racial strife, imperialistic military campaigns, and growing class divides provoked the radicalised thinking of Women's Liberation, Women's Studies emerged just as the basic assumptions of higher education in the US were shifting. The changing economic environment of the 1970s — characterised by retrenchment and subsequent search for 'new markets' for the US academic enterprise — actually helped Women's Studies advocates lay claim to a 'relevant education' (a popular term in the parlance of the times), in ways not dreamed possible before 'student-centred learning' became the hottest trend in US universities and colleges. Add to this the increasing gender parity at the undergraduate level (actually, since 1993, women have outnumbered men at the undergraduate level in the US and the gap continues to grow),[1] and one can begin to account for the field's continued expansion, even in times of conservative backlash and institutional belt-tightening. Given this relative stability, Women's Studies in the US has now begun to show what might be thought of as more subtle signs of maturity, turning a self-reflective eye inward, both to promote itself within the academic hierarchy and to consider how its past successes should relate to its future plans.

A recent development is the proliferation of PhD programmes in Women's Studies, now offered at about a dozen universities, with a handful of joint-doctoral programmes available as well. Its relatively late arrival reflects the typical trajectory of Women's Studies history in the US as a 'bottom up' endeavour: it begins at the marginal locations (like San Diego State), or at lower rungs of the prestige ladder (a few courses at the undergraduate level), and climbs the academic hierarchy from there. This makes sense, given that, in most US institutions, it is undergraduate programmes that offer the most administrative flexibility and room for curricular innovation. Although the PhD was ushered in with a fair amount of hand wringing, even among its advocates,[2] it is proving valuable in building Women's Studies' institutional power. Graduates are getting jobs, and most tenure-track jobs in Women's Studies (not that there are a lot of them), express a preference that candidates hold a doctorate in Women's Studies. Time will tell if this trend toward hiring 'our own' represents a lessening of the porous boundaries that has characterised Women's Studies in the US throughout its history. Administratively, and in terms of its intellectual loyalties, Women's Studies still is arguably the most differentiated, uneven, and multifaceted field of inquiry in the US academy. A PhD won't change that anytime soon.

Thirty-five also seems to be a good age for some earnest self-reflection about future political (in the most expansive sense of that term) strategising for Women's Studies as a field. If one were to just look at numbers of programmes and graduates, the outlook seems rosy. But, of course, it is more complex than that. These complexities have been iterated most recently by a spate of anthologies, special issues in journals, and conferences that attempt to grapple with the meanings and outcomes of Women's Studies' institutionalisation (the PhD being only one facet of it). In other words, what are and have been the consequences of building an academic enterprise out of a social movement that claimed all women, especially the most marginalised women, as its constituency? What are the implications of both living through and theorising about its newly politicised identities (based on gender, race, class, sexuality, nationality, bodily attributes, etc.)? Is the success of Women's Studies a success for women? Or, is our success, by definition, the social movement's failure? How does an unequivocally institutionalised Women's Studies position itself politically within the increasingly corporatised US academy?

Whether these queries lead to a lamenting of an activist past when it all seemed less complicated, or questioning whether such activist pasts are the nostalgic constructions of the retiring first-generation practitioners, the debate about what Women's Studies is and should be has never been more contentious ... or more interesting! Robyn Wiegman (Duke University in

North Carolina), for one, has been especially influential in raising concerns about the apparent necessity of setting the course for Women's Studies' future based on a wistful longing for its pasts.[3] This is at a time when so many in Women's Studies' first generation are composing their memoirs and offering advice to the next generation.[4] This has made for some truly fascinating theoretical and generational disputes.

Taken together, these two trends — greater institutional power and increased theoretical reflection on Women's Studies itself — have meant that the critical discussions about the field are taking place, for the most part, at the highest rungs of the academic ladder with little attention paid to how drastically different Women's Studies looks from, say, a community college populated with first generation, working class, and/or immigrant students, versus an endowed chair at a major research university where the holder is responsible for teaching one graduate seminar per semester. The grassroots orientation has given way to a palpable class-based pecking order.[5] On the one hand, it should come as no surprise that those who speak in the name of Women's Studies tend to be located more and more in a context with the highest publishing demands. On the other hand, it means that the field's exercise in self-reflection is skewed somewhat by a failure to account for its own diversity.[6]

One final item worthy of an extended note: although I have consistently used 'Women's Studies' to refer to the field and its programmes, its use is a matter of convenience and brevity rather than accuracy. 'What's in a name?' seems to be a key question for some surprisingly low-key and short-lived debates as a number of programmes quietly change their letterhead to read: 'Women's and Gender Studies' or, simply, 'Gender Studies.' The reasons are multiple, complex and, in most cases, local. For conservative university administrators who hold the purse strings and might shy away from the field's roots in women's liberation, 'gender' seems less exclusively about, well, women. For male students who sense — rightly or wrongly— that feminist intellectual activity targets their behaviour for analysis and critique, 'gender' provides them with an invitation into our classrooms and justifies their perennial demand: 'what about the men?' Yet, for many Women's Studies practitioners who have been greatly influenced by postmodern analyses of Women's Studies' object of analysis ('women') and the compelling insights of queer theory, 'gender' promises a more radical revisioning of the field's libratory potential to include *all* gendered expressions. Talk about polysemic! 'Gender' seems to promise something for everyone; no wonder the fuss has been so minimal. Whether the name change will deliver on everyone's demands will, of course, differ from location to location and over time. Stay tuned for those assessments.

These are just a few observations from the perspective of someone whose research project is about (in case you hadn't guessed) Women's Studies' disciplinarity, and is now comfortably tenured in an appointment that is 100% in the College's Women's and Gender Studies Programme (yes, we made the name change too!). Other US-based Women's Studies folks would tell different stories, no doubt. Obviously, so much is left unsaid in such a short piece: I have not spoken of the field's growing focus on global processes and flows, the expanding interest in physical disability as a lens of analysis, the new approaches to women and the environment, the continuing struggle to address issues of white supremacy in our own programmes and promote women of colour into leadership positions, the renaissance of the one and only national organisation dedicated to the field — the National Women's Studies Association, the potentials and pitfalls many of us have discovered about doing Women's Studies through distance-learning programmes, or the emergent phenomenon of transitioning (as in, female-to-male or male-to-female) students who arrive on our campuses looking to Women's Studies programmes for intellectual and emotional sustenance. All for another time, I suppose.

Notes

1   *Chronicle of Higher Education*. 49 (42) 27 June 2003: A30.
2   Forum on the Women's Studies PhD in *Feminist Studies* 24. 2 (1998). See, especially, the contributions by Susan Standford Friedman. Vivian M. May, 'Disciplinary Desires and Undisciplined Daughters: Negotiating the Politics of a Women's Studies Doctoral Education.' *NWSA Journal* 14.1 (2002): 134-159.
3   See, for example, Robyn Wiegman's 1999 response to Susan Gubar's lament of contemporary feminist literary criticism: 'What Ails Feminist Criticism? A Second Opinion.' *Critical Enquiry* 25.2 (1997): 107-36, as well as her 'On Location,' Wiegman's introductory essay in *Women's Studies on Its Own: A Next Wave Reader in Institutional Change* (Durham: Duke UP, 2002), 1-44.
4   See, for example, *The Politics of Women's Studies: Testimonies from 30 Foundling Mothers*, Florence Howe, ed. (New York: Feminist Press, 2000).
5   For example, about 75% of the essays in Wiegman's anthology, *Women's Studies on Its Own*, were penned by Women's Studies practitioners located in doctoral-granting, extensive universities (formerly called 'Research I' institutions). Since its publication in 2002, a number of the remaining 25% moved to doctoral-granting, extensive universities.
6   For a more extensive explication of how the class politics of the field affect the representations of Women's Studies in the US, see, Catherine M. Orr and Diane Lichtenstein, 'The Politics of Feminist Locations: A Materialist Analysis of Women's Studies.' *NWSA Journal* 16.3 (Fall 2004): 1-17.

References:

Boxer, Marilyn Jacoby. *When Women Ask the Questions: Creating Women's Studies in America?* Baltimore: Johns Hopkins UP, 1998.

Braithwaite, Ann, *et al. Troubling Women's Studies: Pasts, Presents and Possibilities.* Toronto: Sumach Press, 2004.

Caughie, Pamela L.,ed. 'Forum: Graduate Education in Women's Studies: Paradoxes and Challenges.' *Feminist Studies* 29.2 (2003): 405-47.

Differences: A Journal of Feminist Cultural Studies. Special Issue. 'Women's Studies on the Edge.' 9.3 (1997).

Howe, Florence, ed. *The Politics of Women's Studies: Testimony from 30 Founding Mothers.* New York: Feminist Press, 2000.

Wiegman, Robyn, ed. *Women's Studies On Its Own: A Next Wave Reader in Institutional Change.* Durham, NC: Duke UP, 2002.

Women's Studies Quarterly. Special Issue. 'Women's Studies Then and Now.' 30. 3 / 4 (2002).

CAULDRON

Rebecca Pelan

Women's Studies Centre
National University of Ireland, Galway

Women's Studies in Ireland

To date, no university in Ireland has made a substantial enough commitment to Women's Studies to allow us to say that it is established, institutionally, as a securely defined field of study. Certainly, feminist analyses are now part of much scholarly work across disciplines throughout Ireland, but the development of Women's Studies as a discrete interdisciplinary subject is still embryonic. Whatever success the field has had – and that is not insubstantial – has been the result of dynamic individuals who have worked hard to bring explicit feminist politics into the academy. Of the nine Irish universities[1] – Queen's University, Belfast (QUB); University of Ulster (UU); University College Dublin (UCD); Trinity College Dublin (TCD); Dublin City University (DCU); University College Cork (UCC), National University of Ireland, Maynooth (NUIM); National University of Ireland, Galway (NUIG); University of Limerick (UL) – six offer Women's Studies programmes at some level (QUB, UCD, TCD, UCC, NUIM, NUIG, UL), while four have Women's Studies Centres with dedicated academic staff. No department of Women's Studies exists in Ireland, and there is no professor or Chair in the field,[2] and, as in many other places, it remains contentious as to whether departmental status would be a positive or negative development. However, all Centres and Women's Studies staff in Ireland remain attached to departments – most often, Sociology or History – although this is often more of a structural requirement ('host' department), than one that demands a dual role in terms of work.

In 1998, a US-based philanthropic organisation invited the six Irish universities in which Women's Studies is taught to submit funding applications, with the aim of injecting the field with sufficient funds to advance staffing and resource levels. Historically, Women's Studies in Ireland, as elsewhere, has struggled against a variety of blocks to its progress: for instance, it had 'fitted' into existing, traditional academic structures by whatever means it could, and had relied heavily on voluntary labour from personnel who were prepared to give their time and intellectual energy to the cause. Women's Studies at QUB, which was then structurally attached to the Department of Sociology, was beaten to the funding by a new Centre for the Advancement of Women in Politics, established through the Department of Political Science; Women's Studies at TCD (Centre for Gender and Women's Studies) and UCD (Women's Education, Research and Resource Centre/WERRC) were defeated in their efforts by institutional decisions not to apply. UCC does not have a Centre as such, but, rather, individual academics who work from within different departments and, again, no proposal was submitted. Only UL and NUIG actually submitted proposals, and both were successful.

The current situation is that, in all six of the universities where Women's Studies exists, there are various pre-graduate (Certificate/Diploma), undergraduate and postgraduate programmes available. QUB (under the Directorship of Myrtle Hill), for instance, offers undergraduate Women's Studies degrees as single, major, joint or minor Honours, but they currently have no pre- or postgraduate programmes. UL (co-ordinated by Breda Gray) offers an interdisciplinary BA (with History, Politics, Sociology and Social Sciences) with Women's Studies as a major or minor subject, as well as a pre-graduate Certificate/Diploma and postgraduate MA in Women's Studies. At NUIG, we have pre-graduate (Certificate and Diploma), and postgraduate programmes (MA, M.Litt and PhD), but can only offer modules to visiting students at the undergraduate level, while Women's Studies in UCC (co-ordinated by Sandra McAvoy) offers pre-graduate Certificate/Diploma programmes, as well as postgraduate (MA and PhD). Women's Studies at Trinity College Dublin (under the directorship of Maryann Valiulis) offers a Diploma and M.Phil, as well as an M.Litt and PhD, while the largest of Ireland's Centres, WERRC at UCD (Ailbhe Smyth, Director), offers a range of programmes, including a pre-graduate Certificate (Access), an undergraduate Diploma, a BA (Modular), a Higher Diploma, MA, M.Litt, and PhD. In other words, the programmes across the different universities are extraordinarily uneven to say the least, especially for such a small country. Overall, however, the pattern of development of Women's Studies programmes in Ireland has been one of 'top down', with postgraduate programmes being introduced first, followed, less often, by some undergraduate offerings.

This means that the development of the programmes has had quite a different history from those in both North America – where a 'bottom-up' approach has been the pattern – and from Australia and New Zealand where interdisciplinary programmes at the undergraduate level formed an early basis in the field. In Ireland, Women's Studies at postgraduate level (either taught MA or research-based PhD) is widely available. One of the major obstacles to the development of Women's Studies in Ireland has, in fact, been the difficulty in trying to get a foothold at undergraduate level.

But another major obstacles rests with the continued resistance, most often at departmental level, to the idea of Women's Studies as a discipline. Women's Studies practitioners and theorists have long labeled our field of research and our teaching practices as interdisciplinary – something useful as a means of breaking down the institutional barriers of the academy. Yet a closer examination of interdisciplinarity in Women's Studies programmes in Ireland, reveals that a paradoxical result of its twenty-five year institutional history is that its interdisciplinary goals remain, largely, unrealised. In truth, most Women's Studies programmes remain multi-disciplinary, rather than interdisciplinary. But multi-disciplinarity is qualitatively different from interdisciplinarity, since the former usually involves scholars from various disciplinary backgrounds collaborating, with very little integration occurring (not to mention their having to pay attention to the demands of 'home' departments in terms of resources), while interdisciplinarity is generally understood to be a means of moving beyond the political and intellectual limitations of disciplinary boundaries and, ideally, allowing a re-assessment of such things as the university as a political space. More often than not, the resistance to recognising Women's Studies as an emerging discipline (albeit an interdisciplinary one) has related less to disciplinary concerns than to departmental/territorial ones. Often, there is a clear suspicion that interdisciplinarity, such as that aimed for in Women's Studies, is a means of undermining, eliminating or weakening the disciplines, when it should, in fact, be seen as a means of strengthening them. From a Women's Studies viewpoint, the lack of active engagement with interdisciplinary principles has made it difficult to generate new research that moves away from the traditional disciplines, and this has played into the misguided notion, held by many, that Women's Studies is simply about 'studying women.' All of this is not to underestimate the equally difficult hurdle faced by feminist academics in leaving behind a 'home' discipline, not least because of the uncertainty of their position within an institution that still clearly recognises and rewards, primarily, those with clear discipline-specific expertise.

Women's Studies in Ireland has no national association or organisation, although, given the small size of the country and the relatively few designated staff working in the field, this presents much less difficulty than might be the case elsewhere. The main representative body for women's groups in Ireland, is the National Women's Council of Ireland (NWCI), which has approximately 150 affiliates, and which would include most, if not all, Irish Women's Studies staff and Centres. The NWCI currently represents over 300,000 women, and remains an important body in the context of feminism and Women's Studies in Ireland, not only because of its size, but because it retains a commitment to the principles of women's equality, sometimes to its cost.[3]

In addition to the challenges within the discipline itself, however, there are shifts in other contexts that have impacted on the development of the field. Ireland, for example, is a significantly different place now from what it was in the 1970s, and feminism in Ireland has become functionally quite different from what it was even ten years ago: a significant part of feminist activity today involves a form of institutionalised vigilance to resist the erosion or de-politicisation of those women's issues that have already entered the mainstream of social and political life, especially in the face of conservative restructuring agendas that are currently active in Ireland, and which have exposed the vulnerability of various subjects, not only those like Women's Studies that retain a commitment to interrogative politics, but also many that constitute core areas that sit at the heart of the university as a concept, historically: classics, physics, and many of the languages, for instance.

In addition, topics of ethnicity and (anti)racism have overtaken feminism in Ireland with a sense of urgency, and there are those – some of whom were once supporters and practitioners of Women's Studies – who now reject the field on the grounds that Chandra Mohanty's cry that, "beyond sisterhood there is still racism",[4] embodies a failure on the part of feminism and Women's Studies to address growing racism in this country. The entirely inadequate response is that not only does racism thrive beyond the sisterhood, so too does poverty, disability and other inequities in our society. For many of us, however, this can never justify a turning-away from the need for a separate space in which to examine and address the lives and needs of women today as a larger group subject to all forms of oppression and inequality – in Ireland and beyond.

Notes

1   QUB and UU are in Northern Ireland and, consequently, constitute UK universities, complete with compliance to the Research Assessment Exercise (RAE), which is quite a different form of academic assessment from that which

exists in the Republic of Ireland. However, their Women's Studies history and personnel form part of the overall field on the island of Ireland, and so they are included here.

2   An indication of just how changed the map of Women's Studies is today, compared with its early start, is the fact that the University of Ulster was the first university in Ireland to introduce the subject in the late 1980s. In an even more extraordinary move, the university appointed Professor Celia Davis as professor of Women's Opportunities in 1987. Professor Davis was charged with an academic brief to develop teaching and research, and to undertake a commentary on the university's policies as they affected its female employees. Despite such an optimistic start, however, today, the University of Ulster has no Women's Studies programmes and no dedicated Women's Studies personnel.

3   In 2005, the NWCI refused to endorse the current Social Partnership agreement with the State, because the agreement "contained minimal progress for women's equality." The result was that the NWCI has been excluded from the consultation process relating to the Social Partnership agreement. NWCI Report to Members, July 2005.

4   Chandra Mohanty, 'Under Western Eyes: Feminist Scholarship and Colonial Discourses.' *Feminist Review* 30 (1998): 61-88.

Learning the Craft
i.m. James Plunkett

Everything was new
No. Everything was in tatters.
The old film centre falling
down around us.

I was new, up from College
seeking another life,
with a secret compulsive
desire to write.

Five or six people
round a table. Quiet.
The writer began to speak
in a kind aloof manner.

One woman wrote
a story about an artist's model.
'What am I as?'
she asked the painter
in his studio of a morning.

That moment you could sense
she had struck something.
'What am I as?' the writer nodded.
'Good question.'

Sheila Phelan

Cooking from the Recipe

I am a barely-ripe pear, waiting to be poached in red wine. Boiled, more like it, in crimson water with sugar, cloves, lemon peel, curled cinnamon sticks, and vanilla pods sliced open. You take a firm hold, scathing your blade over my apical ends, my rounded curves. Your thumb guides the edge over my soft, fleshy prone; up and down, up and down.

I'm laid on the cutting board, rolling a bit on the brown-speckled, seventies-style counter top you were too cheap to replace. You move the pot of spicy-sweet, wine-water from the heat then show me, what you called, a melon-baller. You demonstrate how it is to be used – on me, I'm assuming – with Hollywood cackles and rough thrusting motions. I wanted to say, 'I don't think it's supposed to be used that way, your melon-baller, and I'm not one for pleasure through pain.' But what could I do? I mean, I was the one on the cutting board, you had the baller and the recipe calls for it.

So, with your primitive tool, you tore open my fruit, dug down to my centre, my core. I screamed with your irreverent invasion, which, I was beginning to realise, you believed was an entitlement. I knew this was my end, as you scooped out my seeds in the hollow of your device – 2/3 to be exact.

After the wine was drained through a sieve, you threw me into an imitation China bowl and poured the boiling liquid all over my raw, shorn flesh. The memories of clove buds, stout sugarcane, and Madagascan vanilla permeated my pores, and slowly simmered everything I had lived for.

Lying limp on a plate, you tell me with sweaty excitement that I look delicious, and then serve me with a dollop of your own, homemade *crème fraiche*. But I forgot to tell you one thing: I've been rotting from the inside since you plucked me before ripe. *Bon appetite.*

Adrienne Anifant

Niamh Hehir

'The Perfect Narrative Nature of Blue': Memory and the Chora in Medbh McGuckian's *Marconi's Cottage*

Locating the Revolution in Poetry

In an interview with Rebecca E. Wilson, Medbh McGuckian remarked that, "I was brought up in Belfast. I wouldn't have been a poet, I don't think, if I had lived anywhere else. I don't write about 'The Troubles' but in 1968 the conflict did filter into me."[1] Medbh McGuckian's poetry emerges from a context of political conflict that has clearly had a profound influence on her work, but since McGuckian chooses not to write about 'the Troubles' directly, this influence is often implicit rather than explicit in her poetry. How, then, do we understand the filtering and internalisation of political events that affects McGuckian's poetry on such a fundamental level? The work of Julia Kristeva offers a means of identifying the effects of this implicit politicisation in McGuckian's work. In particular, Kristeva's concept of the semiotic and the chora offers a reading of McGuckian's poetry that reveals a fundamental political dimension; one that challenges the constructs of identity and community, which are central to the politics of Northern Ireland.

In *Revolution in Poetic Language*, Kristeva suggests that the political in language is not bound to an expression of a particular subject or theme, but may be embodied in the language structure of the text. Kristeva's understanding of the function of the semiotic in language identifies an act of revolution in the disruption of the symbolic order and the consequent dismantling of the logic that underscores this structure in language. In this respect, Kristeva suggests that, "In 'artistic' practices the semiotic – the precondition of the symbolic – is revealed as that which also destroys the symbolic, and this allows us to presume something about its functioning."[2] What we presume here is a protest against the symbolic order and an implied challenge to the ideology that supports this order: "In this respect modern poetic language goes further than any classical mimesis … because it attacks not only denotation (the positing of the object) but meaning (the positing of the enunciating subject) as well."[3] The intrusion of the semiotic within symbolic language, thus, becomes a revolt against both the structure and logic of symbolic language. Poetic language that includes this intrusion of the semiotic can be seen to "engage in an intra-ideological debate" that calls into question "the very principle of the ideological."[4] In Medbh

McGuckian's poetry, the political can be located at this fundamental level where language revolts against the logic of its own foundations. The symbolic is, thus, rejected as a representation of the ideologies that support and sustain the conflicts that create a divisive society. An analysis of McGuckian's use of memory, as a means of evoking the chora, in her collection *Marconi's Cottage* illustrates this political dimension as deeply embedded in McGuckian's poetry.

Approaching an analysis of the chora from the perspective of memory advances our understanding of both these concepts in language. In particular, we begin to appreciate the significance of the spatial dimension of memory and the implications of this space for our construction of identity and subjectivity. In this respect, the images of rooms and houses in McGuckian's work can be seen as spaces that contain memories and simultaneously exist as echoes of the first *house* of Kristeva's chora. Kristeva suggests this approach to memory in her analysis of both the temporal and spatial aspects of memory in Marcel Proust's, *A La Recherche du Temps Perdu*. Kristeva, thus, explores the "space of memory" and the concept of an "embodied time" in Proust's work.[5]

Kristeva also explores the relationship between memory and subjectivity with the suggestion that Proust "uses time as his intermediary in the search for an embodied imagination: that is to say, for a space where words and their dark, unconscious manifestations contribute to the weaving of the world's unbroken flesh, of which 'I' is a part."[6] In exploring this connection between memory, space and subjectivity in McGuckian's poetry, the chora, as a representation of the 'space of memory', becomes significant. In this analysis, the link between memory and the chora reveals a connection between both the function and the form of these elements in language. In this respect, the function of memory in a text offers a parallel to the process by which the semiotic operates in language. It is this connection between memory, space and subjectivity, and the chora as the manifestation of the 'world's unbroken flesh' that I explore in this analysis of memory and the chora in *Marconi's Cottage*.[7]

When considering this connection between memory and the chora, I was reminded of an excerpt from Virginia Woolf's diaries in which she describes memory as a 'tunnelling device' that she employed to *reveal* her characters when writing the novel *Mrs. Dalloway*.[8] There seemed to be an interesting connection here between Woolf's understanding of the function of memory and Kristeva's concept of the chora that offered a potential reading of the difficult issue of memory in Medbh McGuckian's poetry. I describe this as a difficult issue because of the context from which McGuckian's work emerges. Writing in the North of Ireland during 'the Troubles' would surely make one keenly aware of the potency of remembrance, reminiscence and nostalgia and the dangers of a sentimental approach to the past. It is interesting, then, to briefly compare the representation of memory in Seamus Heaney's collection *North* (1975) with McGuckian's approach to memory in *Marconi's Cottage* (1991).

In a climate where, as Heaney suggests, 'Whatever you Say, Say Nothing', it would be difficult to ignore the problems associated with memory, particularly if one attempts an articulation of a shared or communal memory.[9] The community envisaged in McGuckian's poetry differs greatly from that evoked in Seamus Heaney's work, and the contrasts here provide some interesting perspectives on the difficulty of articulating a shared line of prescribed memories from which any community derives its sense of identity. In this respect, we are reminded of McGuckian's warning in the poem 'Time-Words' that, "Saying we is dangerous" (5). Indeed, any study of the relationship between memory and identity would suggest that it is hard to evoke one without manipulating the other. This brings us to the connection between memory and subjectivity, which I explore in this analysis in terms of a historical or communal construction of identity. Again, the context of the North of Ireland lends an intense immediacy to the discussion of group identities and the construction of a sense of shared subjectivity. The community envisaged in McGuckian's poetry differs greatly from that evoked in Seamus Heaney's work, and the contrasts here provide some interesting perspectives on the difficulty of articulating a shared line of prescribed memories from which any community derives its sense of identity.

Memory, Caves and the Chora

Let us return, then, to Virginia Woolf's description of memory as a tunnelling device in literature. In her diaries, Woolf suggests that this application of memory allowed her to "dig out beautiful caves behind my characters."[10] This enabled Woolf to circumvent the restrictions of the single-day time-span she employs in *Mrs. Dalloway*, and to provide a space where another time could be referenced and contained. What is most interesting here is the spatial imagery Woolf offers in her description of the process of memory. In envisaging a space that accommodates the time shift implied in recollected memory, Woolf acknowledges the necessary connection between time and space that is central to our understanding of memory.[11] Woolf's choice of a 'cave' as the spatial aspect of memory, is evocative of Kristeva's chora and, of course, of Plato's cave from which Kristeva derives the term.[12] In this respect, the chora may be seen to represent the space of memory in McGuckian's poetry.

Both Kristeva and Woolf recognise a distinction between the linear model of time and the fluid and cyclical experience of *another* time, which Kristeva describes in 'Women's Time.' There is a clear connection between Woolf's distinction between historical and psychological time, that we find in *Mrs.Dalloway*, and Kristeva's discussion of the process of a different "modality of time" where "cycles, gestation, the eternal recurrence of a biological rhythm ... imposes a temporality" that shares a "regularity and unison with what is experienced as extra-subjective time."[13] Woolf's understanding of a duality in the function of time was influenced by the publication of *Time and Free Will* by Henri Bergson, which dealt with "the difference between historical time, which is external, linear, and measured in terms of the spatial distance travelled by a pendulum or the hands of a clock; and psychological time, which is internal, subjective, and measured by the relative emotional intensity of a moment."[14] Woolf's understanding of the function of memory as a disruption of the linear experience of time is echoed in Kristeva's description of memory as a series of 'revolutions' in Proust's work that emerge from his understanding of the impossibility of placing memories "in succession to one another."[15]

The process by which memory functions as a means of rupturing linear time suggests a metaphorical model for our understanding of the process by which the semiotic functions in language. Both memory and semiotic language are referenced by our experience of a past time and place; in the case of memory, a particular past event, and in the case of the semiotic, an evocation of our past experience of the chora. Through memory and the semiotic, these places, times and phases are temporarily re-visited by the process of creating a rupture, tunnel or break in the linear or symbolic continuum. These ruptures are contained as pockets of resistance to the structure of syntax in symbolic language and the linear progress of historical or chronological time. If we extend this analogy between memory and the chora, we reach a clearer understanding of how the semiotic functions and of the consequent effect on the linear order of symbolic language. In this analysis, syntax becomes the ordering force in language in the same way that historical time places a structure on the flux of psychological time. Kristeva suggests this imposition of order when she describes the process by which the semiotic is 'restrained' in language: "Indifferent to language, enigmatic and feminine, this space underlying the written is rhythmic, unfettered, irreducible to its intelligible verbal translation; it is musical, anterior to judgement, but restrained by a single guarantee: syntax."[16] This guarantee creates an order in language that contains the semiotic within a symbolic framework, in the same way that memory necessarily functions within a linear time-frame. The chora and the semiotic can thus be seen to function *like* a memory, but also *as* memories that impact on our understanding, not just of time, but also of space.

The Chora as an Embodied Space

It is worth thinking about the implications for our understanding of space in this analysis of the function of memory, the chora and the semiotic. When considering the impact of memory on the process of linear time, we must also consider the spatial dimensions of memory – if we understand memory to be an evocation of another time, must it not also involve the evocation of another space? In 'Women's Time', Kristeva begins her discussion of the question 'Which Time?' with a quotation from Joyce: 'Father's time, mother's species' and comments that "indeed when evoking the name and destiny of women, one thinks more of the *space* generating and forming the human species than of *time*, becoming or history."[17] Since we understand the chora in terms of space rather than time, this seems to suggest an association between the female body as the facilitator of the semiotic stage and the spatial dimension of the chora. Kristeva suggests this connection when she remarks that, "Located elsewhere, distant, permissive, always already past: such is the *chora* that the mother is called upon to produce with her child so that the semiotic disposition might exist."[18] If the mother is integral to the *production* of the chora, then the semiotic, as an evocation of the chora, offers the possibility of a gendered space in language. In Kristeva's use of the term 'embodied time', in relation to Proust's text, she suggests the body as the source of sensations that accompany our recollections of past times.[19] If we understand the chora to be an *embodied* space, could we not similarly suggest the existence of a physical memory of sensations that are located in the experience of the female body as the 'receptacle' of this experience of the chora? In this sense, the semiotic may be seen to create a space in language that is evocative of a female space in its ability to circumvent the structure of linear time and syntax, and in the shape and form of the space created as a cave/womb of creativity.[20]

The Chora as a Source of Creativity

Kristeva suggests that, "The chora is a modality of significance in which the linguistic sign is not yet articulated as the absence of an object and as the distinction between real and symbolic."[21] In this sense, the chora is characterised as an experience of unity with the mother that precedes our unawareness of our separation from others. In this state of unity we have, as yet, no experience of desire as 'the absence of an object', and, as such, have no need for the intermediate structure of language. Once we become aware of a separation between self and other and experience desire for an absent object, we enter the thetic phase that acts as a threshold between the semiotic and the symbolic stages in our development. Our experience of the thetic phase is necessary for our acquisition of language, providing as it does "the precondition of the difference between signifier and signified, denotation and connotation, language and referent; in effect the basis of all theses and antithesis, of all oppositions."[22]

What is significant is Kristeva's understanding of the semiotic as a continuing influence *after* our initiation into the symbolic or linguistic order. The semiotic in language is then identified by Kristeva as that which "underlies figuration and therefore specularization, and only admits analogy with vocal or kinetic rhythm."[23] Kristeva identifies poetic language as the place where we most often encounter the semiotic in language and, as such, she suggests that we "establish poetic language as the object of linguistics' attention."[24] How, then, can we characterise this relationship between the experience of the chora and the semiotic element in language, particularly in relation to poetic language? John Lechte suggests that the chora acts as "the locus of the drive activity underlying the semiotic."[25] In this analysis, the chora is identified as the source of the semiotic, and the origin of the elements in poetic language that resist the *logic* of symbolic language. The problem of translating the essence of the pre-linguistic chora into language then becomes a central element in our understanding of the process by which meaning is communicated in poetry. This suggests a kind of creative conundrum that is energised and sustained by the impossibility of its own solution – how can you talk about an experience that is marked by an absence of language? This is a problem that Kristeva encounters in her attempts to describe the chora. As Toril Moi suggests, this makes Kristeva "acutely aware of the contradictions involved in trying to theorize the untheorizable chora, a contradiction located at the centre of the semiotic enterprise."[26] This dilemma is significant as it situates Kristeva's analysis of literature within "a discourse which always confronts the impasse of language."[27] In applying Kristeva's theories to an analysis of Medbh McGuckian's poetry, then, we situate our analysis at this point of 'impasse in language.' In this respect, we understand the *dilemma* of McGuckian's poetry to be the search for a language capable of expressing our memory of this pre-linguistic experience of the chora.

Memory and the Chora in *Marconi's Cottage*

In turning to McGuckian's work, I will focus on poems from her collection, *Marconi's Cottage*. It is interesting to note the title of this collection and the reference to Marconi and his invention of the radio. Marconi's ability to create a means of wireless communication that travels via waves rather than tangible structures is significant here since this new approach to communication can be seen to represent a symbolic solution to the problem of communicating the experience of the pre-linguistic chora within a linguistic structure. As Clair Wills suggests, "Marconi's harnessing of electro-magnetic waves suggests a means of communicating between ... body and spirit, and from soul to soul" that can be read as a symbolic representation of McGuckian's efforts to forge new pathways of meaning in her poetry.[28]

When reading *Marconi's Cottage* one is struck by the repetition of images of rooms and houses that seem to resonate with echoes of Kristeva's chora.[29] One of the challenges in analysing McGuckian's poetry is to understand the significance of these structures. In Kristeva's analysis of Proust's work she notes that, "Memory is a cascade of spatial metaphors", which suggests a possible reading of the rooms and houses in McGuckian's poetry as visualisations of the spatial dimensions of memory.[30] If we imagine that these structures are connected to the chora and we understand the chora to be, as Miglena Nikolchina suggests, "the troubled source of the demiurgic activity", then these rooms and houses become the places from which McGuckian's poetry emerges; the source of her creativity.[31]

This description of the chora as the 'troubled source' of creativity is appropriate here. In evoking this experience of the chora in her work, McGuckian relies on a recognition of this experience on the part of the reader for this poetic project to succeed. If the reader fails to remember, then the evocations of the chora become a gesture towards an abstract transcendental space that has no actual resonance for the reader. McGuckian is aware of the possible risk of obscurity inherent in her endeavours to evoke the chora. In the poem 'East of Mozart', she acknowledges the possibility that her poetry may seem inaccessible to her reader: "In one corner of my room, a feeling/With no actual name in language,/Which perhaps does not exist except in me" (2-4). In the poem 'Sky-Writing', McGuckian suggests an awareness of this problem of obscurity that emerges from her decision to "forfeit the world outside/For the sake of my own inwardness" (13-14). It is, however, a project clearly worth the risk for McGuckian, and one that challenges the implied distinction between private and public by suggesting that if we pursue our own inwardness we may revisit the experience of the chora where no such distinctions exist.[32] McGuckian's descriptions of these rooms as places without language, suggests this connection with the chora. In 'The Rosary Dress', McGuckian says "there are no words, there are reds/In the farthest of my three rooms" (45-46). The problem of translating the experience of the pre-linguistic chora into language is apparent in poems like 'The Oval of a

Girl' where McGuckian struggles to articulate, "A kind of forlorn frenzy leaking over into sound/for whose unpronounceable blue I am an ear" (8-9).

The Chora as the Colour Blue

The use of colour in McGuckian's poetry may also be seen as an example of synaesthesia – in this case the conversion of colour into sound. This approach to colour is again evocative of the chora, where, according to Elizabeth Grosz, "The dual narcissistic and identificatory structure of imaginary relations is synaesthetic."[33] It is interesting to note here the significance Kristeva places on the colour blue in her analysis of painting in 'Giotto's Joy.' Here Kristeva suggests that "all colours, but blue in particular, would have a non-centered or decentering effect, lessening both object identification and phenomenal fixation. They thereby return the subject to the archaic moment of its dialectic, that is, before the fixed, specular 'I'."[34] In the poem 'Breaking the Blue', McGuckian suggests a similar understanding of blue as evocative of a place before "the fixed specular 'I'", when she suggests that the introduction of subjectivity, in this case 'You', will destroy the *decentering* effect of blue: "Deluged with the dustless air, unspeaking likeness:/You, who were the spaces between words in the act of reading,/A colour sown on to colour, break the blue" (1-3).

In this sense, blue becomes evocative of the chora, and the source of the sound McGuckian wishes to articulate in her poetry. A similar tendency towards representations of blue is evident in the work of Ruth Carr, another poet writing in the North of Ireland. In a recent interview with Rebecca Pelan, Carr suggests that, "I would see it as a blue – of nature, of the sky over everybody – and blue as trying to escape those binaries."[35] McGuckian makes a similar connection with blue and the sky in the poem 'The Invalid's Echo', where she also implies a link with memory, in this case an experience of blue as a moment of forgetting: "That having forgotten/Everything he will imagine the sky/In its second appearance as/ The quintessence of blue" (51-54). As a place of escape from binaries, the sky as "the quintessence of blue", is evocative of the chora. In this sense, the sky becomes representative of a transcendental space above and beyond the binaries that divide and structure our everyday realities. It is interesting to note Virginia Woolf's use of the sky in *Mrs. Dalloway* as a point of triangulation between different subject positions, which allows her to switch from one character narrative to another. In one particular sequence, Woolf describes the effect of a sky-writing aeroplane on the crowds in and around Regent Park: "All down the mall people were standing and looking up at the sky. As they looked the whole world became perfectly silent."[36] In the poem 'Sky-Writing', McGuckian seems to suggest sky-writing as an image for what she aspires to in her poetry. The poem ends with the plaintive question, "Shall I ever again be caught up gently/As the rustle of a written address by the sky?" (23-24).

In the poem 'Swallow's Wood, Glenshesk', McGuckian writes, "We do so need a blue sky" (19). It is interesting to look, then, at what the blue sky represents for McGuckian, and why it is important that her poetry *emerges* from blue. In the poem 'The Unplayed Rosalind', McGuckian offers a possible answer to this question:

> I have lived on a war footing and slept
> On the blue revolution of my sword;
> Given the perfect narrative nature of blue,
> I have been the poet of women and consequently
> Of the young; if you burned my letters
> In the soiled autumn they would form two hearts. (14-19)

The "perfect narrative nature of blue" offers a moment of neutrality in its association with the sky and in its evocation of the chora. As a source of creativity, blue becomes the colour of the chora, the point of poetic origin, which, as McGuckian suggests in the poem 'Turning the Moon into a Verb', represents "the experience/when the sky becomes a womb" (20-21).

The Chora as a House Without Subjects

The experience of the chora can be linked to the room/house image in McGuckian's poetry where, as she states in 'The Carrying Ring', "The conceived or recollected/Room is the beginning of life" (5-6). This structure is described as a kind of past utopia in the poem 'Journal In Time', where McGuckian reasserts the connection between the house and the chora: "As a child's first and most satisfying/house where everyone is repeated in everyone else" (22-23). In this respect, the chora exists as an image of unity and satisfaction that precedes our initiation into the symbolic or linguistic order. McGuckian's work evokes this experience of the chora as a place before separation, distinction, and the development of the kind of identities that divide and structure our adult communities. It is a place where even our own identity and subjectivity remains un-constituted, a place where, according to Kristeva, "the subject is both generated and negated."[37]

In *Marconi's Cottage* there are repeated examples of a fluid and unfixed subjectivity. This experience of fluid subjectivity is described in poems like 'The Cloth Mother', where the speaker shifts from one subject position to another: "Later, I played I was my own daughter for a year" (10). In 'On Her Second Birthday', McGuckian reminds us that we originated in the chora where there is no fixed subjectivity: "In the beginning I was no more/than a rising and falling mist" (1-3). The ability to release ourselves from the bind of a fixed subject position becomes more than a gesture of empathy in this poem and is seen to be an essential aspect of our ability to understand the world:

> It seems as though
> To explain the shape of the world
> We must fall apart,
> Throw ourselves upon the world,
> Slip away from ourselves
> Through the world's inner road,
> Whose atoms make us weary. (10-16)

By evoking this memory of fluid subjectivity and, also, suggesting that we may revisit this state within the symbolic structure, McGuckian challenges our perception of subjectivity as a fixed and unyielding construct. This aspect of our memory of the chora provides a startling contrast to the divided and identity-orientated reality of the society McGuckian experiences in the North of Ireland. In this sense, McGuckian's evocation of the chora as the original experience of unity with another, challenges our allegiance to the fixed code of subjectivities that underpin the fractured and inflexible nature of community in Northern Ireland.

Memory in Seamus Heaney's *North*

It is interesting here to briefly contrast the nature of the memories evoked in McGuckian's poetry with the representations of memory we find in the work of Seamus Heaney. Again, the context of the North weighs heavily on the burden of offering a speaking position that articulates the memory of a collective past. In his collection *North*, Heaney attempts a kind of archaeology of shared tribal memories as a means of indirect commentary on the politics of Northern Ireland. This brings to mind Annette Kuhn's observation that, "Telling stories about the past, our past, is a key moment in the making of our selves."[38] In *North*, Heaney endeavours to capture this key moment that makes a connection between the past and the construction of a present-day tribal or communal identity. The image he employs to create this connection is of the perfectly preserved corpses found during excavations of the bogs in Denmark. In this sense, the bog comes to represent the depths of racial memory, and the bodies found preserved within become the relics of communal memory.

Heaney suggests in the poem 'North', that memory offers a means of "incubating the spilled blood" (28). In this sense, memory allows Heaney to find a continuum that recreates community, sacrifice and revenge as the emblems of identity. Memory, then, acts like a bog, capable of preserving the victims of violence and providing shelter from the amnesia of time. The idea that the victims will not be forgotten becomes a source of comfort in the 'Grauballe Man', when Heaney writes, "But now he lies/perfected in my memory" (37-38). Here, the corpse becomes a symbol for the existence of this continuum, guaranteed by memory that connects us to past communities and past conflicts. By the close of this poem, the Grauballe man's corpse becomes loaded "with the actual weight/of each hooded victim/slashed and dumped" (46-48). In creating this association between past and present victims, Heaney suggests the existence of a pattern of violence in society that is an inevitable and, perhaps, necessary aspect of the community that, as Elmer Andrews suggests, may even offer "the possibility of renewal resulting from violence."[39] In the poem 'Punishment', Heaney implies an almost genetic communal propensity for violence when he suggests that, despite declarations of "civilised outrage", we are able to "understand the exact/and tribal, intimate revenge" (42-44). The memories Heaney evokes are tribal in nature, representing a collective history of community that reflects and repeats the experience of community in the North. In this respect, memory preserves and confirms our sense of community and the idioms of identity that are capable of inciting a community to violence.

Conclusion

Both Heaney and McGuckian access memory as a means of locating origins, of finding the bedrock of a shared past that makes sense of the present. The contrast in their frames of reference provides an interesting commentary on the approach to the concept of community in the work of these two poets. McGuckian returns to the first stage of our psychological development, while Heaney looks to a historical past to derive his sense of community. In both cases, the past is an imagined place, impossible to confirm, that is moulded by our experience of present-day reality. In *North*, the past offers Heaney the possibility that violence is not specific and futile, but that it is part of a pattern of existence that communities are bound to repeat. In McGuckian's work, this shared past is a time before language, separation and difference, and the necessity of articulating the nuances of a particular community and the idiomatic language of identity.

We begin to appreciate the political dimension of this evocation of the chora in McGuckian's poetry within the context of Kristeva's understanding of the destructive power of the semiotic in language. Kristeva's exploration of the nature of revolt in poetic language, from *Revolution in Poetic Language* to *The Sense and Non-Sense of Revolt*, challenges our limited definition of what constitutes the political in poetry. In redefining our understanding of the term 'revolt', Kristeva endeavours to "wrest it, etymologically, from the overtly narrow political sense it has taken in our time."[40] It is interesting, then, to consider the alternative definition of the word revolution: "a movement in or as if in a circle."[41] This circular motion is significant in that it differs from the trajectory of linear motion by virtue of its containment within a given space. Is this circular space of revolution, then, evocative of the chora? In the poem 'The Unplayed Rosalind', McGuckian talks about "the blue revolution of my sword" (15), a description that combines the blue of the chora with the circular motion and political dimension of revolution. So much in language is linear, that the insertion of a circular spatial dimension, through an evocation of the chora and the cave of memory in a text, may thus be seen to constitute an act of implicit revolution.

In this context, we understand McGuckian's approach to language and meaning in her poetry, which is often described as difficult and obscure, to be a revolt against symbolic language and the ideologies that it represents. If the thetic phase introduces the "precondition of difference" as "the basis of all thesis and antithesis", then the semiotic counters this reliance on a structure of binary oppositions with a recognition of the unifying potential of our common experience of the chora.[42] In this respect, Kristeva's observation that Roland Barthes work contains a "negativity that works against the transparency of language and the symbolic function in general" may be similarly applied to a reading of McGuckian's poetry.[43] As Kimberly S. Bohman suggests: "Though she [McGuckian] may appear obscure, the virtue of her form is the subversion of the conventional comfort level of how to read poetry."[44] The *subversion* Bohman identifies here represents a political dimension, often overlooked in McGuckian's poetry, that challenges the fundamental structures at the core of symbolic language. In this respect, McGuckian's evocation of the chora represents a central aspect of this positing of alternatives that constitutes the political in her poetry.

In the context of the North, McGuckian's refusal to confirm the divisions and distinctions that denote identity and subjectivity becomes a gesture towards universality, a desire to find a 'common ground.' In the poem 'Almond', McGuckian suggests the route we might take to achieve this:

> To follow the road
> On which we lose the power

>   Of explaining ourselves
>   Back ever more deeply
>   Is to mix in the earth
>   Or soil as a ferment
>   To redissolve the hazards
>   Of our own growth
>   Like the very flower of matter
>   Woven into the common ground. (40-49)

The experience of the chora offers McGuckian a representation of this 'common ground.' Significantly, this is an experience characterised by an absence of subjectivity, which precedes our separation into distinct individual and communal groupings. McGuckian's poetry may, thus, be seen to offer us the sanctuary of an undifferentiated place. In this sense, McGuckian uses memory in her poetry to remind us of the chora and what she describes in the poem 'Marconi's Cottage', as the experience of, "A pure clear place of no particular childhood" (2). The power of this evocation lies in its ability to suggest the existence of a common origin that might dissolve differences by offering a new perspective on identity, subjectivity and community. In the poem 'In the Rainshadow', McGuckian expresses this desire to unite through a recollection of our shared memory of the chora when she suggests the existence of place, "At the deepest moral note where people/Can still press together/What they both remember/Till it joins" (58-61).

Notes

1. Rebecca E Wilson, *Sleeping With Monsters: Conversations with Scottish and Irish Women Poets* (Dublin: Wolfhound Press, 1990), 2.
2. Julia Kristeva, 'Revolution on Poetic Language' in *The Kristeva Reader*. Toril Moi, ed. (New York: Columbia UP, 1986), 103.
3. *ibid*, 109.
4. *ibid*, 112.
5. Julia Kristeva, *Proust and The Sense of Time* (London: Faber and Faber, 1988), 6 & 24
6. *ibid*, 5.
7. Medbh McGuckian, *Marconi's Cottage* (Oldcastle: The Gallery Press, 1991). All future in-text references to McGuckian's poetry refer to this edition.
8. Virginia Woolf, *A Writer's Diary: Being Extracts from Virginia Woolf* (London: Hogarth Press, 1953), 263.
9. Seamus Heaney, *New Selected Poems 1966-1987* (London: Faber and Faber, 1990), 78. All future in-text references to Heaney's poetry refer to this edition.
10. Virginia Woolf, *A Writer's Diary: Being Extracts from Virginia Woolf* (London: Hogarth Press, 1953), 263.
11. Virginia Woolf's understanding of the relationship between time and space indicates her awareness of advancements in scientific thought. In her book *Open*

Fields: Science in Cultural Encounter (Oxford UP, 1996), Gillian Beer explores the influence of science on Woolf's writings and concludes that, "ways of viewing the world are not constructed separately by scientists and poets; they share the moment's discourse", 171.

12 Julia Kristeva, *Desire in Language* (Oxford: Blackwell Press, 1989), 133. "Plato's Timeus speaks of a chora, receptacle, unnamable, improbable, hybrid, anterior to naming, to the One, to the father, and consequently, maternally connoted to such an extent that it merits 'not even the rank of syllable.'"

13 Julia Kristeva, 'Women's Time' in *The Kristeva Reader*. Toril Moi, ed. (Oxford: Blackwell Press, 1986), 191.

14 Elaine Showalter, 'Introduction to Mrs. Dalloway' in Virginia Woolf, *Mrs Dalloway*. (London: Penguin Books 1992), xx.

15 Julia Kristeva, *Proust and The Sense of Time* (London: Faber & Faber, 1988), 23.

16 Julia Kristeva, 'Revolution in Poetic Language' in *The Kristeva Reader*. Toril Moi, ed. (Oxford: Blackwell Press, 1986), 97.

17 Julia Kristeva, 'Women's Time' in *The Kristeva Reader*. Toril Moi, ed. (Oxford: Blackwell Press, 1986), 190.

18 Julia Kristeva. *Desire in Language* (Oxford: Blackwell Press, 1989), 286.

19 Julia Kristeva, *Proust and The Sense of Time* (London: Faber & Faber, 1988), 24.

20 The question of the existence of a gendered form of writing or the semiotic as a gendered space in writing cannot be fully explored here. For an expanded discussion of this subject see Noelle McAfee's recent publication, *Julia Kristeva* (Routledge, 2004).

21 Julia Kristeva, 'Revolution in Poetic Language' in *The Kristeva Reader*. Toril Moi, ed. (Oxford: Blackwell Press, 1986), 94.

22 John Lechte, *Julia Kristeva* (London & New York: Routledge Press, 1990), 135.

23 Julia Kristeva, *Revolution in Poetic Language*. Trans. Margaret Waller. (New York: Columbia UP, 1984), 24.

24 Julia Kristeva. *Desire in Language* (Oxford: Blackwell Press, 1989), 25.

25 John Lechte, *Julia Kristeva*. (London & New York: Routledge Press, 1990), 129.

26 Toril Moi, ed. *The Kristeva Reader*. (Oxford: Blackwell Press, 1986), 13.

27 *ibid*, 10

28 Clair Wills, *Improprieties: Politics and Sexuality in Northern Irish Poetry* (Oxford: Claredon Press, 1993), 185.

29 Indeed, of the 60 poems in this collection, 46 contain references to rooms or houses and of the 14 that don't, 6 describe implied rooms with their references to windows and doors.

30 Julia Kristeva, *Proust and The Sense of Time* (London: Faber and Faber, 1988), 48.

31 Miglena Nikolchina, 'The Lost Territory: Parables Of Exile In Julia Kristeva' in *The Kristeva Critical Reader*. John Lechte and Mary Zournazi, eds. (Edinburgh: Edinburgh UP, 2003), 164.

32 This poetic journey inwards is not exclusive to McGuckian's poetry and was seen, for example, to be a defining characteristic of Symbolist poetry. Edmund Wilson suggests a similar risk of obscurity in this endeavour: "Symbolism, indeed, sometimes had the result of making poetry so much a private concern of the poet's that it turned out to be incommunicable to the reader." Edmund Wilson, *Axel's Castle* (Great Britain: Collins Fontana Press, 1959), 23.

33 Elizabeth Grosz, *Jacques Lacan: A Feminist Introduction*. (London and New York: Routledge, 1990), 158.

34   Julia Kristeva, 'Giotto's Joy' in *Desire in Language*. (Oxford: Blackwell Press, 1980), 225.
35   Rebecca Pelan, Unpublished Interview with Ruth Carr. Cited with approval of Pelan and Carr.
36   Virginia Woolf, *Mrs. Dalloway* (London: Penguin Books, 1992), 21.
37   Julia Kristeva, 'Revolution in Poetic Language' in *The Kristeva Reader*. Toril Moi, ed. (Oxford: Blackwell Press, 1986), 95.
38   Annette Kuhn, *Family Secrets: Acts of Memory and Imagination* (London & New York: Verso, 2002), 2.
39   Elmer Andrews, *The Poetry of Seamus Heaney* (New York: Columbia UP, 1998), 109.
40   Kristeva, Julia, *The Sense and Non-sense of Revolt*. Trans. J.Herman, (New York: Columbia UP, 2000), 3.
41   William T. McLeod, *The New Collins Dictionary and Thesaurus* (Glasgow: HarperCollins, 1991), 857.
42   John Lechte, *Julia Kristeva* (London & New York: Routledge Press, 1990), 135.
43   Julia Kristeva, *The Sense and Non-Sense of Revolt*. Trans. J.Herman, (New York: Columbia UP, 2000), 210-211.
44   Kimberly S. Bohman, 'Borders or Frontiers: Gender Roles and Gender Politics in Medbh McGuckian's Unconscious Realm.' *Irish Journal of Feminist Studies* (Spring 1996): 120.

Little Paper Bag of Sweeties

From the very beginning,
I wouldn't listen to her:
she liked to feel cottontail clean;
she didn't like the bleachy smell;
she hated the hungry things he said:

"You can do better than that, little lady!"
Like a horizontal John Wayne impressionist,
he would urge her on, his pointed tongue stuck sideways
between his rodent teeth.
"Come on, little lady …
Swallow me up! Swallow me up!"

But, I wouldn't listen to her
or her whimpering;
I was a grown woman, and she was just a
skinny, freckle-faced virgin I'd left
at a Pendle Hill party sometime
back in January 1975.

"If I'm going to survive this plastic cup
of homemade *sake* called adult life,
I mustn't listen
to you anymore!" I warned her.
Sometimes, I let her cry when the porch lights were off.
"Shhh!" I would threaten her,
her pale face like a pasty moon,
flat and half transparent in the dark …
"This will just have to be

our little secret."

Philomena van Rijswijk

Hanna Herzog and Agate Krauss

Women's Knowledge: A Resource and Policy Research Centre as a Lever for Discursive Change

This paper provides an analysis of women's knowledge production in a knowledge-based society. It uses the Resource and Policy Research Centre of the Israel Women's Network (IWN) as a case study of convergence between research activities and social activism.[1]

The Resource and Policy Research Centre (RPRC) was established within the framework of the Israel Women's Network (IWN) in 1996.[2] The founding of the Centre, in which feminist researchers from diverse disciplines, as well as professional women and feminist activists in various public spheres, were involved, enabled the creation of another locus of influence in the feminist struggle for social change in Israel. The establishment of the RPRC was an additional step in broadening and deepening IWN activities with the aim of producing new knowledge in order to constitute social publics and promote social advocacy for new social agendas and policies. Although we see the Israeli experience as part of a larger change in patterns of citizens' involvement in governance and the introduction of new policies emerging from citizen-based knowledge, our focus is on feminist knowledge and politics.

An analysis of the Israeli case demonstrates how changes that take place in the world are adopted and assimilated in local practices. The RPRC is situated at a junction where changes in concepts of knowledge sources, particularly feminist knowledge sources, intersect; for example, changes in the concept of ways of governance and forms of civic participation, especially of women in today's society. The nomenclature used to describe the current society varies according to the theoretical emphasis of researchers, hence it is variously labelled a post-industrial, post-modern, high-risk, global, information based, network society, and of late, a knowledge-based society.[3] Naturally, it is impossible to discuss at length each of these terms and processes within the limits of one article, particularly in light of the broad and complex discussion existing in the literature.[4] However, a common thread of these analyses is the collapse or gradual dissolution of traditional social arrangements and social categories.

Our discussion will focus on the main tendencies underlying the project of creating knowledge within the Israel Women's Network, particularly the basis for the RPRC's growth and the basic ideas which guide its work. Our main claim is that the RPRC is an attempt to develop feminist knowledge and feminist politics in an era of continuous processes of the dissolution of boundaries, dividing of identities, and decentralisation of power and knowledge sources. We claim that the RPRC, as a think tank forum, strives to act as an institutional site for the creation of transversal knowledge and politics.

Feminist Production of Knowledge: Call for Change
Feminist critiques, Black and Ethnic Studies, and postcolonial conceptions maintain that social knowledge based on hegemonic science ignores the life experience of powerless and marginalised groups, including women.[5] According to this argument, the concept of 'human' grounded in hegemonic science has been perceived as abstract, universal, and neutral. As an abstract, universal and neutral hu-man supposedly represents all individuals, regardless of race or gender. Yet, in practice, the generalisations pertaining to 'hu-man' represent the experience of the male, white, bourgeois human being while ignoring gender, class, racial, and other differences, and their way of viewing, experiencing, and reconstructing social realities.[6] Feminist and other radical critiques call, not only for a discovery of 'others', but for the 'others' to express a voice of their own. It is a call for a reflexive and critical production of knowledge.

Since Simone de Beauvoir coined the term 'Woman, The Other' in *The Second Sex*[7] (1949), Women's Studies has developed this idea in conjunction with other critical schools, such as race/ethnic-based feminisms, postcolonial, and postmodernist theories. In myriad ways these critiques determine that the social order is no longer conceived as natural or universal but, rather, as socially constructed and as time, position, and culture context-dependent.

The different insights gained from women's life experiences and from their designated social positioning based on dominant social arrangements – known as women's knowledge – are widely accepted in feminist writings, though at the same time intensively discussed and debated.[8] Much recent feminist writing agrees that a woman cannot be represented as simply a matter of bodily difference, nor as a social position or an ontological basis of community. As women are located in every class, race, culture, and sexuality, they vary in their positionings and standpoints.[9] These multiple locations vary and negate each other as women find themselves subjected to men's domination, but, at the same time, sub/dominating (by) other women. In light of the multiple positioning of women and the compound production of situated knowledge, the possibility of developing a Feminist knowledge and a Feminist politics (with capital letter) that applies to all women is questioned, or as Yuval-Davis asks, "Are effective politics and adequate theoretical analysis inherently contradictory?"[10] The answer is no. Using feminist imaginations, like the title of Bell's book and paraphrases on it, many women's scholars and activists are suggesting alternative ways to conduct politics in ambivalent, conflictive, and changing situations.[11] In a departure from the premise that knowledge produced from specific positioning is never complete,[12] the need for dialogue between knowledge producers is emphasised.[13] Knowledge production is shifted to 'the social.'

Feminist imaginations search for new tools and venues for political activities such as *ad hoc* coalition politics suggested by Young,[14] creating "epistemic communities" in line with Assiter's notion that subjects from differential positionings and identities share the same values,[15] and transversal politics suggested by Yuval-Davis.[16] The common denominator of these perceptions is the focus on a dialogue that makes it possible to transcend the differential positionings and identities that lead beyond situational differences: "While situatedness is always embodied and multiple, the dialogical process usually involves only those dimensions of the specific situatedness that are considered/imagined to be the most relevant to it and to the politics involved."[17] It is, thus, possible to avoid essentialising woman as a social category and, at the same time, to develop identity politics, deconstruct social identities, and create a social agenda based on cultural politics of social tolerance and difference.[18] By adopting *ad hoc* 'strategic essentialism', to paraphrase Spivak's[19] term, transversal politics seeks to develop a bridge to enable women to work together. Yuval-Davis[20] emphasises that transversal politics, based on dialogue, "does not assume that the dialogue is boundariless, and that each conflict of interest is reconcilable. However, the boundaries of such a dialogue are determined by the message, rather than the messenger."[21]

These perceptions coincide with those on the essence of power and ways of governance in the postmodern society, particularly with the nature and role of knowledge in such a society, which is now frequently referred to as a knowledge-based society.[22]

Knowledge is Power: From Government to Governance in a Knowledge-based Society

Among the characteristics of the postmodern society are globalisation, accelerated growth of economic networks and of communications, global migration of work and capital, the decline of the nation-state, the sprouting of new categories of identity, and the rise of new topics on the daily agenda.

Common to them all is the crossing of social boundaries and institutionalised social categories. Here, too, the emphasis is on 'the social.'

One of the important shifts to 'the social' is marked by the transformation from 'government' to 'governance.' As Foucault argues, power is not simply located in the state, but rather in social relations and, as such, it permeates into the social.[23] While governing suggests the management of society by the state, governance means that social actions are structured by discursive strategies. Determining the rules of the discourse lies at the foundation of power. Power resides in social relations and is shaped in particular discursive contexts. Foucault used the equation power/knowledge primarily to deconstruct the disciplinary power of institutions, mainly state institutions. This is not surprising, since he analysed the forms of power in the modern era, when the state was the most powerful political power and social regulator.

However, with the transition to the postmodern era we are witness to the rise of new patterns of political activity and a decline in the power of the state.[24] Foucault's ideas that subversion, resistance, and an alternative 'gaze' are forms of power that reside in society provided the foundation for a concept of the postmodern society. These ideas have been taken far by feminist groups, which developed what Castoriadis calls the "radical imaginary"[25] and what Delanty[26] calls "the radical discourses of creativity, reflexivity and discursivity"[27] (also, see discussion above). By localising, fragmentising, and dissolving given dominant social categories, and transversing others, feminists have been expanding the discursive and democratic spaces.[28]

The substitution of the old term 'government' with 'governance' is not just a language game; it reflects changes taking place in governing modes and culture. Whereas 'governing' assumes control of knowledge and the existence of hierarchic, top-bottom political arrangements, 'governance' stresses multi-focal changing political processes and the various sources of knowledge. New forms of relationship between the state and non/citizens emerge.[29]

Social actors are guided by a multitude of interests, sometimes conflicting, and by an awareness that is not organised or coordinated in a coherent, unified manner. The social differentiation into political categories is fluid in itself and enables more organisations, divisions, and inner conflicts, as well as greater simultaneousness. This is a crowded and ongoing political arena with many participants and positions, as well as politics from below and sub-politics.[30] Such a description suits Castells diagnosis of a network society in which social relations are increasingly shaped by the flow of information.[31]

The diffusion of information technology thrusts economic production into the political domain of power and into the sphere of experience and identity. Access to information exchange, cultural codes, and symbols is at the heart of power. Delanty, though, accepts Castells' analysis of the information society and suggests the use of the term "knowledge society."[32]

> Knowledge is a wider category and pertains to experience, communication and identity; it is primarily social and has many levels, ranging from everyday knowledge to scientific knowledge. The important point is that, as a cognitive practice, knowledge is also a form of experience and is, therefore, a medium of cultural reproduction. Knowledge is manifested in the three levels of information, communication, and reflexivity.[33]

The concept of a knowledge-based society suggests a multi-actor arena where different players contest, discuss, and dialogue over the cultural model of society itself, and address the discourses around the debated issues.

Some criticise these developments, claiming a loss of solidarity[34] and social responsibility, though others deliberately emphasise the option of building trust and solidarity. Different groups are taking part in rebuilding the political dialogue. At the heart of this discussion is the creation of knowledge and its introduction into the public dialogue and into the consciousness of decision-makers. Not only is feminist thinking, like many feminist practices of the third wave of feminism (during the 1980s and until today), an inseparable part of postmodern being, but, in many cases of Women's Studies, the feminist dialogue, as discussed above, and practices of creating knowledge have preceded the theoretical analyses of the postmodern society. Reflexivity, discursivity, and creativity have become the basis of modern feminist thinking. Therefore, in a sense, as Delanty notes, feminism played a central role in creating the concept of a knowledge-based society.[35]

The alternative view of governing modes, concomitant with the alternate view of knowledge sources and the assumption that research and knowledge areas (including the social sciences) must contribute significantly to the general welfare of societies and to the quality of life of citizens as individuals and groups, leads to the conclusion that this contribution is only possible through the creation of a dialogue between these groups and the State, and among these groups themselves. The dialogue must also include the inputs of citizens in producing knowledge about themselves and their needs. We suggest that think tanks are one of the many social sites that enable such dialogue to take place.

Think Tanks: Institutional Setting for Creating Dialogue Knowledge

The study of think tanks has only recently begun to develop, though it is not developing at nearly the same pace as the phenomenon itself in the public arena.[36] Existing literature has difficulty defining the phenomenon. The term was borrowed from the military jargon of World War II for strategic planning, was broadened in the 1960s and '70s to include private research groups or groups partly associated with government and public bodies that dealt with policy analysis, and, during the last two decades of the twentieth century, became a lively arena with a strong orientation of advocacy for groups of independent civil organisations not reliant on government or on economic organisations. Today, the category of think tanks subsumes a multiplicity of organisations, varying in size, organisational character, goals, level of independence, and innovativeness aspired to.[37]

Think tanks are committed, in many cases, to producing applied knowledge geared toward policy and social change. Unlike academic institutions, which declaratively avoid normative claims, think tank studies directly address normative issues. They consider knowledge as mediating between social structure and individual and social agencies. Think tanks are meant to operate on the borderlines of ideas, existing political situations, social occurrences, and social change. They are concerned with ideas and concepts which underlie policy, and they question conventional wisdom. They often operate through a network of researchers from academia who are willing to participate in the 'real' world. Many think tanks act as a bridge between academia and decision- makers, while concomitantly playing a central role in interpreting studies and disseminating them worldwide. They bring the result of social research to the world at large by diversified means, such as reports, conferences, seminars for the general public, and policy papers.[38]

In a knowledge-based society, think tanks open space for a radical reflexivity in the contemporary culture of multiple, unstable interlocking identities and politics. One of many 'spaces' is cyberspace. It does not take a great deal of surfing on the Web to discover that there are hundreds of sites that exist or report their activities on the Internet. Among these sites women's networks and/or networks dealing with women's issues constitute a significant presence. This is certainly a phenomenon of the information society. However, it is not only a matter of creating and transferring information; great emphasis is placed on knowledge as a cognitive practice and on the social process of creating knowledge as an ongoing dialogue and practice for social change. In this manner, the Demos site, for example, defines itself as a think tank designed to be used as a virtual meeting place for "researchers, thinkers, and practitioners ... [a] greenhouse for new ideas, open resources of knowledge and learning that operates beyond traditional parties, identities and disciplines."[39]

As such, think tanks create social sites for constructing an epistemic community with strong social responsibility. This epistemic community is comprised of experts and social activists who are collectively connected through common ideas and values and whose aim is to translate their belief system into policy and public programmes, which, in effect, constitute political projects. To gain and consolidate political influence, the epistemic community requires the cooperation of issue networks, advocacy coalitions, and political communities. In the coming pages, we shall analyse the work of the Resource and Policy Research Centre (RPRC) of the Israel Women's Network and show how the Centre strives to promote feminist politics by creating women's knowledge while contending with the challenges that a diverse, often disputatious, multi-identity society presents.

Some Remarks on Feminist Dialogues in Israel

From its very inception, even before the establishment of the state, the feminist movement in Israel was forced to deal with delegitimising processes and the demand for national mobilisation and the closing of ranks. Later feminist organisations have continued to cope with the unremitting demand for nationwide enlistment and the insistence that 'particularist' claims be deferred in light of the Palestinian-Israeli conflict.[40] Yet, notwithstanding the difficulties facing women in Israel, a lively feminist dialogue exists in the country.

Since the late 1970s, but more emphatically in the past decade, there has been an outburst of voices: secular and religious women, Mizrahi women, Palestinian women living in Israel, lesbians, single mothers, mothers of soldiers, women with political views from the right and left, such as Women in Black (on the left), Women in Green (on the right), liberal, Marxist, and radical feminists, as well as women who consider gender an essentialist social category and others who see it as a socially constructed category. All these voices are involved in the public political discourse, some loudly, some whispered, and others in deafening silence.[41]

The logic of feminist thinking, which is widely accepted in Israeli feminisms, rules out the possibility of delegitimising any of that choir of voices. If gender is a result of power-oriented social construction, then any concept of a single, all-inclusive gendered identity must contain a coercive element. Attempts to describe this identity and to act in its name are defined as power-driven, normalising, and exclusionary. Attempts to speak in the name of 'The Women' have been negated in Israel as they have in many global discourses. As a result, feminist politics in Israel, as in many other places, searches for alternative forms of organisation. Examples are the *modus operandi* of the Women's Network (see later discussion); Women in Black, which agreed on a single slogan, 'End the Occupation', and refused to debate other feminist issues;[42] or other attempts to set up an *ad hoc* coalition (like Icar, an international coalition of women's organisation that struggles for solution for agunot – chained women (women who cannot be divorced according to Jewish religious law because of their husbands' refusal).

The feminist voice is growing ever more diverse, preventing the formation of a uniform feminist identity that can unite women around it and crystallise into a single political force. The multi-vocal, non-unified participation of feminist organisations in the formal, institutionalised political arena leaves feminist women's organisations outside the power centres of decision-makers. Within this fragmented, conflictual, and competitive social arena, the RPRC, as a think tank forum, strives to serve as an institutional site for the creation of transversal knowledge and politics.[43]

The Israel Women's Network as an Example of a Policy Oriented Knowledge Production Organisation

The Israel Women's Network (IWN) is a civil organisation that aims to promote policy furthering women's equality. The network seeks to combine advocacy for legislation and policy with the creation of new critical knowledge as the basis for policy, as well as initiatives to engender change. At the same time, in contrast to think tanks that function *vis-à-vis* an amorphous public, the IWN aims to create socially conscious publics and mobilise them to advance newly generated ideas. As members of a feminist women's movement, IWN members engage in a continuous dialogue among themselves, while IWN as an organisation is in dialogue with similar bodies worldwide. Though absorbing ideas from the international community, much of IWN's knowledge production is situated in the Israeli context and derives from women's experiences there. As such, women's knowledge can be described as 'glocal' (global+local) knowledge. It draws on and is influenced by feminist ideas originating in different parts of the world but, at the same time, is anchored in the unique reality of Israel – a nation-state that has no separation of religion and state and in which a multiplicity of ethnic and national groups live in the shadow of the ongoing Israeli-Palestinian conflict – all of which influence the status of women in Israel.[44]

The IWN was established in 1984 as an independent and non-partisan organisation for social change, more specifically with the aim of enhancing women's status through parliamentary lobbying, legislation, raising public awareness, education, and research. IWN members and activists hold diverse political and religious outlooks,[45] but are united in their determination to promote the status of women so that Israel will become an egalitarian state for all its citizens, irrespective of gender.[46] The IWN's Resource and Policy Research Centre functions as a think tank. From its inception, the IWN aimed to build a new body of knowledge of and about women in Israel. It should be noted that among its founders are a large representation of women from academia who chose not to remain in the 'ivory tower' but to become involved in processes of social change.[47] At the time, none of the Israeli universities had Women's Studies or Gender Studies programmes.[48] The influence an organisation such as the IWN can exert, and the effectiveness of its activities, depend in large measure on its level of independence. Based on three principles, this autonomy accords the organisation its legitimacy and influence:[49]

1. Political independence with the aim of cultivating the IWN's identity as an organisation striving to serve the public interest. For example, avoiding involvement in political party intrigues or identification with sector or party interests, apart from a total commitment to an agenda of women's needs.
2. Autonomy in the intellectual-research sphere. The IWN's internal agenda is dictated solely by the feminist epistemic communities created around each issue that is addressed in the think-tank activity.
3. Funding sources – the organisation is not dependent on the bodies that underwrite its activities. As a non-profit organisation, the IWN is funded by contributions and grants. Manifestly, funders wish to promote the goals to which the IWN is committed; however, they are precluded from influencing the organisation's outputs or the positions it takes.

Adhering to these principles on a day-to-day basis is very complex, not least because of the wide range of sectors and political parties represented in the IWN. Over the years, the population represented within the IWN has expanded to become more inclusive. Whereas in the first years most of the activists were Ashkenazi women from the middle class and academia, in time, more Mizrahi women (of Middle Eastern and North African descent), as well as Arab women became involved in the organisation. Moreover, the IWN's target population (of knowledge consumers) has also broadened and its marketing patterns have changed accordingly. The target population ranges from specific Knesset (parliament) members and cabinet ministers of both sexes, in order to influence policy, to all women in society with the aim of creating awareness and shaping public opinion.

The IWN's target population can also be mapped by examining the outputs produced by its Policy and Resource Centre (which actually act as two separate segments), legal department, media centre, and project coordinators. We will focus on the first three bodies, which are at the forefront of the IWN's knowledge production and serve as the basis for engendering change and for its implementation in practice.[50]

The Policy Research Centre as a Basis for the Production and Dissemination of Knowledge

The Policy Research Centre (PRC) was established in 1996 with the aim of analysing existing data and producing new information by conducting studies and analysing the implications of their findings as the basis for creating knowledge that is an alternative to what is disseminated by dominant social institutions. The PRC conducts its activities in the form of think tanks so that as many voices as possible can be heard. Operating alongside the PRC is a steering committee comprised of experts and professionals, mainly women, from the field under study; women researchers, mostly from academia, and from diverse disciplines; and women's activists. Steering committee members strive to express their positions through projects conducted by the Centre. In the course of negotiating and discussing a given issue, the steering committee creates an *ad hoc* epistemic community. Furthermore, a designated temporary (*ad hoc*) steering committee is formed in connection with the subject on the agenda, consisting of different partners each time. Though in the final stage the research is conducted by academic researchers, the research questions are formulated in a think tank process. Although the research is financed by the IWN, there are no normative constraints other than the demand to represent women's interests, deriving from the definition of an advocacy think tank The PRC also produces policy recommendations. Every issue investigated is examined from the perspective of public policy implications. Accordingly, each study includes policy recommendations stemming from the study's conclusions as adduced by the researcher, the *ad hoc* steering committee, and the PRC steering committee.

The PRC's activity is a multi-layered project: it serves as a dialogue arena for knowledge creation, it acts as a facilitator of new publics through conferences and seminars, and it addresses the media. At the same time, the knowledge produced serves as a basis for political activities. Many of these activities are carried by new *ad hoc* organisations and/or advocacy work of the IWN aimed at policy makers. Although it is very difficult to assess the influence or impact of think tanks on policy making,[51] the examples of PRC activity that follow are indicative of its social relevance and effectiveness.

Research Activities

The PRC's research areas are varied. Each research topic represents a different group of women, in an effort to give voice to women's needs in a range of areas. The four examples below illustrate this approach and suggest criteria for assessing the impact of the Centre's work.

Trafficking in Women

In the wake of the steep increase in the number of cases of women held unwillingly for purposes of commercial prostitution in Israel in the 1990s, a research report, 'Trafficking of Women in Israel and Enforced Prostitution', written by Martina Vandenberg (1997), examined the scope of the phenomenon and its handling by the public sector. It is important to note that the victims of white slavery in Israel include many new-immigrant women as well non-citizen migrant workers and, in the past, women from the occupied territories as well. The publication of the report led to the establishment of the Coalition Against Trafficking in Women, consisting of representatives from a variety of organisations. Its efforts brought about the establishment of a parliamentary commission of inquiry on trafficking in women, which suggested several amendments to existing laws, among them an amendment to the Penal Code prohibiting trafficking in humans, which was passed by the Knesset.

Daycare Centre Subsidies

A study conducted by Naomi Shefer – 'Government Policy Toward Subsidizing Daycare Centres: Implications for Women's Entry into the Workforce',[52] examined the government's declared policy concerning subsidised daycare and encouragement of women to enter the workforce. While daycare centres relate to most women's (families') needs, underprivileged groups need subsidisation more urgently. By exposing the gap between government declarations and reality – aims and actuality – with respect to this issue, it will be possible to influence government policy so that women and their family members will find it worthwhile to seek employment.

Women and Poverty in Israel

The study 'Poor Women in Israel' was conducted by Professor Haya Stier from the Department of Sociology and Labor Studies at Tel Aviv University and Dr. Aliza Lewin from the Department of Sociology at the University of Haifa.[53] The purpose of the study was to examine, for the first time, the scope of poverty among women in Israel, as well as the social and economic characteristics related to the probability of women to fall into poverty, with the aim of influencing policy planning and implementation to reduce this form of poverty. The IWN held a symposium on the topic and published the research findings with the intention of raising public awareness of the issue and placing it on the public agenda. These activities in themselves constitute an output with social impact, regardless of whether the change occurs immediately.

Palestinian Israelis in the Textile Industry[54]

The textile sector, which epitomises the 'old economy', has declined steadily in Israel under the impact of globalisation. About 70 percent of the employees in the textile industry are women, most of them Palestinian Israelis. The industry has been a major employer for Palestinian Israeli women because workshops were set up in villages and it was culturally acceptable for women to work at these facilities, because they could do so while remaining under the close supervision of male relatives. Although these jobs are poorly paid, studies have shown that they helped empower women within their families. Consequently, the loss of work has had a profound impact on them. The study, initiated by a PRC think tank, seeks to examine the implications of the industry's decline on these women, and asks whether they have found other sources of employment, what alternatives the state provides, and what can be done within the framework of public policy to re-incorporate them into the workforce. In addition to experts in the field, the think tank group included Palestinian women as well, to enable the voices and needs of those directly involved to be given expression.

The Resource Centre as a Source of Data Collection, Preservation, and Dissemination

The IWN Resource Centre was established in 1988. Its aim is to expose the public to unknown sources of documentation concerning the history of Israeli society and to encourage discussion of women's status and gender inequality with the aim of advancing processes of change. Data collection itself is an important mission, because 'if there are no documents – there is no history', a condition which existed for thousands of years.

The Centre is active in three areas: archival documentation, the establishment of a library specifically dedicated to women's issues and women in Israel, and data compilation. The Centre's spheres of activity areas accord it and the IWN a central place with respect to gender knowledge in Israel. Many consumers utilise the Centre, particularly journalists, women's organisations, Knesset members, high-school and university students. Each consumer, with her or his specific use of the information, becomes a social agent involved in a dialogue created between social actors with or in opposition to the state and its agents.

Data sources generated by the Policy Research Centre, in collaboration with the Resource Centre, indicate the wide spectrum of women's knowledge that is produced:

Women in Israel

A compendium of up-to-date data and information on the status of women in Israel in various areas within a specific time frame. The first comprehensive sources of information about the status and progress of women in Israel, the book is a tool used by researchers as well as by journalists and the general public. A notable feature of the volume is a comprehensive chapter on the status of women under Israeli law – information that every woman may find of general interest or of assistance in advancing her needs.

Women's Health in Israel

With data from 1998-1999, this book was produced in collaboration with Hadassah USA, Hadassah Israel, and the National Centre for Disease Control. It was written and edited by Anika Yifrach[55] from the National Centre for Disease Control in the Ministry of Health. Its goal was to compile existing data on women's health in Israel, identify areas in which data are lacking, and formulate preliminary recommendations for research, policy, education, and health service initiatives based on the findings.

The information in the book serves as an alternative to government data in international conferences on women. For example, the first official report of the State of Israel submitted to the UN Committee on the Elimination of Discrimination Against Women was based on the Compendium of Data on *Women in Israel* for 1996,[56] and the National Report on the Status of Women in Israel, 'BEIJING +5',[57] drew its information from the 1999 volume of data in *Women's Health in Israel*.

The Legal Department – Creating Dialogue as a Source of New Knowledge

The legal department of the IWN has become a hothouse for new discourses on women's rights and social status. By questioning the 'common-sense' that underlies the existing laws and reframing them, the legal department creates new knowledge. Moreover, promoting legislative reforms in the Knesset and representing women's causes in the High Court of Justice in order to advance women's rights, generates a new discursive order. Such activity creates dialogue between the state and its institutions, brings about the emergence of civil groups, and arouses lively debate among women.

A striking example of this process is H.C. 4541/94, Alice Miller v. the Minister of Defense and Others. The petition to the High Court of Justice was filed in 1994 on behalf of Alice Miller, a lieutenant in the Israel Defense Forces (IDF), requesting the court to order the IDF to summon Miller to the admission exams of the Air Force pilots' course. The aim of the petition was to open the course to women with suitable qualifications, thus enabling them to realise their basic right to gender equality. The petition was sponsored by the Israel Women's Network in cooperation with the Association for Civil Right in Israel and supported by MK Naomi Chazan. The High Court ruled that the IDF must admit servicewomen or defence service candidates to the pilots' course – a precedent-setting decision with respect to women's participation in the course. The court's ruling paved the way for the enactment of Amendment No. 11 to the Defense Service Law. The amendment traverses gender boundaries and gives female defence service candidates the opportunity to compete for almost all military professions.

The structural changes currently taking place in the IDF are the most fundamental outcome of the amendment. As the IDF is, in essence, a military organisation based on an androcentric culture, this process of change is highly significant and will have a ripple effect on other social institutions due to the centrality of the IDF in Israeli society.

The Alice Miller case rekindled the debate concerning the deep-seated gender structure of the IDF,[58] and the IWN initiated a public debate on the issue.⁵⁹ Indeed, the case raised many questions going beyond women's place in the army, not least of which is the question of the army's place in Israeli society. Thus, for instance, feminist groups have voiced the view that because the army is an inherently male framework, women's enlistment cannot constitute a genuine feminist act. Other groups claim that the struggle over the role of women in the army effectively silences the feminist voice, which is trying to create deeper change and civil-ise Israeli society and, especially, to oppose the oppression of Palestinians in the West bank and Gaza strip by Israel.⁶⁰

The Amendment to the Family Courts Law of 1995⁶¹ equalised the status of Muslim and Christian women with that of Jewish women, enabling them to apply to civil family courts in matters related to alimony, child support payments, and child custody. The amendment is an example of activities that have a direct influence on the normative institutional structure which supports the supremacy of men or the 'sacredness' of the family discussed by Ben Eliezer.⁶²

Another example is H.C. 104/87, Nevo v. The National Labor Court, the Jewish Agency and Others, in which the High Court ruled that a different retirement age for men and women – 65 and 60, respectively – constitutes unlawful discrimination. Subsequently, the Equal Retirement Age for Male and Female Employees Law of 1987 was passed, prohibiting mandatory retirement of female employees at an earlier age than males. The law provides female employees the option of early retirement from the age of 60.

H.C. 453,454/94, The Israel Women's Network v. the State of Israel and Others, known as H.C. Directorates, is a further example of our contention. This High Court of Justice ruling established the principle of affirmative action and the importance of its enforcement as an instrument for eliminating discrimination against women. Following this ruling, Amendment 18 to the Government Companies Law was passed, mandating due gender representation in the composition of boards of directors of government companies and application of the instrument of affirmative action until due gender representation is attained.

A follow-up study conducted from 1993 to 2000 by Dafna Izraeli from Bar-Ilan University⁶³ showed that the amendment to the Government Companies Law passed in 1993, and particularly the High Court ruling, contributed to a significant increase in the representation of women on boards of directors of government companies. Although due gender representation as mandated by the amendment has not yet been achieved, a trend of increased representation is evident. In the case of legislation concerning affirmative action in government companies, the IWN played an active and central role in various stages of the law's formulation as well as in advocacy efforts promoting the issue. The continuous and complex struggle this process involves, together with the centrality of the IWN in it, is analysed in an article by Izraeli.[64]

Although the initiative affected mainly elite groups of women, and was duly criticised as such, it acted as a catalyst for the discussion of affirmative action for other groups, and for claims of other groups, particularly Arabs in Israel.

Ben Eliezer[65] claims that legislation, even if enforced, will not make a difference as long as the overall normative-institutional structure, also comprising state institutions, supports male supremacy. This is correct. However, a broader perspective suggests that the numerous activities described in this paper are both influential and instrumental in producing a gradual change in the normative institutional structure. Although no immediate results have been produced, the process has implications for the future and its outcome will become evident in the long run. Legislative initiatives are no less influential than legislative achievements in vastly increasing the chances of fomenting a dialogue between the state and civil groups, as well between various other groups. This dialogue constitutes a source of new knowledge and serves as a basis for discursive change. The discourse between women concerning various legislative initiatives is a constant wellspring of different and renewed women's knowledge and provides a model for the creation and utilisation of social capital, as demonstrated by Izraeli.[66] Moreover, it creates *ad hoc* women's coalitions and networks. According to Izraeli, the overall process of applying the instrument of affirmative action could not have come about had it not been for the activities of women who acted together through social networks both within and outside the public sector.

An additional indirect contribution of this High Court ruling was the debate it fomented over the IWN's legislative and operational priorities. The upshot was that the IWN expanded its activities in issues bearing on weak groups (women and poverty) and within these groups (Ethiopian women, young women, women's employment in the textile industry and other industries, Arab women). The dialogue between women who hold different social positions affords a better understanding of women's differing needs and led the IWN to become more active in creating transversal knowledge and politics in Yuval-Davis's terms.[67]

Conclusion

The concept of a knowledge-based society suggests a multi-actor arena where different players contest, discuss, and dialogue over the cultural model of society itself, and address the discourses around the debated issues. The case study of the Israel Women's Network points to a site in which new knowledge is produced and from which a dialogue is conducted while crossing boundaries of social categories and the social location of knowledge producers.

Our main argument is that the Israel Women's Network, with its departments that deal with creating knowledge, especially the Resource and Policy Research Centre, exemplifies an attempt to develop feminist knowledge and feminist politics in an era of continuous processes of the dissolution of boundaries, the fragmentation of identities, and the decentralisation of power and knowledge sources. The Resource and Policy Research Centre, as a think tank forum, serves as an institutional site for the creation of transversal knowledge and politics.

At its inception, the IWN aimed to represent women as a social category. With the emergence of critical feminist discourses, mainly concerning who the knowledge producers are and whose interests are represented, the IWN changed its policy toward transversal modes of organisation. It has created flexible, changing dialogical sites for knowledge production. The dialogical process usually involves only those dimensions of the specific situatedness that are considered/imagined to be the most relevant to it and to the politics involved. It creates *ad hoc* multi-epistemic communities, which, each in its own way, contribute to the changing discursive culture as a whole. It is a quilt work, to use a feminine metaphor, in which each part is different and unique though, at the same time, is part of the whole.

Notes

1. We met while working together to promote the activities of the Resource and Policy Research Centre. The idea of writing an article examining the significance of the Israeli experience to produce women's knowledge emerged from our personal encounter, which embodies, to a large extent, the convergence we set out to analyse: the meeting of research activities and social activism.
2. The IWN Policy Research Centre was established by Prof.essor Alice Shalvi, the founder of the IWN.
3. Anthony Giddens, *The Consequences of Modernity* (California: Stanford UP, 1990); David Held, D McGrew, D. Goldblatt, and J. Perraton, eds. *Politics Global Transformation, Economics and Culture* (Stanford: Stanford UP, 1999); Ulrich Beck, 'The Reinvention of Politics: Towards a Theory of Reflexive Modernization' in Ulrich Beck, Anthony Giddens, and Scott Lash, eds. *Reflexive Modernization* (Stanford: Stanford UP, 1994); Manuel Castells, *The Information Age: The Rise of the Network Society*, Vol. 1 (Oxford: Blackwell, 1996).
4. For a comprehensive discussion see Gerard Delanty, *Social Theory in a Changing World: Conceptions of Modernity* (Cambridge, Malden, MA: Polity, 1999).
5. Michael Foucault, 'Question on Geography' in C. Gordon, ed. *Power/Knowledge, Selected Interviews and other Writing 1972-1977* (New York: Pantheon Books, 1980), 96-70; bell hooks, *Yearning- Race, Gender, and Cultural Politics* (Boston, MA: South

End Press, 1990); Sandra Harding, *Whose Science? Whose Knowledge?* (Ithaca, NY: Cornell UP, 1991); Sylvia Walby, 'Beyond the Politics of Location.' *Feminist Theory* 1.2 (2000): 189-206; Homi K. Bhaba, 'The Other Question: Difference, Discrimination and the Discourse of Colonialism' in R. Ferguson, M. Gever, T.T, Minhha, C. West, eds. *Out There: Marginalization and Contemporary Cultures* (Cambridge, Massachusetts: MIT Press, 1990); Leela Gandhi, *Postcolonial Theory, A Critical Introduction* (New York: Columbia UP, 1998), 81-101.

6 Carole Pateman, *The Sexual Contract* (Stanford: Stanford UP, 1988); Chandra Mohanty, 'Under Western Eyes: Feminist Scholarship and Colonial Discourses'. *Feminist Review.* 30 (1998): 61-88; Floya Anthias, 'Rethinking Social Divisions: Some Notes Towards a Theoretical Framework.' *The Sociological Review* 46.3 (1998): 506-535; Linda Nicholson, *Feminism/Postmodernism*. (New York: Routledge, 1990).

7 Simone De Beauvoir, *The Second Sex*. Trans. H. M. Parshley. (New York: Alfred A. Knopf, 1949, 1980).

8 See, for example, Harding, *Whose Science?* For a concise overview of the theoretical debate see, Marcel Stoetzler & Nira Yuval-Davis, 'Standpoint Theory, Situated Knowledge and the Situated Imagination.' *Feminist Theory.* 3 (2002): 315-333.

9 See some of the much discussed works, Chandra Mohanty, 'Under Western Eyes'; bell hooks, *Ain't I A Woman? Black Women and Feminism* (Boston, MA: South End Press, 1981); Harding. *Whose Science?* .

10 Nira Yuval-Davis, 'Beyond Differences: Women, Empowerment and Coalition Politics' in N. Charles & H. Hintjens, eds. *Gender, Ethnicity and Political Ideologies* (London and New York: Routledge, 1998), 179.

11 Vikki Bell, *Feminist Imagination* (London, Thousand Oaks, New Delhi: Sage Publications, 1999).

12 Patricia Hill Collins, *Black Feminist Thought: Consciousness and the Politics of Empowerment* (London: Harper Collins, 1990).

13 Donna Haraway, 'Situated Knowledges: The Science Question in Feminism and the Privilege of Partial Perspective.' *Feminist Studies.* 14 (1988): 575-599; Walby, 'Beyond the Politics of Location.'

14 Iris M. Young, 'Gender as Seriality: Thinking about Women as a Social Collective.' *Signs: Journal of Women in Culture and Society* 19 (1994): 713-738.

15 Alison Assiter, 'Feminist Epistemology and Value.' *Feminist Theor.* 1 (1996): 329-345.

16 Nira Yuval-Davis, 'Beyond Differences' 168-189.

17 Stoetzler, & Yuval-Davis, 'Standpoint Theory' 328.

18 Linda J. Nicholson and Steve Seidman eds. *Social Postmodernism: Beyond Identity Politics* (Cambridge: Polity, 1995).

19 Gayatri Chakravorty Spivak, *Post-Colonial Critic: Interviews, Strategies Dialogues*. (New York: Routledge, 1990).

20 Yuval-Davis, 'Beyond Differences.'

21 *Ibid*, 186.

22 Nico Stehr and Richard V. Ericson, eds. *The Culture and Power of Knowledge: Inquiries into Contemporary Societies* (Berlin: W. de Gruyter, 1992).

23 Michael Foucault, 'Question on Geography' in C. Gordon, ed. *Power/Knowledge, Selected Interviews and Other Writing 1972-1977* (New York: Pantheon Books, 1980), 96-70.

24 Held, *et al. Global Transformation.*

25 Cornelius Castoriadis, *The Imaginary Institution of Society* (Cambridge: Polity Press, 1987).
26 Delanty, *Social Theory in a Changing World*.
27 *Ibid*, 105.
28 While other new social movements adopted similar logics, it seems that feminist movements have developed a wider radical discourse, if only because women are situated in all social arenas.
29 Gerard Delanty, *Citizenship in a Global Age: Society, Culture, Politics* (Buckingham, Philadelphia: Open UP, 2000).
30 Beck, 'The Reinvention of Politics.'
31 Castells, *The Information Age*.
32 Delanty, *Social Theory in a Changing World*, 179-187.
33 *Ibid*, 184.
34 Giddens, *The Consequences of Modernity*; Beck. 'The Reinvention of Politics.' See discussion, Delanty, *Social Theory in a Changing World*, 179-187; Assiter, 'Feminist Epistemology and Value.'
35 Delanty, *Social Theory in a Changing World*, 186.
36 Andrew Denham and Mark Garnett, *British Think-tanks and the Climate of Opinion* (London: UCL Press, Taylor & Francis Group, 1998), 3, 7.
37 Denham and Garnett, *ibid*; James G. McCann, and R. Kent Weaver, *Think Tanks & Civil Societies: Catalysts for Ideas and Action* (New Brunswick, N.J.: Transaction Publishers, 2000); Donald E. Abelson, *Do Think Tanks Matter? Assessing the Impact of Public Policy Institutes* (Montreal; Ithaca [N.Y.]: McGill-Queen's University Press, 2002).
38 Diane Stone, 'Think Tanks, Policy Advice and Governance' in Diane Stone, A Denham & M. Garnett, eds. *Think Tanks Across Nations, A Comparative Approach* (Manchester: Manchester UP, 1998).
39 http://www.demos.co.uk/
40 Hanna Herzog, 'Homefront and Battlefront and the Status of Jewish and Palestinian Women in Israel.' *Israeli Studies* 3 (1998): 61-84; Nitza Berkovitch, 'Motherhood as a National Mission: The Construction of Womanhood in the Legal Discourse in Israel.' *Women Studies International Forum* 20 (1997): 605-619.
41 Hanna Herzog, 'Women in Israeli Society' in Uzi Rebhun and Chaim I. Waxman, eds. *Jews in Israel: Contemporary Social and Cultural Patterns* (Hanover and London: Brandeis UP/University Press of New England, 2004), 206-215.
42 Sara Helman and Tamar Rapoport, 'Women in Black: Challenging Israel's Gender and Socio-Political Orders.' *British Journal of Sociology* 48(1997): 682-700.
43 As in other countries, many think tanks have evolved in Israel in the last two decades. They constitute the emerging discursive knowledge-based society. Among these are the Citizen-Based Consensus Conference initiated by the Zippori Centre, the Jerusalem Institute for Israel Studies, the Israel Democracy Institute, Adva Centre, Van Leer Jerusalem Institute, the Floersheimer Institute for Policy Studies, the Centre for the Study of Israeli Arab Society, and others. While differing in focus and operational modes, the common principle shared by these institutes is the production of policy-oriented knowledge.
44 Barbara Swirski and Merylin P.E. Safir, eds., *Calling the Equality Bluff - Women in Israel* (New York: Pergamon Press, 1991); Herzog, 'Homefront and Battlefront.'
45 The most impressive proof of the diversity of political outlooks in the IWN is the involvement over the years of right-wing activists such as Limor Livnat (Likud;

currently the Minister of Education), MK Naomi Blumenthal (Likud) and Miriam Lapid, an ultra-right activist, alongside left-wing activists, such as former MKs Naomi Chazan and Anat Maor (Meretz), Tamar Gozansky (-Communist Party-Hadash), Yael Dayan (Labor), and many others.

46 Tali Rozin, *What is Feminism Anyhow?* (Tel Aviv: Zemora-Bitan 2000), (Hebrew).

47 The IWN was headed by Alice Shalvi (an educator and professor of English literature). Among the founders were Professors Dafna Izraeli (sociology), Marylin Safir (psychology), Frances Raday (law), Rivka Bar-Yosef (sociology), and Galia Golan (political science).

48 The relation between academia in general and Women's Studies and grassroots feminists in particular, touches upon questions of epistemologies of science and are beyond the scope of this article. For a comprehensive discussion of the subject, see Liz Stanley, *Knowing Feminisms: On Academic Borders, Territories and Tribes* (London; Thousand Oaks, Calif.: Sage Publications 1997); in the Israeli context see Hanna Herzog, 'Knowledge, Power and Feminist Politics' in Hanna Herzog (ed.) *Society in Reflection* (Tel Aviv: Ramot Publication, 2000), 269-293. (Hebrew).

49 Arik Carmon, 'Think Tanks: The Israel Democracy Institute as a Model' in David Nachmias and Menachem Gila, eds., *Public Policy in Israel* (Jerusalem: The Israel Democracy Institute, 1999) (Hebrew).

50 The IWN has been involved in various women's knowledge initiatives. The intent of this paper is not historical documentation of IWN's activities and, therefore, most of the examples refer to the Network's activities in recent years.

51 Donald E. Abelson, *Do Think Tanks Matter? Assessing the Impact of Public Policy Institutes* (Montreal; Ithaca [N.Y.]: McGill-Queen's UP, 2002).

52 Naomi Sheffer, *The Israel Government's Policy in Subsidizing Daycare: Its Implications for the Work of Women Outside the Home* (Jerusalem: The Israel Women's Network, 1999) (Hebrew).

53 Haya,Stier and Aliza Lewin, *Poor Women in Israel* (Jerusalem: The Israel Women's Network, 2000) (Hebrew).

54 This study was in process at the time the paper was written.

55 Anika Yifrach, ed., *Women's Health in Israel* (Jerusalem: The Israel Women's Network, 1999) (Hebrew).

56 Implementation of the United Nations Convention on the Elimination of All Forms of Discrimination Against Women (CEDAW) 1997.

57 The report was produced by the Authority for the Advancement of the Status of Women in the Prime Minister's Office, 2000.

58 Dafna N. Izraeli, 'Gendering Military Service in the Israeli Defense Forces.' *Israel Social Science Research* 12(1997): 129-166.

59 The Israel Women's Network, 'Women and Military Service: Reality, Desire and Vision. Symposium.' (Tel Aviv, Tel Aviv University in cooperation with The Forum for Women's Studies, 1995) (Hebrew).

60 For an example of such a group see new profile movement at http://www.newprofile.org/. On the relation between peace movements and feminism in Israel see Sara, Helman, and Tamar Rapoport.,'Women in Black: Challenging Israel's Gender and Socio-Political Orders.' *British Journal of Sociology*. 48(1997): 682-700; Emmett, Ayala, *Our Sisters' Promised Land: Women, Politics, and Israeli-Palestinian Coexistence, Women and Culture* (Ann Arbor: The University of Michigan Press, 1996).

61 The IWN's legal department, in collaboration with associations, non-profit organisations, and Knesset members of both sexes spearheaded the activities that led to the amendment's enactment.
62 Uri Ben Eliezer, 'Is Civil Society Emerging in Israel? Politics and Identity in the New Associations.' *Israeli Sociology.* 2.1 (1999): 51-98 (Hebrew).
63 Dafna N. Izraeli and Hillel Rachel, 'Women's Representation on Board's of Director's of Government Companies – Changing Trends 1993-1997-2000.' (Bar Ilan University, 2000) (Hebrew).
64 Dafna N. Izraeli, 'Gender Politics in Israel: The case of Affirmative Action for Women Directors.' *Women's Studies International Forum.* 26.2 (2003): 109-128.
65 Ben Eliezer, 'Is Civil Society Emerging in Israel?'
66 Dafna N. Izraeli, 'Gender Politics in Israel: The Case of Affirmative Action for Women Directors.' *Women's Studies International Forum.* 26.2 (2003): 109-128.
67 Nira Yuval-Davis, *Gender & Nation* (London, Thousand Oaks, New Delhi: Sage Publication, 1997).

Rain

Mother,
you have been crying
a long time.
What can I do
but cry
along with you?
You have been plundered
more than is bearable,
still give
bounty today,
Autumn trees,
singing birds,
small cold apples
in forgotten gardens,
a butterfly
trapped by a plastic window.
It's time Father Sun
became a hero
and smiled
on you.

Jungle

From my Window

The first butterfly
lands on a dandelion
this day
before summer.

My dilemma –
looking out
on this gorgeous
jungle
of old gardens,
safe from developers
and unreachable
from my high window.

Kathleen O'Driscoll

Yvonne McKenna

A Gendered Revolution: Vatican II and Irish Women Religious

Josephine's family and friends did not react positively to her decision, made at nineteen years of age, to enter religious life. Her mother, in particular, "thought that being a nun[1] was a *total* waste of time." Elaborating, Josephine said, "you see, you didn't see religious as women, as such. You just saw them as this kind of neutered gender wandering around the place. But you didn't think of them as women!" This was 1970 and attitudes to religious life in Ireland had changed. Economic advancements made in the 1960s had precipitated socio-cultural change also. Opportunities for women in Ireland improved and religious life began to be regarded as a less attractive life path to follow. Reversing a pattern set in the nineteenth century, declining vocations from the late 1960s on were proof positive of this. At a more fundamental level, falling vocations reflected the redefinition of Irish womanhood that was taking place. Women in Ireland, sometimes acting collectively, sometimes not, had begun to challenge the dominant discourse of Irish womanhood as de-sexualised and self-sacrificial, if not self-effaced. The position of women religious became increasingly anomalous in an era of modernising womanhood. Concurrently, however, the Catholic Church was, in the form of Vatican II, undergoing a process of renewal and redefinition itself, one which would have a profound impact on the lives of consecrated women.

Drawing on collected oral history narratives of Irish women religious,[2] this paper explores the impact of Vatican II on their lives. Giving voice to a group of women whose experiences of womanhood tend to be ignored, the assertion made in this paper will be that for women religious, Vatican II was fundamentally and experientially, though not always consciously, about gender and the kind of women women religious should or could claim to be. In addition to shedding light on a neglected group, this paper draws attention to the dynamics of contestation and negotiation that occur around gendered subjectivity and identity, not only between women and the wider societies they inhabit, but amongst women themselves.

Placing the Accounts
Between 1962 and 1965, over four sessions, which each lasted about two months, the Second Vatican Council met to consider and clarify the Catholic

Church's position with respect to a changed and changing world. The outcome of Vatican II, as it was known, was sixteen published documents on a range of issues from ecumenism to education, revelation to liturgy. Footnotes aside, they ran to over 103,000 words. One of the documents, *Perfectae Caritatis*, aimed specifically at the renewal of religious life, would, over the course of time, render that life utterly altered. Such was the impact Vatican II had on the practice, form and expression of Catholicism that a 'before' and 'after' narrative has materialised amongst not only religious themselves, but the Catholic laity in general.

The women whose oral testimonies form the basis of this paper were most certainly of a pre-Vatican II generation. Born and raised in Ireland between 1910 and 1950, they entered active, which is to say not enclosed, religious congregations between 1930 and 1970 and have lived as religious in Ireland, England and elsewhere since. Only one of the women, Josephine,[3] joined religious life after Vatican II had officially ended. Notwithstanding this exception, owing to the time it took for changes to filter through, it can be said that all of the women in this study were familiar with the system of governance that prevailed before Vatican II and that most were influenced, if not formed, by it. In order to fully appreciate the impact of Vatican II on them, however, it is necessary not only to consider the women's lives in religious previous to it, but the lives they had before they entered religious, and the society they left in order to do so.

Growing Up

Reflecting the demographic makeup of vocations to the religious life in Ireland during the period more generally, the women of this study came from predominantly rural, middle or lower-middle class backgrounds. The Irish society they grew up in was itself predominantly rural. Not until the late 1960s would a majority of the Irish population be registered as urban dwellers.[4] In addition, post-independence Ireland was economically depressed. Not until reforms introduced under the administration of Sean Lemass bore fruit in the 1960s, did Ireland's economic fortunes take an upturn.[5] Previous to this, in its short life, the young state had witnessed record unemployment and levels of emigration not recorded since those associated with the Great Famine of the nineteenth century.

Social conservatism and religious devotion were the other hallmarks of Irish society in the period the women of this study were born and raised in. In the context of a culturally insular, if not stagnant, society, religion – predominantly Catholicism and especially the Church itself – provided a social glue as much as it did a social structure around which society was organised. Numerically, Catholics dominated the independent state. When independence was achieved in 1922, over ninety-two per cent of the population were Catholic, rising to ninety-five per cent in the 1960s.[6] The importance of Catholicism to the women as girls was a conspicuous and recurrent theme in their accounts.

Because they devoted themselves to God and the Church, but also for the services they provided the state, religious themselves were a revered and accepted part of Irish society, especially priests, but also nuns and brothers. Their buildings were dotted across the villages, towns and cities of Ireland and religious themselves were a familiar sight and a fundamental part of society, both individually and institutionally. Nuns far outnumbered their male co-religious. Four years after independence was achieved, there were 14,790 registered religious attached to the Irish Catholic Church, of which almost 10,000 were female religious. When figures for all categories of religious (priests, brothers and nuns) reached a peak in 1967, there were just short of 34,000 religious in Ireland, of which over 19,000 were women.[7]

As noted by Inglis[8] and O'Connnor,[9] post-independence Irish society was largely sex-segregated. Whether due to a depressed economy, gender-specific legislation or underlying socio-religious assumptions, the state that was shaped in the wake of Irish independence worked hard to maintain a distinction between the private (female) and the public (male) sphere. Women were regarded first and foremost as wives and mothers, and their primary place was judged to be within the family and the home. Consequently, opportunities outside of it were limited. Importantly, the state's views on womanhood coalesced with that of the Church and its conception of women exclusively in terms of married motherhood and the domestic space found expression in the constitution. Not only did *Bunreacht na hEireann* formally recognise 'woman's life within the home', but the terms 'woman' and 'mother' were used interchangeably, thus implying their synonymity.[10] It was as they were growing up that the women of this study became aware of the gendered nature of Irish society and the particular roles women and men, girls and boys had within it. Josephine, for example, observed that she "was expected to do things that the boys were never expected to do." The lives of their mothers provided a model of marriage and motherhood for the women. It was by helping them, and sometimes taking over the job of mothering themselves, that the women became intimately familiar with the occupation and subject position they were expected to take on later in life: "My mother was worn out with child-bearing so she used to take to her bed … and I ran the house. I did. I knew how to do it" (Margaret).[11]

Arguably, the most important model of womanhood outside married motherhood was religious life. Certainly it was the only other form of womanhood the Catholic Church publicly espoused.[12] Significantly, it was one the state benefited from also. There were important similarities between married motherhood and religious life, at least in the way the Church and state conceived of them. Idealised notions of each were associated with piety, demureness, self-sacrifice and devotion to others. While Catholic motherhood tended not to be connected to sex or sexuality,[13] religious were, according to the teachings of the Catholic Church, asexual.[14] There was no apparent contradiction between married motherhood and religious life: mothers and nuns were each defined by the institutions to which they belonged, not only asexualised, but de-personalised also.[15] Neither the iconic figure of the Irish Mother nor the Irish Nun left much space for the individual behind it.

MacCurtain describes the image of the nun in mid-century Ireland as "a docile and submissive figure clad in a black or white or blue sweep of garment with a medieval headdress who rarely raised her voice or eyes."[16] At the same time, however, religious were public figures with demanding and important jobs. They were teachers and headmistresses, nurses and matrons, foreign missionaries. To many of the women in this study, that sweep of garment symbolised professionalism, responsibility and power. For some, it signified perfection and purity. Religious embodied an alternative life path, one that offered a life of spirituality, devotion to prayer and service to God, implicit in it also was the possibility of further education or training, work and travel. It was this path the women of this study chose in preference to married motherhood. Reflecting attitudes to religious more generally, with the exception of Josephine, the women's families responded positively – with joy, relief, excitement, pride and respect – to their daughter's religious vocation, though many were also pained by the separation it inevitably entailed.

Religious Life, Pre-Vatican II
While fundamentally part of the wider society, religious in the pre-Vatican II era lived distinct from it. Though 'active', sisters lived under a system that imposed monastic restrictions upon them, which limited their movement outside the convent as well as their lives and relationships within it. Presided over by the absolute authority of the superior, religious life was organised according to an elaborate set of rules ('the rule'), strictly enforced, which governed every aspect of a religious sister's life, from work and prayer to appearance and deportment, to behaviour and thought. By the time the women of this study entered, the rules had become the faith:

> The sacred collection of rules ... was the be all and end all. You had this idea, 'keep the rule and the rule will keep you'. [There was] no [other] judgement of how you were doing. [Francis][17]

As women were not born nuns, they had to become them. The process by which they were to be 'transformed' involved a rejection of the secular world and their secular selves. In the context of a theology preoccupied with sin, which tended to stress the darker side of human nature and its inclination towards evil,[18] aspirants were expected to transcend their imperfect earthly selves, suppress their own human nature and personality. Individuality, in any guise, was frowned upon and legislated against. In its place, conformity to community was imposed. Religious dressed alike, had no personal possessions and a large part of their daily activities were carried out in common. Essentially, this was an identity project, involving the breakdown of one identity and its replacement with the congregational identity set out in the rule book. Moving into the convent, wearing a habit and replacing one's baptismal name with that of a saint were all metaphorical symbols by which the secular, individual self was put to death and the women were 're-born', together, into religious life.

As a process, it was thoroughly gendered. The secular self that religious were expected to overcome was most certainly gendered, while the identity they were expected to replace it with was also gendered, based on the ideal of the Virgin Mary. Through repression and denial, acting 'against nature', the worldly female self would become subjugate to this 'otherworldly', but still very much female, religious self. Fundamental to the transformation of women was control over their bodies and minds. Various techniques were employed to aid the process. These included, but were not confined to: the religious habit which hid the female form; rules around deportment which restricted expression; heavily-laden timetables designed to keep the women busy, either in work or prayer; and the elaborate controls placed on relations religious had with seculars, with each other and with themselves.

While the objective of the pre-Vatican II regime was transformation, its basis was the Christian tradition itself, which regarded women as mentally weaker and less rational than men. Of feeble mind, women's bodies were regarded as potentially powerful and dangerous and were especially connected with sexuality and reproduction. While the figure of the Virgin Mary suggested the possibility of female perfection, women themselves were regarded as intrinsically flawed. This is not to suggest, however, that it was a system women themselves, including the women of this system, neither invested in nor benefited from.

Difference based on sex was a basic tenet of the system of 'Natural Law', the laws of God which, according to the teachings of the Catholic Church "everyone is subject to...from birth."[19] It was equally so within consecrated life. The purpose, role and identity of nuns was considered distinct from male religious and their lives reflected this. Though male religious, especially brothers, did live according to a system of rules and regulations, it was not as extensive as the one women were subject to. While the Church's largely negative interpretation of 'human nature' affected both male and female religious, the fact that this interpretation was also gendered meant that it applied differently to them.

In explaining their perception of religious as gender-neutral, Josephine remarked that her family and friends were "operating out of [their] school days", referring to the pre-Vatican II era. In fact, however, gender was vital to the organisation and lived experience of religious in the pre-Vatican II period. Everything about the lives of women religious – from the clothes they wore to the work they engaged in, from their living arrangements to the reading and prayer material they were permitted access to – was contingent upon their sex. Women religious were constantly being marked out as women, precisely through a process which denied them any investment in femininity.

Vatican II: A Gendered Revolution for Some

As part of a wider project of reformation, the Vatican Council of the Catholic Church issued its decree on religious life late in October, 1965. *Perfectae Caritatis* called upon religious congregations to renew themselves by jettisoning rules and rituals deemed archaic and irrelevant, while maintaining the 'essentials' of religious life.[20] Religious life had changed little in the one hundred and fifty years prior to Vatican II, a revision of Canon Law in 1917 serving only to further entrench the monastic restrictions under which nuns lived. Though some changes had been introduced prior to Vatican II (for example, many congregations dispensed with the formal distinction between lay and choir sisters), the life was, generally speaking, "very constant" (Elaine).[21] Indeed, the notion of change was anathema to the principle of religious as fixed and divine. Now, religious were being directly asked to question, and consider altering, what had become the fundamentals of religious life: rule and adherence to rule; abidance and obedience; rigidity, inflexibility and permanence. What is more, religious congregations were being asked to do this themselves in consultation with their members, though any changes made would ultimately have required ratification by Rome.

Changes introduced to religious life as a result of Vatican II included the introduction of a simpler habit, many congregations later discarding it altogether, and greater access to scripture and theology. Congregational charisms were reinterpreted, which expanded the work of individual congregation and the work opportunities for women within them. Regulation and controls on relations between women in religious life, and between them and the secular world, including with their families, were loosened. At the same time, alterations in the living arrangements of religious enabled sisters to move out of large convents into smaller communities, often in residential housing. Generally speaking, religious were given greater freedom of expression as the strict hierarchical and authoritarian regime of the pre-Vatican II period began to be relaxed. Through a convoluted process that was faster or slower depending on congregations themselves as well as individuals within them, religious life became less 'scripted.' If not change itself, then the prospect of change began to replace decades of tradition.

The reinterpretation of religious life that occurred in the wake of Vatican II affected women in religious life especially. Many of the women described it in retrospect as a necessary rite of passage, a process which allowed, but also forced them to mature into adulthood. Irene,[22] for example, described the condition of religious prior to Vatican II as "almost childlike … we had a kind of infantile mentality.' In as much as Vatican II was a revolution, and this was how many chose to describe it, for some, the revolution was gendered. Frances, for example, defined Vatican II as the means by which she "became a woman." As such, Vatican II became not just a rite of passage, but a gendered rite of passage. Significantly, and in contrast to what had held previously, Vatican II gave the women an opportunity to claim a more positive identity as women, something Margaret had, as she put it, "denied for so long." For her, this was the "most important" thing about Vatican II "and [now] that's what I value most, is my womanhood." For those that wanted to and could, there were various ways to negotiate, reclaim or, indeed, claim an identity as women.

Renaming

One significant way in which women redefined themselves in terms of gender in the wake of Vatican II was in the apparently simple gesture of re-naming. After Vatican II, many congregations gave women the opportunity to revert to their baptismal name. Of the twenty-one women in this study, sixteen reverted to their secular names, three chose to keep their name in religious, and two were obliged by their congregation to do so. Reverting to their baptismal name reconnected the women with their birth family and their secular selves, the gendered person they had been expected to repress. Moreover, it required them to think fundamentally about their self-identity and who they were.

Equally, the women of this study renegotiated their gendered identity in the forms of address they chose to use for themselves. During the course of the interviews, each of them was asked the labels of identity they might use to define themselves, the ones they would privilege above others and the ones they would shy away from using. The terms 'sister', 'nun', and 'women' were proffered, along with others relating to work, congregation, ethnicity, age, etc.. For some of the women, (among them Frances, Josephine, Lillian, Joan, and Irene),[23] the titles 'religious' and 'woman' were of equal importance: "being a woman, being a religious … would [both] be very high … sort of a level pegging" (Joan). Claiming an identity as women alongside that of a religious demonstrated a re-negotiation of 'nun/sister' as a complete or total identity in itself. Some women (including Geraldine, Teresa, Sarah, Vera, Margaret and Catherine),[24] chose to privilege their identity as women above that of sister, usually due to the associations they felt other people made around religious:

> The sister comes out on top – that's the way people perceive me principally … and *then* Irish and *then* a woman! [But] I put woman first … Irish second and sister third! … I preferred to be anonymous. [When people know you're a religious], they put you in a pigeon-hole, the 'Sr. Geraldine' pigeon-hole. And you don't feel a human-being in relation to them. You're something different. [Geraldine]

Dress

Dress was another significant means by which the women claimed an identity as women. The more simple habit was less cumbersome and less likely to completely hide the female form than its predecessor. Hair protruded from the smaller veil, while the shorter dress revealed that nuns did, indeed, have legs. Of course, habits continued to distinguish religious from secular women and emphasised their identity as religious. When the opportunity arose, many of the women chose to abandon their habit altogether. The predominant reason given for this was the desire to 'fit in', but it also gave religious some space in which to express a female self-identity. Teresa was "absolutely delighted" about changing into secular dress because "it made me feel [like] a woman."

The Body and Femininity

Vatican II enabled women religious to think about themselves and their bodies in new ways, a fact reflected in modern rulebooks which make far fewer references to the shame surrounding the female body and the need for it to be covered. Several of the women commented on their appearance during the interviews. For example, Irene remarked on the size of her hips (getting bigger, a bad thing), while Margaret talked about the possibility of getting a perm. Lillian apologised for her clothes (jeans and jumper) when we met and mentioned them again during the interview, remarking "the state of me now! I mean, I'm not even respectable!" Although these comments were made casually during the course of our conversation, they revealed an investment in femininity not possible, or perhaps necessary, previously. The opportunity to make such an investment was something many of the women valued as a means of positively repositioning themselves as women, as exemplified by Teresa:

> I was aware [after Vatican II] of some liberation around myself as a woman, you know? I [had] missed the things ... like clothes, like perfume, like hair-dos. All of that [was] part of the sacrifice ... But there has been, over the last X number of years, [the opportunity] to re-claim that sense of care for myself as a woman and ... the femininity bit of me.

Collective Gendered Identities

Vatican II gave many of the women the opportunity to work in new areas of employment and some chose to work specifically with other women.[25] The desire to work with women often reflected a gender-based collective identity. Josephine referred to herself and the other members of a local women's group she was involved with as 'us' or 'we', making no distinction between herself as a religious and them as seculars, while Margaret found working as a therapist for women "very satisfying" because "I understand women better, obviously, [because] I'm a woman myself." For Margaret, a collective gendered identity was based on a shared experience of patriarchy, and she defined her work in terms of women's empowerment:

> I particularly want to work with women and for women ... I think women get an awfully raw deal, [they're] discriminated against, they're set aside. And I know what that feels like because I feel that, as a woman, I've been discriminated against in the Church ... I can get angry about that ... it's something I know about. So I suppose from that point of view, that's why I want to work with women. Even though [therapy] isn't consciousness raising,

not overtly anyway, it is helping women to get some insight into their own situation and take some control over it.

Sarah expressed similar sentiments when describing her work in female adult education classes as advancing the 'liberation' and 'empowerment' of women. Josephine formed gender-based communities with other Irish women she knew in England (not professed, some not Catholic), while both Vera and Margaret used gender as the means to transcend ethnic boundaries. Vera abandoned her identity as Irish in preference for "cosmopolitan ... professional woman" while Margaret preferred to think of herself as belonging to the "human family" rather than being 'just' Irish. She qualified this with the following statement, which echoed Virginia Woolf's remark that "as a woman, I have no country":[26]

> We have an awful lot in common ... Especially women ... It's like belonging to the woman family! ... Because I associate with women naturally, it's like belonging to this human, feminine group. And we all have the same difficulties and struggles. It's kind of universal.

Sexual Identity

Since Vatican II, the Church's teaching on sexuality has changed. It now recognises that religious are not a-sexual, thus enabling women religious to claim a sexual identity for themselves. Some of the women did so in the interviews. Margaret called religious "sexual beings, like everyone else" while Lillian described herself as a "perfectly normal heterosexual woman." These women presented their celibacy as a sexuality of choice, not denial. This was reflected also in a number of the modern rule books which tended to place much less emphasis on the 'dangers' of sexuality. Some congregations highlighted the importance of religious discussing their sexuality, including any difficulties they might be experiencing with their vow of celibacy. A number of the women had attended workshops or courses on sexuality and seemed quite comfortable speaking about it with someone who was a relative stranger. Indeed, the language they used and their purchase on sexuality generally seemed unusual for women of their generation in Ireland.[27]

Though it was changes in the Church's teaching that had given the women an opportunity to claim a sexual identity, some of the women expressed views about sexuality that were at odds with the Church's official line. Lillian, for example described a friend's lesbian relationship as "perfectly natural" while Rebecca[28] disagreed strongly with the Church's attitude to contraception, remarking, "I feel the church needs to move on [but] I think if I said all I feel, I would be excommunicated!"

Feminist Identities

The desire to renegotiate their identity as women and occupy the category 'woman' differently, as some of the women clearly did, suggests a consciousness as women, if not feminists. While only two of the women described themselves as feminists (Margaret and Pauline), many were aware of feminist ideology and used terms popularised by feminism, such as "patriarchy" (Lillian), "female subservience" (Frances), and "women's liberation" (Frances, Teresa and Sarah) to talk about their own experiences.[29] This was not surprising since Vatican II had coincided with the second-wave feminist movement. Both congregations and individuals were influenced by it and incorporated elements of it into their redefinition of religious life. Indeed, many of the women drew attention to the pioneering work of women's religious congregations in the areas of education, health and social work, depicting the strict pre-Vatican II regime as anathema to the original ideals of active religious. As Pauline put it, "By the time I entered [in 1948] … we were very obedient [but] religious aren't meant to be that kind of person at all." Although Annette[30] did not describe herself as a feminist, she was "very proud" that nuns had been responsible for the education of "very feminist" women such as Germaine Greer and Benazir Bhutto. A woman-centred consciousness was sometimes discernible at an institutional level too. A publication by the St. Mildred congregation, for example, based on a Chapter held in the mid-1990s, made several references to the commitment of the congregation to women's issues and the empowerment of women.

Differing Responses

Congregations and individuals within them responded differently to Vatican II. Some women felt their congregation moved too fast, others that it did not respond fast enough. Despite their varied responses, however, the women of this study chose to remain within religious life. Many of their co-religious did not. Though the changes brought about by Vatican II were introduced neither at one time nor to the same extent in all religious organisations, it sent an immediate psychological shockwave throughout religious life and precipitated a haemorrhage from it. The exodus consisted of those who found in change the freedom to realise they did not have a vocation, as well as those who "were lost … couldn't cope [when] the structures were removed" (Kate).[31] Others leaving made the process of change difficult for those who stayed: "It was very, very tough … because that was when a lot of our friends left and you'd wonder … should I do the same?" (Irene). Even those who never doubted their own vocation found transition difficult. Francis, for example, believed in hindsight that the "constraints [were] really burdensome…reform absolutely necessary", yet still experienced Vatican II and its aftermath as "a very painful process. Because it's extremely difficult to undo something that has been so sacred." Vera, also fully supportive of the changes, was frustrated by the lingering influence the pre-Vatican II regime had on her:

> Even though I say I kicked against the regime for a quite a long time, it's amazing the impact it's had on me and how in certain respects, even though I seem to be free of it, I am *not* free. I'm *not* free of the yolk of religious life that was imposed.

Reservations

Unsurprisingly, some women were positively traumatised by Vatican II and tried as much as possible to hold on to what was familiar to them. As Elaine put it, "I have remained very much what I was [with no] need to … strike out for a different type of life." Of all the women, Elaine seemed least comfortable about change, her hesitancy in the following remark gives the impression that it is herself she was trying to convince of the benefits of change more than anyone else: "I wonder is [change] a good thing, you know? You just, but I think it is. 'All things worse to good', if you've heard it, if you love God."

In fact, Elaine employed interesting tactics to deal with Vatican II, which included telling herself that she must adapt to the changes under her vow of obedience. An example of this was her attitude to home visits. According to the rule of her congregation, Elaine had been forbidden to visit home after she entered religious life in 1945. This rule was changed in the 1960s, but Elaine was reluctant to "break the promise I had made." Eventually, in the late 1970s, she felt compelled to relent on the basis that, "You felt the odd one out and you were sort of saying, now you *must* go home. This is the regulation. And you feel this was obedience too and you *have* to." Other women, (most noticeably Bernadette),[32] though aware that Vatican II had taken place, appeared not to have let it affect the way they lived their life to any great extent. These women were reluctant to talk about their feelings and continually used language that emphasised a collective, communal identity.

For the most part, a less than positive reaction to Vatican II was expressed through ambiguity and reservation: the fear that something crucial was being lost in the rush to reform, a case of 'modernisation at any cost.' As Kate put it "I thought it was a bit stupid. Some of [the changes] were not for the best … I think sometimes you can throw out the baby with the bath water." Women who were ambiguous about the changes chose to cling on to elements of the pre-Vatican II religious identity in less totalising ways. For example, by continuing to wear the habit, but taking advantage of the opportunity to retrain or return home more frequently. Annette, Bernadette, Elaine, Hannah[33] and Kate each chose to wear the habit, or some approximation of it, as a visible reflection of their religious status. For these women, the habit was not an unnecessary encumbrance associated with religious life, but a fundamental element of it. Not only did it publicly affirm the women's decision to follow the path of religious life over others, it made religious instantly recognisable to those who might be in need of them.

This way of thinking emphasised, from the women's point of view, the necessity of religious as much as the obligations associated with religious life. Though it exposed her to possible abuse, verbal and otherwise, Annette felt it was important to wear the habit in public because "it's a kind of mission going out with the habit on … It makes you feel what the blacks feel … the people who are persecuted feel." Moreover, she believed that by abandoning the habit in favour of 'civvies', religious were allowing themselves to be silenced by the spread of secularism, acquiescing in the "banish[ment] of God from the streets." This was an interesting take on the modernising impact of Vatican II, suggesting that, through it, religious were giving up their rebellious, counter-cultural position for the security and safety of fitting in with the masses. These same women, along with May[34] (though she wore secular clothes), identified themselves first and foremost as religious, maintaining that identity as the one which subsumed all others within it, including their identity as women, the option of which they tended to ignore. Annette identified 'sister' as her "proudest, proudest title" while Kate seemed unable to countenance the idea of an alternative identity at all. When asked if she felt people in England positioned her any differently because she was Irish, Kate remarked, almost in exasperation, *"but I was a sister"* suggesting that, for her at least, religious identity negated all others

Tension
Tensions naturally arose between those sisters who desired change and those who regarded communal conformity as the essence of religious life and relied upon it to define themselves as religious. Humorous, but dismissive, remarks were made about 'modern' nuns to the effect that they

had "no faith" (Bernadette) or took "no vows" (Annette). Others, choosing not to wear the habit, also created problems:

> I preferred people to know I was religious ... I think it's important ... I mean, I laugh at some. We had some people who didn't want to wear a veil at any cost. As soon as they could, [they] gave it up. And then they got all dressed up to be scout mistresses or whatever... in their hats and their uniform. I said, 'why do you wear that if you're not prepared to wear a veil?' "Well, you have to be recognised". I said, "that's why I'm wearing *this*!" ... Yes, I think there was a certain amount of unease and tension. [Hannah]

Those women who chose to wear the habit tended to dismiss religious who wore secular dress as cowardly or less brave than themselves. They regarded secular clothes as representing a refusal to take on the demands and responsibilities of religious life, especially in the more trying circumstances of contemporary society. For some, it was important that religious present a united front. Tensions also arose because some women were claiming greater independence within community life, thinking in terms of 'I' rather than 'we.' One way this manifested itself was with respect to personal possessions. Prior to Vatican II, religious owned nothing and held all goods in common. Hannah, in particular, was incensed by what she saw as the rise of proprietorship within community:

> Possibly because of the rapid changes after Vatican II, people said, well, they [can] have their own cars and their own things. What they don't realise is that [it's] *not* your own car. It's for the use of the community. Or for the use of your work ... I was sick of people talking about 'my, my, my, my'.

The communal, congregational identity that Hannah and others were trying to hold on to was undermined by other's claims to individuality. It was impossible to be 'one' in religious life with differing and apparently incompatible notions of what religious life meant. Simply put, communal identity relied upon the community defining it similarly.

The incidences related here point to a wider tension amongst the religious of this study over the extent to which women religious wanted, remained or could claim to be intrinsically 'distinct' from seculars in the post-Vatican II period. Equally at issue was gender: the 'kind' of women religious were and the extent to which they could claim to be different from other women. The desire to renegotiate their identity as women and to occupy the category 'woman' differently reflected, at heart, a desire to be seen to be 'just' like other women (whatever that might mean) and to be treated as such. In essence, the women were demystifying and demythologising religious life in favour of a more realistic notion of themselves as women. Some of these women retrospectively regarded difference negatively. For them, the habit marked them out as religious, highlighted their inferior status *vis-à-vis* male religious and prohibited their acceptance as 'normal' women: "The habit made you stand out like a sore thumb ... I'd love to have said, 'look, in spite of the way I look ... I'm *not* a freak!'" (Margaret). For others, however, difference remained the very essence of religious life and they wanted to distinguish themselves from women who did not have a vocation, had not entered religious life and had not taken holy orders.

In addition to the *kind* of women religious debated defining themselves as, in thought and deed if not verbally, the extent to which they as a group were able, expected or wanted to embrace 'modern' womanhood was also an issue around which conflict emerged. In as much as some women were frustrated by the Church's hesitancy to embrace more progressive gender politics, the same could be said for their own congregations or co-religious. Likewise, others were uncomfortable with the influence feminism had had on modernisation within religious life. May, for example, was "irritated" by women "going to town with inclusive language."

Beyond The Convent

It was not only inside religious life, but outside it too that religious encountered difficulties claiming the subjectivities they wanted to. For those who held on to more traditional notions of religious life, revered by a diminishing proportion of an ageing section of the population, they felt irrelevant to a growing majority of it. At best ignored, at worst, they felt regarded as potential abusers. On the other hand, for those who had embraced Vatican II and the opportunity to redefine themselves in its wake, having that self accepted by others proved problematic also. First, some felt pressurised to conform to more conventional notions of what religious 'should' be like, in terms of dress, work and/or behaviour. As Lillian did, several of the women spoke of being treated as a child in this respect:

> My mother's friends now, they're dreadful! They drive me mad! 'Are you all out of the habit?' It's all 'what's religious life coming to?' ... My aunt used to talk about me as though I wasn't in the room ... They treat you like a child. I used to get so angry and I still do. That they feel free to pass comment on you because you're not conforming to whatever image they have.

Refusing to don the 'traditional' cap did not necessarily grant them access to 'ordinary' womanhood, however, especially when admittance to that category was dependent, as Josephine suggests in the follow quotation, on coping with the difficulties of being a wife and mother:

> My mother's qualification for knowing anything is having a mortgage and children. *That's* work. We don't have any worries. That's responsibilities. We don't have any worries. They talk as if we're eejits … Honest to God! Just 'cause we haven't got kids we know sweet all. We're non-persons … If you eschew [marriage] and you don't have children, I mean, what the hell do you know? You don't know what goes on in the real world.

Notions of womanhood in Ireland traditionally coalesced around sacrifice and devotion to others – either in the form of 'proper' religious life or married motherhood. Conforming to neither of these stereotypes, the women found themselves dismissed as juveniles. At the same time, claims to more modern notions of womanhood proved equally difficult to legitimate. Francis remarked:

> Now, I tell you. I find it a little bit irksome … that I am not accepted just as a woman. There are … snide [or] jokey … ways of talking about 'this sister' … You're treated as though you haven't quite got the hang of what Women's Lib is, that you haven't got the right kind of insights.

Frances and Lillian reasoned their perceived exclusion from the category 'woman' on the basis that, as religious, they were not considered to be either familiar or concerned with patriarchy or the liberation of women. This suggested that religious' right to claim a feminist identity was also one they felt others questioned. The associations made around religious – as Lillian put it "of repression, denial of who we are, of our sexuality. Of pretending to be holier than thou, and that sort of crap" – prevented others, from the women's point of view, from seeing past their identity as religious. As Josephine said, "they still have this thing of you're a nun first. Or a religious. *Then* you're a woman – if you graduate to that level, of which you're not at all certain!"

Conclusion

Women religious formed the largest and most powerful group of professional women in Ireland until the 1970s. In addition, they have also played a significant, if unacknowledged, role in the construction of Irishness and Irish womanhood. And yet they remain curiously under-explored, both in explorations of Irishness and Irish womanhood. The women whose oral histories this paper has drawn from were born and grew up in a society with particular and particularly well-policed notions regarding acceptable behaviour for women and respectable life paths for them to follow. They entered into a system which further regulated and controlled them on the basis of their sex. Though it gave them opportunities not easily available to women outside it, religious life in the pre-Vatican II period aimed to transform women into nuns, imposing on them a particular and totalising gendered subjectivity. It was one few thought to question, but from which many derived meaning and value.

The subjective understanding and expression of religious identity by and amongst Irish women religious is an under explored area of research, no more so than in relation to Vatican II. The aim of Vatican II was to identify and clarify the position of the Catholic Church with respect to the changed and changing realities of the modern world. *Perfectae Caritatis*, the document aimed at religious life, was not expressly designed to elicit a gendered revolution, but, for many women religious, this was how it was experienced. For these women, Vatican II liberated them from the strictures of a gendered subjectivity based on denial and repression, allowing them to claim a more positive identity as women in its place. For those less enthusiastic about the changes, Vatican II was experienced as an attack on their identity as religious – and as women.

Women religious have tended to be ignored *as women*, though religious life both before and after Vatican II has continued to sex and gender them in particular ways. Drawing on their oral history testimonies, this paper has explored the significance of *Perfectae Caritatis* in the lives of Irish women religious: how they lived and interpreted it but, most especially, the impact it had on their sense of self as women. In so doing, it has given voice to a group of women previously ignored and highlighted the contested and contingent nature of gender identity and subjectivity, as well as pointing to some of the negotiations that occur around it.

Notes

The author would like to acknowledge funding in the form of a post-doctoral fellowship received from the Irish Research Council for the Humanities and Social Sciences. I would also like to thank an anonymous reader for helpful comments on an earlier draft of this paper.

1   The terms 'nun' and 'sister' have distinct meanings in canon law (the law of the Catholic Church). Strictly speaking, 'nuns' are members of religious orders, take formal vows and are enclosed, while 'sisters' are members of religious congregations who take simple vows and are not enclosed, thus allowing them to work and move outside their congregation. The distinction is rarely maintained in the vernacular, however. For stylistic reasons, 'religious', 'sister' and 'nun' are used interchangeably throughout this article, although the focus of the research is on 'active' religious.

2   The oral histories upon which this article is based were collected for a broader piece of research which explored gendered, religious, ethnic and migrant identities amongst Irish women religious. The twenty-one women interviewed entered five congregations, none of which were Irish. One of the congregations was English (involved in teaching), another English, though French in origin (whose charism was the care of the elderly and orphaned). The remaining three were French. Two of these were teaching congregations, one was involved in nursing. All the women have lived some, and some all, of their religious life outside Ireland. The respondents were contacted by way of an introductory letter sent to several religious organisations known to have houses in Ireland, in the greater London area. The sample was largely self-selecting: seven of the women responded directly to the letter or a follow-up telephone call, the remaining fourteen were found through contact with the original seven. At the time of the interviews, thirteen of the women were living in England, while eight had returned to Ireland to live. All names, including those of congregations, are pseudonyms.

3   Josephine was born in 1950, came from a rural background and had six siblings. She entered a French teaching congregation (the Sisters of St. Marie) in 1970.

4   Terence Brown, *Ireland A Social and Cultural History, 1922-2002* (London: Harper Perennial, 2004), 246. (First published 1981).

5   J.J. Lee, *Ireland, 1912-1985* (Cambridge: Cambridge UP, 1989), 341-370.

6   John H. Whyte, *Church and State in Modern Ireland, 1923-1979* (Dublin: Gill and Macmillan, 1980), 3.

7   Anonymous, 'Survey of Catholic Clergy and Religious Personnel.' *Irish Journal of Sociology* (March 1972): 137-234.

8   Tom Ingis, *Moral Monopoly, The Rise and Fall of the Catholic Church in Modern Ireland* (Dublin: University College Dublin Press, 1998). (First published 1987).

9   Pat O'Connor, *Emerging Voices, Women in Contemporary Irish Society* (Dublin: Institute of Public Administration, 1998).

10 Bunreacht na hEireann, *The Constitution of Ireland* (Dublin: Government Publications Office, 1937), 136. Of course, ideologies of womanhood in Ireland at the time did not differ substantially from other European countries.

11 Margaret was born in 1942, came from a rural background and had eight siblings. She entered the St. Marie congregation in 1960.

12 Bronwen Walter, *Outsiders Inside, Whiteness, Place and Irish Women* (London: Routledge, 2001), 18.

13 See, for example, Liam O'Dowd, 'Church, State and Women: The Aftermath of Partition' in Chris Curtin, Pauline Jackson and Barbara O'Connor, eds. *Gender in Irish Society* (Galway: Galway UP, 1987), 13; and Angela K. Martin, 'The Practice of Identity and an Irish Sense of Place.' *Gender, Place and Culture, A Journal of Feminist Geography* 4.1: 101.

14 Jenny Beale, *Women in Ireland, Voices of Change* (Bloomington and Indianapolis: Indiana UP, 1987), 174.

15 Lee, 42.

16 Margaret MacCurtain 'Godly Burden, Catholic Sisterhoods in Twentieth Century Ireland' in Anthony Bradley and Maryann Gialanella Valiulis, eds. *Gender and Sexuality in Modern Ireland* (Massachusetts: University of Massachusetts, 1997), 245-256.

17 Frances was born in 1930, came from a rural background and had ten siblings. She entered an English teaching congregation (the Sisters of St. Mildred) in 1948.

18 Louise Fuller, *Irish Catholicism Since 1950, The Undoing of a Culture* (Dublin: Gill and Macmillan), 119. (First published 2002).
19 John A. Hardon, *Modern Catholic Dictionary* (London: Robert Hale, 1980).
20 Walter M. Abbott, *The Documents of Vatican II* (London: Geoffrey Chapman, 1965), 466-482.
21 Elaine was born in 1922, came from a rural background and had five siblings. She entered the St. Mildred congregation, as a lay-sister, in 1948.
22 Irene was born in 1939, came from a rural background and had one sibling. In 1956, she entered an English congregation, which was French in origin (the Sisters of St. Cecile) devoted to care for the elderly and orphaned.
23 Lillian's background was rural. Born in 1947, she had five siblings and entered the St. Marie congregation in 1965. Joan, born in 1930, from a rural background and with two siblings, also entered the St. Marie congregation in 1949.
24 Geraldine was born in 1945, came from a rural background and had five siblings. She entered the St. Mildred congregation in 1945. Teresa was born in 1944 and also came from a rural background. She had one sibling and entered the St. Marie congregation in 1961. Sarah was born in 1944, was from a rural background, had at least three siblings (perhaps more) and entered a French teaching congregation (the Sisters of St. Louise) in 1961. Vera was born in 1931, came from a rural background and had eight siblings. She entered the St. Mildred congregation in 1955. Catherine was born in 1941, came from a rural background and had three siblings. She entered the St. Cecile congregation in 1959.
25 Sarah, Josephine, Eileen, Pauline and Margaret each worked on gender-based projects, while Lillian, Norah, and Teresa expressed a desire to do so. Eileen, from a 'large' family, was born in Dublin in 1932 and entered the St. Mildred congregation in 1952. Pauline had one sibling, was born in Dublin in 1930 and entered the St. Mildred congregation in 1948. Norah was in the St. Marie congregation. Born in 1922, she came from a rural background and had seven siblings.
26 Virginia Woolf, *Three Guineas* (London: The Hogarth Press, 1938), 125.
27 See, for example, Inglis, 1998.
28 Rebecca was born in 1918, came from a rural background and had one sibling. She entered the St. Mildred congregation in 1938.
29 As the women were not asked specifically if they would identity themselves as feminists, it is not possible to guess how many would choose to do so.
30 Annette was born in 1919, came from a rural background, and had one sibling. She entered the St. Louise congregation in 1939.
31 Kate was born in 1936, came from a rural background and had one sibling. She entered the St. Louise congregation in 1955.
32 Bernadette was born in 1911, came from a rural background and had seven siblings. She entered a French nursing order (Sisters of St. Nadine) in 1931.
33 Hannah was born in 1933, came from a rural background and had one sibling. She entered the St. Mildred congregation in 1951.
34 May was born in 1920 in Dublin. She had one sibling and entered the St. Mildred congregation in 1938.

Melpomene

To watch a sister suffer and to be
no Athena or Calliope,
to have only these tears of my own.

Now once a year I must crush
them into visibility,
as every month my fingers push
and probe each bead and welcome bone.

Why this maiming of the innocent?
Aunts, aunts on each side going back
for generations, and no precedent
for this catastrophe,
and no panacea
in battle-shield or epic grief.

Every year in an X-ray
of each tear-shaped, vulnerable sac
the spectre of death
the joy of relief
and, for now,
the hostage future given back.

Kathleen Vejvoda Chaplin

In Tune

The old reel-to-reel captured breathy voices,
one stops mid-rhyme to ask "Mammy what's a chamber?"
An infant's spirited rendition of The Boston Burglar
belies its gory end. In the beginning I was a mere wail,
a backdrop as the others mouthed, halting, the notes and words,
Dad on the harmonica helping out, filling in the gaps.

Deirdre our adored cousin sang like an angel,
The Rose of Aran Mór, flawless, then taught me
numbers by The Stones, Sonny and Cher,
pulling the elastic of my Sunday hat beneath my chin
Paint it Black, My Baby Shot me Down.

Uncannily, a world fills the room as the tape
winds round and round the spool, bringing
snapshots of interiors from the inside out;
I find I know the words of every one
and mouth them now with the child
the way my father did, as if to say
"Yes, keep going, sing your song".

Lorna Shaughnessy

Kitchen sink

*I fed you so much rope
you should've been hanging for days...*
(Aimee Mann)

There's a kettleful of anger steaming up the kitchen,
she says nothing but peels the potatoes
gauging out each eye with surgical precision,
slices the carrots from top to tip
then pours cold water on the lot
and turns up the music.

Back to the future

As the train pulled out they realised
their seats were facing backwards.
They were pulling away from the future
and accelerating towards a past
they thought they had escaped.

As they pulled into the station
they were tempted to step
backwards onto the platform
like a film rewinding,
and with this double negative in motion
make a new departure of their arrival.

Lorna Shaughnessy

Retrospective

BARRY LAVERTY CASTLE

Barry Laverty Castle was born in Dublin in May 1935, the daughter of the acclaimed (yet highly neglected) writer and playwright Maura Laverty. Barry attended the Dublin Art School (whose teachers included Sean Keating, Maurice MacGonigal and John Kelly) between 1950 and 1952, where she met her lifelong friend, Pauline Bewick. She then met and married English artist Philip Castle (who sadly passed away this summer). Barry Castle began painting seriously in 1968, and over the last four decades has created the most striking and haunting images (some of which are reproduced here).

'What Animal Am I?' 1989. Oil on board, 31.5 x 23.5 inches

"All they do is spend the day going around the place with their bottoms encased in trousers", Professor Sean Keating said about Barry Laverty and Pauline Bewick. According to Bewick, "Maurice MacGonigal would burst into the room loudly shouting 'symmetry makes design.' Barry and I just sat on the hot pipes gossiping about hops."

'Woman and Young Fox.' 2000 Oil on board, 80 cm x 60 cm

"Barry's mother, Maura Laverty, gave up on Barry settling down to painting. Then Barry married a Trinity physics student called Philip Castle. He was also an amazing artist who painted sophisticated scenes of Dublin city with its canal and pub walling. Barry admired Philip's detailed painting technique. One day when Philip was away (Barry was about 30 at this time) she took up his brushes and paints and a huge urge took over her to paint and she hasn't stopped since ... Her paintings are of strange dreamlike places, people existing in a still shadowless world. She would get huge waves of humour. One year she painted and wrote *Cooking for Cats* ... Then another year she spent doing paintings called 'we are what we eat' – a man with a bunch of carrots for a head and a fine carrot for his penis. She has now got to be more serious. A heavy lidded woman holds a goat or a bird, flowers around her head, life still – still life".

Pauline Bewick, RHA, 1998

'Hiding Out.' 1990. Oil on board, 32 x 40 inches

'Bang Bang, You're Dead.' 1990. Oil on board, 23.5 x 31.5 inches

Barry Castle has written and illustrated *Cooking for Cats* (Methuen, 1985), and illustrated *Cry Wolf and Other Aesop Fables* (Methuen, 1988). She has also illustrated two books by her mother, the first of which was a reissue of *The Cottage in the Bog* (TownHouse, 1992). In 1995, Poolbeg published *The Queen of Aran's Daughter*, previously unpublished Laverty stories recently discovered amongst manuscripts in the National Library and illustrated in full colour by Barry.

"Glance in a 'hand glass' with Barry Castle illustrations and you are instantly transported elsewhere. The journey is to magic lands, to that place which lies 'over the hills and far away.' Reflected there we can see, not so much society as it is, but the world as we might like it to be. Here is reflected neither ugliness, nor fear …

"When rereading these stories and looking again at the pictures which Barry provides for us, I wish that time could be folded like a telescope and that Maura Laverty still lived among us. For each of Barry's pictures, whether on the page or on the wall has a distinct melody, is a song without words. Maura Laverty would have known the words just as Barry harmonises so perfectly to the tune on her mother's pages."

Dr Pat Donlon, 1998

'Playing With Hares.' 1995. Oil on board, 31.5 x 48 inches

"Symbolism has been mentioned in connection with my paintings. I didn't intend this but I'm glad if the viewer finds symbols in what to me is reality. I paint at night so it may be that my reality isn't everybody's. The colours I use are the colours in my memory, not as I see them by daylight. Sometimes I'm surprised to find nature darker than I had remembered."

Barry Castle, 1993

'Self Portrait.' 1987. Oil on board, 31.5 x 23.5 inches

'Three Women Fishing for the Salmon of Knowledge.' 1986. Oil on board, 31.5 x 23.5"

"Barry Castle is an unusual artist; a visionary of rare inventiveness and a technician of a high order whose ensembles leave a lasting impression on age groups as wide as eight to eighty. She is the Grimm of the painted panel."

Thomas Ryan, PPRHA, 1998

"Barry Castle's covetable pictures are more than works of art. They are a living presence. There is an almost tactile pleasure to her intense engagement with nature. Castle creates a lush paradise where insects become jewels, snakes become beautiful pods, leaves are veined more sensuously than human skin ... Barry Castle paints an inverse garden of Eden with knowing animals and plants pulsating with primal force, but humans wistful, submissive, innocent as angels ... She draws us into the picture, almost into the act of creation or evolution, exhibiting the intricacy, humour and glamour of the natural world ... You can almost feel the warmth in Castle's paintings. Influenced by the works of the Renaissance, and by her homes in Tuscany and the South of France, she has brought a radiant and joyful clarity to her colours ... When I first came across Castle's work, I was delighted by the humour as well as the exactness and insight. But there is wistfulness too. Sometimes a small window inside a picture shows a patch of sun, some hills, bright rooftops, suggesting a freer world beyond the scene, some different journey, another place to discover. No matter how long you own them, how often you look at them, none of her paintings are ever quite familiar. Revisiting them becomes one of life's pleasures."

Clare Boylan, 1998

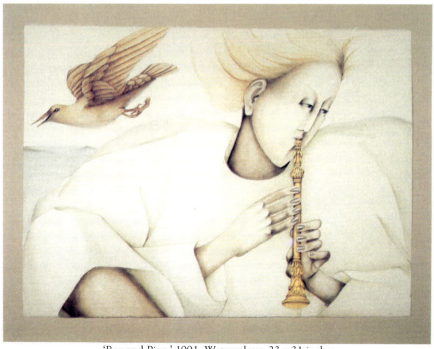

'Boy and Pipe.' 1991. Watercolour, 23 x 31 inches

'Clown.' 1980. Oil on board, 23 x 19"

'1 A.D.' 1992. Oil on board, 11 x 18"

Barry Castle's paintings are held in public and private collections throughout the world. The artist can be contacted at barry.castle@cegetel.net

'Aspects of Love.' 1976. Oil on board, 46 x 48"

'Lucian in Tuscany.' 1998. Oil on board, 40 x 48"

Origins

Feminist Publishing in Ireland, 1984

Samples of books in the Irish Feminist Publishing Collection

1984 was an important year for publishing in Ireland, being the first time that three feminist publishing houses were active here: namely Arlen House, Women's Community Press and Attic Press. This situation reflects well on the strength of the feminist community in Ireland. Across the water in the United Kingdom with its vastly bigger population there were also three feminist publishers (Virago, the Women's Press and Pandora) alongside a couple of smaller, niche feminist houses (Onlywomen and Sheba, radical lesbian publishers). While the output was, of course, of far greater quantity in the UK, Irish publishers in 1984 produced a small number of high quality, ground-breaking titles. The Irish Feminist Publishing Collection at NUI, Galway preserves this material and we represent some pieces from that collection in this feature.

Women's Community Press had been established in 1983 during a training course in publishing for women, run by Roisín Conroy of Irish Feminist Information. It followed a co-operative model, using a non-hierarchical structure and sharing work equally. The original aim of the press was to open up the print medium to people and groups usually denied access to it. As they stated in 1983 "we believe that the culture and creativity of groups such as working people, unemployed people, women, travelling people, children, prisoners, those without literacy skills and so on, have been denied expression through the established channels of communication. We use the term 'community publishing' to describe our efforts to rectify this." Their main contribution to publishing feminism in 1984 came with *The Irish Feminist Review '84* which appeared at the end of the year.

Feminist postcards originated by Women's Community Press

The Irish Feminist Review '84 was a new departure in publishing, being an attempt to turn an academic format into an easy-to-read, political survey of feminist activism that would appeal to a general readership who would never have looked at anything 'academic.' Beautifully produced, with lots of cartoons and photographs, it attempted to cover events of relevance to women activists, with the articles actually written by women involved in feminism throughout the whole island. The book looked at women fighting for control over their own fertility, the right to choose movement, fighting sexual harassment at work, lesbian discrimination, prison as a feminist issue, women and the law, and writing and publishing. The WCP collective sought to record the recent history of feminist activism and provoke constructive debate within the women's movement. They felt the book went some way towards "rectifying the lack of documentation and analysis of women's activities in recent years … [providing] a forum for discussion and exploration of issues relevant to our lives."

Women's Community Press also reissued an anthology in 1984 of women's creative writing from the Kilbarrack community in Dublin, *If You Can Talk … You Can Write*, stating that, "women have been writing about their lives and experiences as far back as writing began, but without female critics or publishers most of their work was doomed to obscurity. Our efforts, written and published by women, will help break through the silence surrounding us, and will encourage other women to try something similar, after all, if you can talk, you can write."

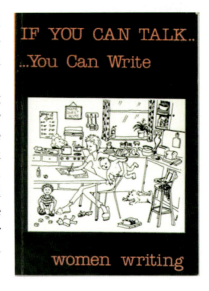

The press initiated a series of feminist postcards which helped them address a large number of political topics in a funny and provocative manner, and also generated a steady cash flow. Two of the best in the series included a representation of a young girl and boy, both looking down each others' pants, and the girl saying, "so that's why you get paid more than I do." There was also a nativity scene, with the three wise men arriving laden down with gifts, to the holy birth and discovering "it's a girl!" Unfortunately, original copies of these two postcards have not yet been traced for preservation in the Irish Feminist Publishing Collection.

Arlen House, 1975-1987
(relaunched in 2000)

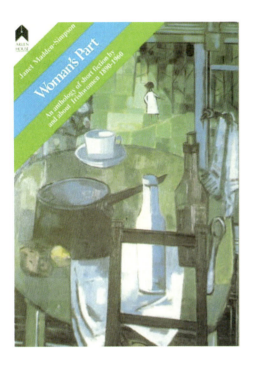

Janet Madden-Simpson,
Arlen House literary editor,
and compiler of the anthology
Woman's Part, published in 1984

Arlen House's main contribution in 1984 was in the form of literature, new and re-discovered. Arlen editor Janet Madden-Simpson compiled *Woman's Part: An Anthology of Short Fiction By and About Irishwomen 1890-1960*. Included in this beautifully produced anthology were stories by the well-known (Edith Somerville, Elizabeth Bowen, Mary Lavin) alongside many women who had been forgotten (Maura Laverty, Geraldine Cummins, Jane Barlow, Dorothy Macardle, Elizabeth Connor and Norah Hoult). Subsequently two of Maura Laverty's novels were reissued by Virago in their Modern Classics series and Arlen House republished Norah Hoult's *Holy Ireland* in 1985 as part of its Modern Classics series. According to Madden-Simpson, "these stories provide a link with the present explosion of writing by women and also they illuminate the yet to be explored riches of the past. This book is not only an invaluable reference, but it provides an original and stimulating introduction to the hitherto unexplored territory of Irishwomen's social and literary history" (cover blurb). This rescue work by Arlen House editors Eavan Boland, Louise Barry and Janet Madden-Simpson and publisher Catherine Rose was to change the nature of Irish publishing and was a "major step in the rewriting of the Irish literary canon" according to Anthony Roche (*Ordinary People Dancing*, Eibhear Walshe, ed. Cork University Press, 1993).

Arlen House also published two more volumes in its Modern Classics series, *Bridie Steen* by Anne Crone and *The Maiden Dinosaur* by Janet McNeill. The final publication of the year was a new edition of Eavan Boland's feminist poetry collection, *Night Feed*, first published in 1982.

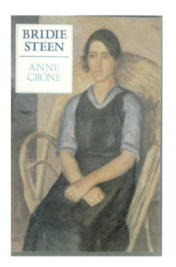
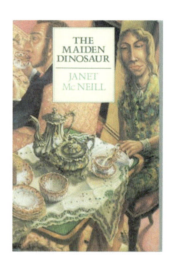

The newest addition to feminist publishing arrived in October 1984 when Irish Feminist Information announced a new imprint, Attic Press, co-founded by Roisín Conroy and Mary Paul Keane. Attic's first books were *Smashing Times* by Rosemary Cullen Owens, the first history of the Irish suffrage movement and Nell McCafferty's *The Best of Nell*, a collection of her articles from a wide variety of sources over a period of fourteen years. In this book, the author gives her own, very strong analysis of Irish society.

IRISH FEMINIST INFORMATION LAUNCHES A NEW FEMINIST PUBLISHING IMPRINT.

New and forthcoming titles

THE BEST OF NELL: A Selection of Writings Over Fourteen Years *Nell McCafferty.*

Introduced by Eavan Boland The Best of Nell is a funny and sad book, which will place Nell McCafferty alongside the top international journalists whose work deserves to be recorded in the more permanent book form.

£10.00 hb.   ISBN 0 946211 05 1
£3.95 pb.   ISBN 0 946211 10 8
             Publication November '84

SMASHING TIMES: A History of the Irish Women's Suffrage Movement 1889-1922 *Rosemary Cullen Owens.*

Who were the women involved in the early women's movement? How did they set about obtaining their objectives? How were they viewed by the Irish public, priests and politicians? What was achieved? **Smashing Times** *traces the development of the early feminist movement in Ireland and attempts to answer some of these questions.*

£10.00 hb.
£4.96 pb.
(illustrated)
ISBN 0 946211 07 8
ISBN 0 946211 08 6
Publication November '84

1985 IRISH WOMENS GUIDEBOOK & DIARY (6th ed,)

Highlights the achievements, struggles, events, campaigns, during the International Decade for Women 1975-1985.

£2.95   ISBN 0 946211 13 2
        Publication October '84

WOMEN STUDYING WOMEN: Collected Essays in Womens Studies *Edited by Liz Steiner Scott.*
£15.00 hb.   ISBN 0 946211 09 4
£5.95 pb.   ISBN 0 946211 10 8

AROUND THE BANKS OF PIMLICO *Mairin Johnson*
£4.95 pb (illustrated)   ISBN 0 946211 15 9

Attic Press,   Representation
48 Fleet Street,   Fergus Corcoran
Dublin 2   87 Haddington Road, Dublin 4
Phone: 716367   Phone: 682103

Roisín Conroy, co-founder of Irish Feminist Information (1978-1997). Co-founder and publisher of Attic Press (1984-1997).

McCafferty's article on the tragedy of Anne Lovett explored and exposed one of the biggest scandals in 1980s Ireland. Other articles looked at Northern Ireland, the law and church and state, bringing a sense of immediacy, pathos and humour to these subjects. *The Best of Nell* has recently gone into its ninth printing and she became Attic's most successful author with sales of an estimated 100,000 copies of her books over the coming years.

From its early beginning Attic grew dramatically, building strong literary and political lists, beginning the careers of a number of women writers and provoking much commentary on controversial subjects. The sale of the press in 1997 to Cork University Press, and subsequent actions taken at UCC, has ultimately seen Attic's influence decline considerably .

The Irish Feminist Publishing Archive @ NUI, Galway

Celebrating the work of
Arlen House, Women's Education Bureau,
Irish Feminist Information Publications,
Women's Community Press & Attic Press

The Women's Studies Centre at NUI, Galway has a long-term commitment to documenting the Irish feminist movement and collecting, conserving and compiling a documentary record of original material in the form of published books and journals, archival material and oral history.

For further information please contact Alan Hayes, Irish Feminist Publishing Collection, c/o Women's Studies Centre, NUI, Galway. Email alan.hayes@nuigalway.ie

stitch-up

an exhibition of contemporary paintings by martina hynan

**Siobhán McKenna Lecture Theatre
Arts Millennium Building
NUI Galway**

9.00am-5.30pm daily
5th July-23rd July 2005

in association with the Women's Studies Centre Galway
sponsored by AXA Insurance

Martina Hynan
Stitch-up
An Exhibition of Contemporary Paintings

...exhibition notes...

I returned to Ireland from the UK, for the second time, at the end of May, 2004.

Shortly after my return I met with Co. Clare Arts Officer, Siobhán Mulcahy, who offered me a show in the de Valera Gallery, Ennis, to coincide with International Women's Day 2005.

During the exhibition I met women from backgrounds in both visual arts and Women's Studies. They were intrigued to see so many different images of women thinkers sharing the same space.

Due to the interest in this initial exhibition, the Women's Studies Centre, NUI, Galway, invited me to show this work as part of their 2005 conference, *Feminisms: Within and Without.*

The experience of showing this work 'within' the university context has raised many issues for me.

I was both delighted and apprehensive to have been asked.

Delighted because those working 'within' Women's Studies would see the work. Apprehensive because I was reminded of the acute sense of dislocation that I feel, from academia, from Women's Studies, and from Irish society.

I have felt, and still feel, at a great distance from where I am.

"Sexual difference is probably the issue in our time which could be our 'salvation' if we think it through."

Luce Irigaray

Speaking at the conference launch I was very aware that not only my work was on view, but I was too. The experience was curiously positive. The audience was very receptive and welcoming. I took the opportunity to speak because I felt that it was important to engage with the delegates.

Having created this work in quiet solitude I felt secure in my invisibility, now I had to face the sense of vulnerability that comes with visibility.

The interaction between the audience and myself made a significant difference to my experience of the work.

In particular, I was reminded of just how important context is when showing work.

Having shown the work in three different venues, to three different audiences I now feel ready to ask, and address, some of the questions which have haunted me for years.

As an artist, is there a role 'within' Women's Studies for me ? must I, plough my furrow in a patriarchal art world ? are the worlds separate ? have women artists changed the visual arts ? do the art educational institutions here in Ireland engage with feminist theory ? how is feminist art interpreted and valued in this culture ? is it valued ? who are the feminist artists here ? is the idea of being a feminist artist desirable, or obsolete ?

I am enjoying asking questions, and there are so many to ask.

I want to continue and develop this work.

But how…..

Now the fun begins!

I have experienced feminism as an artist and as an academic and my aim is to unite these two perspectives.

Chandra Mohanty

Feminist art theory and feminist art practice are indivisible.

This exhibition is a very direct and personal engagement with the issue of visually representing women, specifically women thinkers, who have helped me to understand myself and my relationship with society.

The selection process

I decided to revisit my past to connect with the challenging ideas I had studied as part of my postgraduate Women's Studies course. As I re-read my lecture notes, I unearthed the familiar names and faces of the women thinkers who have continued to influence my creative life.

"the abject is 'the place where meaning collapses'."

Julia Kristeva

This is a living feminist archive.

It represents a portrait of our past, present and future.

So far I have painted;

Gloria Anzaldua, Hannah Arendt, Christine Battersby, Rosemary Betterton, Judith Butler, Helene Cixous, Mary Condren, Joan Copjec, Simone De Beauvoir, Katy Deepwell, Elizabeth Grosz*, Donna Haraway, bell hooks, Marie-Helene Huet, Luce Irigaray, Ludmilla Jordanova, Alexandra Kollontai, Julia Kristeva, Michele Le Doeuff, Lucy Lippard, Trinh T. Minh-ha, Chandra Mohanty, Toril Moi, Laura Mulvey, Jo Murphy-Lawless, Ronit Lentin, Lynda Nead*, Linda Nochlin, Griselda Pollock, Adrienne Rich, Hilary Robinson*, Gayatri Spivak, Ailbhe Smyth, Susan Rubin Suleiman, Virginia Woolf, Klara Zetkin.

The names with * indicate that I could not find an image, or, as in the case of Ronit Lentin, the quality and scale of the image was too poor to work from.

"Because of the whole theoretical enterprise into which feminism has launched us, feminist cultural practices have been such a rich and vivid place for development of theory that they can easily be taken over by theory... The idea is to see what theory does for us in terms of practice."

Griselda Pollock

I used the internet to source the images for my paintings. It is fascinating to see who is out there on the Net and who is not.

In most cases, I chose the most repeated image of the woman available. The most 'popular' photographs usually depicted the woman in her 30s.

This raises many questions about the 'acceptable' face of the woman thinker.

How the process developed

I chose to paint on sewing patterns, laid onto paper. These are used symbolically to suggest the transgressive desires of the women I have chosen to represent.

Having first made a drawing from the downloaded image, I then layered sewing patterns over the drawing, which became the template for the finished painting.

The relationship between the liquid substance of the paint and the machine-printed surface of the sewing pattern emphasises the way that these women have transformed the static social boundaries of self into more fluid forms of identity.

"The forms, conventions, and poses of art have worked metaphorically to shore up the female body – to seal orifices and to prevent marginal matter from transgressing the boundary dividing the inside of the body and the outside, the self from the space of the other."

Lynda Nead

"Censor the body and you censor breath and speech at the same time. Write yourself. Your body must be heard."

Helene Cixous

Hanging

I displayed the works on clothes-hangers.

The ephemeral quality of the material lends itself to concepts of separateness, otherness and difference.

The works seem to take on a life of their own. They move as one passes.

The heating system in the de Valera Gallery made paintings move constantly.

On two occasions members of staff had to come in early to disarm the alarm system.

It seems that the gentle subversive presence of these images set the alarm off each time the heating system came on. And so part of the heating system had to be blocked off and also part of the alarm system bypassed for the duration of the exhibition.

"It is thus not lack of cleanliness or health that causes abjection but what disturbs identity, system, order. What does not respect borders, positions, rules. The in-between, the ambiguous, the composite. The traitor, the liar, the criminal with a good conscience, the shameless rapist, the killer who claims, he is saviour."

Julia Kristeva

A selection of the paintings were used to help create a context for the launch of a publication by the Clare Women's Network.

It was interesting to see the work in different contexts. Each venue that the work is shown in subtly affects the interpretation of the work itself.

Choosing quotations

I included a quotation from each of the women represented.

In selecting these quotes I was conscious of de-contextualising each woman. However, I feel that ambiguity and paradox are integral to the exhibition, and so it was on this basis that I made my choices.

In the de Valera Gallery, the quotations were shown in the display cases provided.

At the time of hanging the exhibition, I was unaware that

these display cases had housed de Valera[1] memorabilia and, furthermore, that my exhibition was probably the first time they were used since.

"To mime is not merely a passive reproduction, but an active process of reinscribing and recontextualising the mimicked 'object.' It is to position oneself both within and outside the system duplicated to produce something quite other than an autonomous from it, using recognisable actions for new purposes."

Elizabeth Grosz

I very much enjoyed watching my six-year old daughter's response to the images. It is pleasantly surprising to hear her talk of her favourite images, Julia Kristeva and Mary Condren, and to speculate about the impact that these images may have on her in the future.

"We all return to memories and dreams…again and again, the story we tell of our own life is reshaped around them. But the point doesn't lie there, back in the past, back in the lost time when they happened; the only point lies in interpretation."

Carol Steedman

Location, location, location

Because I have recently returned to Ireland, I am in rental accommodation. In fact, I have moved three times within this past year.

I have just left the cottage where much of this work was made.

The paintings took over the cottage and our lives in the run up to the exhibition. I very much enjoyed the juxtaposition of cultures in our little kitchen.

"I resist genres because in Western tradition to pigeon-hole oneself in a genre is to accept a hierarchy....I resist perhaps because I am a woman, and traditionally women have always had a way of speaking, of expressing themselves artistically rather than simply, coolly, logically, and I don't want to participate in the repression of this mode of expression....I resist genres because, above all, what matters to me is opening new ways of thought."

Luce Irigaray

Where to from here ?

I hope to secure a studio space in the near future, and am looking forward to further developing my work.

I want to explore the work of postcolonial feminist artists from the perspective of an artist working within the world of Women's Studies.

There are many more women I would like to include in this body of work.

I am keen to exhibit the work in other venues.

With thanks...

I am very grateful to the Women's Studies Centre, NUI Galway for their support.
I would also like to thank Siobhán Mulcahy, Arts Officer, Co. Clare.
For supplying sewing patterns, I am indebted to Mary Honan, Kilrush and Hickey's Fabrics, Limerick.
Finally, thanks to AXA Insurance, Galway for their sponsorship.

Contact details:
Martina Hynan, M.Phil, BA (Hons.)
15 The Green,
Lifford, Ennis,
Co. Clare
e-mail: martinahynan@eircom.netT,
mobile: 087 922 4986

Individual works are for sale at €400.00 each

Notes

1 Eamon de Valera (1882-1975) former President and Taoiseach (Prime Minister) of Ireland. Considered to be responsible for the 1937 Constitution. Article 41.2 is now widely considered to have been discriminatory against women, deterring them from entering the workforce and attaining economic independence.

> "Article 41.2: 1. In part the State recognises that by her life within the home, woman gives to the State a support within the home without which the common good cannot be achieved. 2 The State shall, therefore, endeavour to ensure that mothers shall not be obliged by economic necessity to engage in labour to the neglect of their duties in the home."

Women United for an End to Violence (2004)

Living to Tell the Tale
...As Told by Survivors of Domestic Violence

Women United for an End to Violence (2004)

Living to Tell the Tale
...As Told by Survivors of Domestic Violence

Women who have experienced domestic violence rarely have their voices heard on the subject. With this in mind, ten survivors undertook a thirty-week training programme to create a manual on domestic violence. This is an excerpt from their work.

Included are the experiences of younger and older women, settled and Traveller, urban and rural. The authors do not wish to use their names because they fear retaliation and dislike the shame and the stigma of being identified as victims/survivors of domestic violence. They have, however, a voice, and they use that voice here to inform us of the raw reality of domestic violence. […]

Throughout the programme, the women opened their hearts in order to document their stories. What emerged is the knowledge that the years don't dull the pain of testimonies that are unheard or disbelieved. Time doesn't always heal and it doesn't make rape, miscarriage through violence, and physical and sexual assault any easier to bear. Some women recalled events of over 40 years ago, and these painful memories are as fresh for them as if they happened yesterday. [….]

If you think you are living or have lived in a domestic abuse situation, then this book will give you support, advice and information. If you have a neighbour, friend or family member who you think may be abused, then the book will help you to understand the complexities of what they are going through and how you might offer useful support. […]

The issue of justice is absent from this manual as it has been absent from the experiences of the contributors. For all the documented rapes, sexual assaults, beatings and miscarriages through violence described here, not one perpetrator received a conviction let alone a day in prison. If these crimes happened outside the home they would be treated differently. […]

The women chose the title *Living to Tell the Tale,* for most of those taking part carry the memories of near-death experiences and know that they are lucky to be alive. We pay tribute to their lives, their honesty, their hard work, their courage and their commitment to ensuring that things change for the better in relation to domestic violence. They choose to speak out. They are neither victim nor survivor – they are heroic.

Domestic Violence – What it is

"Domestic Violence refers to the use of physical or emotional force or threat of physical force, including sexual violence, in close adult relationships. This includes violence perpetrated by spouse, partner, son, daughter or any other person who is a close or blood relation of the victim."(*Report of the Task Force on Violence Against Women*; 1997: 27). The vast majority of incidents are experienced by women and perpetrated by men.

Domestic Violence is generally understood to include:

Physical Abuse – Slapping, hitting, kicking, burning, punching, choking, shoving, beating, throwing things, locking out, restraining and other acts designed to injure, hurt, endanger or cause physical pain.

Sexual Abuse – Sexual abuse in the relationship can include the following tactics: Forcing someone to have sex when she does not want to; forcing someone to engage in sexual acts she does not like or finds unpleasant, frightening, or violent; forcing someone to have sex with others or watch others; criticism of sexual performance; sadism; anything that makes her feel demeaned or violated. This form of abuse may also include forcing a woman into reproductive decisions that are contrary to her wishes, or forcing her to have sex without protection against disease or pregnancy. Sexual abuse in the relationship often reinforces the subservience of the victim and induces feelings of humiliation and degradation. With sexual violence it is possible to inflict an intense level of pain over a prolonged period of time without killing the woman.

Emotional Abuse – Consistently doing or saying things to shame, insult, ridicule, embarrass, demean, belittle or mentally hurt another person. This may include calling a person names such as fat, lazy, stupid, bitch, silly, ugly, failure; telling someone she can't do anything right, is worthless, is an unfit mother, is undeserving, is unwanted. It also involves withholding money, affection, or attention; forbidding someone to work, handle money, see friends or family, make decisions, socialise, keep property; flaunting infidelity; engaging in destructive acts; forcing someone to do things she does not want to do; manipulation; hurting or threatening children or pets; threatening to abandon; threatening to take the children away. It may also include refusing to help someone who is sick or hurt; ridiculing her most valued beliefs, religion, race, heritage, or class; insulting her family or friends. From *The Domestic Violence Sourcebook*, Dawn Bradley Berry, (1998*)*. […]

Research consistently demonstrates that a woman is more likely to be injured, raped or killed by a current or former partner than by any other person. From *Violence Against Women Information Pack: A Priority Health Issue*, WHO, (July 1997).

Does your partner –
- Control who you see and what you do?
- Put you down and humiliate you?
- Hurt you physically- for example by hitting, slapping, kicking, or biting you?
- Make you have sex when you don't want to?
- Control how the money is spent?
- Not want you to have your own friends?
- Threaten to take the children away?
- Destroy your things or smash up the furniture?
- Threaten to harm himself if you leave?
- Turn into a nice person outside the home?
- Apologise after attacking you and promise he won't do it again – but he does?

Are you –
- Afraid for yourself and your children?
- Feeling guilty or ashamed about what is happening?
- Isolated with no one to talk to?
- Afraid to express an opinion when he is around?
- Hiding bruises or making excuses for injuries caused by him?
- Finding it hard to be enthusiastic about life?
- Always watching what you say or do, so he won't be angry?
- Feeling like you're going mad or wishing it was all over?

If your answer is YES to some of these questions, it is likely that you are living with domestic abuse.

From: *Lean on me – An Information Guide for Women Living with Domestic Violence.* Adapt House, Limerick.

who's afraid of the dark?

I met my husband when I was eighteen. I married him when I was twenty-two and he was twenty-six. Times were hard for both of us with employment, not that he would work anyway. When poverty came in the door love flew out the window. I can remember the first time he hit me. I was head butted and kicked in my body. I had more black eyes than a boxer in a ring.

I could never do anything right for him; it was never good enough. I worked all through my marriage. It was like walking on glass when he was around trying to please him all the time. I had no friends, my money was accounted for, and I had to know what every penny was spent on. I had no leisure time in my life; he controlled everything. Make-up and nice clothes were not allowed. He always belittled me to his family. I was shit on his shoes.

I lost count of how many times I left my husband throughout our marriage. He would always tell me he'd change. He gave me money to buy clothes and then he would burn them. He destroyed the confidence that I had, told me I was fat and ugly. He would force sex on me when he wanted to because he was my husband and that was his right.

Through our marriage I had two miscarriages and was in hospital on numerous occasions with infections. At one stage, when I lost the second baby, I was in hospital for nearly two weeks. When I came home I had to cook and clean up for him. I had had major surgery before all this happened but he forced sex on me a few nights later. The following morning he pulled me out of bed, and I still had stitches. He blamed me for not carrying our babies. It was my fault, and I believed him. My doctor put me on the pill because it was dangerous after surgery, and he wouldn't let me take it.

I finally left my husband after years of emotional, physical and sexual abuse. There is a lot I could write about but I don't want to remember it. When I look at myself - my body, my image, my heart, my brain, I feel every bit of it.

This is why I am afraid of the dark.

(These events occurred within the last 5 years.)

the perfect couple

I was twenty-one when I got married. I always dreamt of getting married in a white dress. That was one wish I had. I had second thoughts on the morning I got married - was I doing the right thing? My heart was telling me one thing and my head was telling me something else. I will never forget that morning. I asked one of my neighbours was I doing the right thing. All he said to me was, "It's your decision. All I can do is wish you good luck." My parents were totally against it.

…We were living in rented accommodation when we got married in a rural town. I was isolated from all my family and friends. I decided to put my name down for a County Council house, but I was told you had to have at least two children before you were even considered. I had another baby and we eventually got a Council house. My husband was asked to collect the key for the house and to sign for the tenancy.

Any excuse and he would go to the pub to celebrate. He would return home at any hour of the night, and expect me to be up and waiting for him. If I wasn't up he would bang the door and shout up the stairs even though the children were asleep. I wouldn't answer him and that used to make him worse. He would come up to the bedroom and waken the children after me having taken some time to get them asleep. He would lift them out of their beds and take them into our room. I would have to wait until he fell asleep and take the children back out. I would be wrecked the next morning.

…I seldom had a social life, as he would spend most of his day in the pub. When he came home he would cause a lot of trouble if I said I was going out with my friends. When he went to bed, I would get one of my family to baby-sit. I would have to take my shoes off coming up the street in case he would hear me. I would have to sleep in with one of the children in case I would waken him. I locked him out one night, as he wasn't home at four o'clock. He threw a brick in the window and said, "I might as well break them all while I am at it." He broke all the windows in our house back and front. He said, "You will open the door the next time." My children were screaming; they were terrified. I had to tell the Council it was done during the night and that I didn't know who did it. Otherwise I would have had to pay for them myself. […]

> *years of hell*
>
> One night when he was at home, he came in. I was in bed. He had drink on him. He got into the bed. I begged him to leave me alone. He wouldn't, and he raped me.
>
> After eight years of hell he came home one day and told me that he had gotten another woman pregnant and that he was leaving us for this other woman. I was heart broken. He left me in April. Then, in August, he decided to come back but I had met someone else as a friend and I didn't want him back.

> *jekyll and hyde*
>
> When I started dating my partner he was a lovely guy. He would give me the earth. He had a little temper problem but that was easily dealt with - or so I thought. When he blew a fuse he broke everything he could lay his hands on, and it was my fault if I didn't do this and that. He was a Jekyll and Hyde character, like two different people.

> *you should get out*
>
> Once a relationship starts becoming abusive it's never going to stop. Before you get too involved you should get out. Once he's put his hand on you or abuses you once, it's going to continue. I don't care what they say about anger therapy and stuff. Personally myself, I don't think that works. I think if it's in them it will be in them.

The Impact of Sexual Abuse

A woman is most at risk from sexual violence and rape:
- When she is pregnant.
- When she is ill and discharged from hospital.
- When she attempts to leave her partner.
- If her partner abuses alcohol or drugs.
- In the first year of marriage.

Within larger society, and even among service providers, there is a myth that 'wife rape' is somehow less traumatic because one's partner is a 'known entity.' The reality is that survivors of wife rape seem to suffer even more traumatic consequences than stranger rape survivors. In her study, Russell found that women who have been raped by their husbands perceived these assaults as having more damaging, long-term effects on their lives than sexual assaults by strangers. From *Rape within Marriage*, J. Russell (New York: Macmillan, 1982).

The physical impact of sexual violence and marital rape are:

- Injuries to the vaginal and anal area
- Lacerations (cuts)
- Soreness and bruising
- Torn muscles
- Fatigue
- Vomiting and nausea
- Headaches

Specific gynaecological consequences of marital rape include:

- Vaginal stretching
- Miscarriages
- Bladder infections and dysfunction
- Infertility
- Potential contraction of sexually transmitted diseases including HIV

Short-term impact includes:

- Anxiety
- Shock
- Intense fear
- Depression
- Suicidal thoughts
- Post traumatic stress disorder

(Bergen, 1996; Russell, 1990)

Long-term impacts include:

- Disordered eating
- Sleep problems
- Depression
- Problems establishing new relationships
- Increased negative feelings about themselves
- Flashbacks
- Sexual dysfunction
- Emotional pain

(Bergen, 1996; Whatley, 1993)

how it changed me

I was like putty in his hands. For a number of years I had to be a doormat, hide my feelings, be seen but not heard.

I had never known what it was like to be beaten. I had never seen it before. My family were never like that. My Dad loved my Mom. There was love there. He never raised his hands to her nor to any of his children. I grew up with love, not hate. I was taught not to be possessive, but not to have a temper and not to be controlled by anyone. My life was stolen and it took a lot of years to get away from it. I tried but failed many times. I had three healthy children and two miscarriages.

From the first beating to the last beating; from the first time he stole a life; from the first time he raped me; it all affected me big time. I kept it for a number of years to myself. There are things that happened that I forgot about, but they do come back to haunt me. I won't sleep in my bedroom, full stop, that's where I got most of my beatings. It has affected me so much my sleep pattern is totally crazy. After 2am I go to sleep and wake up 2-3 times during the night. I'm a night owl, go to bed late and wake up early. I sleep on the couch and sofa bed but not in my bedroom. I painted it, changed the bed and made it nice the way I like it. But all the bed does is hold clothes, another storage area for me. The bedroom is a storage area, full stop. My trust in men is gone. It takes a long time for a man to get close to me, let alone sexual. I push them away. I have lost trust in men.

…For me to break down my wall, I'm not ready. The wall is my protection, to protect myself and my family. I hate what my ex did to me. He ruined my life completely.

i wish…

I wish I hadn't to leave my home that I loved through domestic violence.
I wish I hadn't to go court continually, it is very stressful.
I wish my ex would stop being so bad and not using my daughter as a pawn for access.
I wish I could stop smoking.
I wish there was a light at the end of the tunnel.
I wish I could have a good night's sleep.
I wish I were full of energy and not suffering from stress.
I wish to be healthy and happy in the future.

it's a memory i'll never forget

The day I told him I was pregnant I thought would be the happiest of his life. I should never have told him until I was a few months gone, but by your mistakes you learn.

My ex said, "How do I know the baby is mine? Maybe you are sleeping around. Your body is mine and there is a thing growing inside you." I turned around and asked, "Do you want me to have an abortion?" "Yes", he said, "I don't want to see you looking like a fat whale for nine months." He got mad and went to the pub.

I was delighted to be pregnant. I thought he might change and come around to the idea. Little did I know what was in store for me that night. It was the night he stole the life of my unborn baby.

The banging on the door woke me. Like a fool I let him in. He was hungry so I cooked a big fry up for him. He said, "Sit down and talk to me." I should have gone to bed but like an idiot I stayed.

When he had finished his food he came over and stood beside me. I thought he was going to give me a hug but he gave me a slap across the face and asked who was the father of the kid. I said, "You are." Why would I tell lies? He called me every name under the sun – whore, prostitute, and slut. I was sitting down but I was a little petrified. I said, "If you want me to have an abortion, there's no way I will, otherwise I will leave you." Instead he said, "There's no way you will ever leave me. I won't let you".

He kept slapping me in the face. I had lovely long hair and he pulled it. He dragged me upstairs by the hair. He told me to tell him the truth. As I stood beside the bed I was crying for fear, as this was the guy who said he loved me. He threw me on top of the bed and kept shouting, "Tell me. Tell me." It went on for hours – shouting, slapping, belting, punching, pushing and hitting. You name it, I got it. I did fight back but I got nowhere. He weighed over twenty stones. He flattened me like a pancake. When, after a good few hours, I told him I wanted to go to the toilet he said, "I have a kind heart, I'll let you go." I nearly died when I went to the toilet. I couldn't believe what I looked like. I was covered in blood, my hair was a mess, and my face was brutal with cuts and bruises. I was a prisoner to him, something for him to own, to tell what to do. What had happened to him?

He was shouting, "I'm coming. Hurry up." I was crying at this stage. I never knew what violence was until I met this man. He pushed open the door, caught my hair and pulled me. He said, "Would you fucking tell me who the father of your bastarding baby is?" He was shouting. I was shouting at him.

It's a memory I'll never forget. He got his fist and dug it into my stomach. He shouted, "Can you feel that?" I couldn't even protect my belly. He kept hitting until I passed out. When I woke up the next day I didn't dare go outside for a few days. I phoned work and told them I was sick.

The after effects of the beating were that I lost my baby and I lost my body. I lost me the fighter that I thought I was. When he found out the baby was lost I was to blame. Not him, the bastard who beat me to a pulp. As he said, "You had it coming." Me, who had done nothing wrong, I was just the wrong person.
(These events occurred within the last 14 years.)

i'd pretend to be asleep

I'd go to bed early so that he'd have no one or no reason to start a row. It made no difference. He would come upstairs and sit on my feet at the bottom of the bed to wake me. I'd pretend to be asleep and turn over and then he'd start banging the wardrobe doors and start whistling so as to wake the children. He knew that I would react to that. I was not going to allow him to deprive my children of a night's sleep.

my daughter

I put the ordeal of the rape at the back of my mind and moved on with my life. I gave birth to a lovely baby girl. I breast-fed her. I was the best Mum to her. She was beautiful. She makes me so proud of her. She's got a heart of gold, but she talks about her Daddy and how much she loves him.

I still hate him for what he has done. He destroyed two people's lives that night. He broke me. I'd rather have gotten a heavy beating. It will never leave me. It will always be there no matter how many times I put it in the chest and throw away the key.

It will go to the grave with me what happened.

Impact on Children

Men's violence against their female partners can have many devastating consequences for their children.

- Irish research indicates that two-thirds (64%) of women who experience violence report that their children witness the violence as it occurs. (*Making the Link*, a research report for Women's Aid by Kelleher & Assoc with M. O'Connor (1995).
- Witnessing the violence and abuse is itself an abuse of the rights of the child to live a life free from fear and harm.
- Many children, whose mothers are being abused, are themselves being directly physically, sexually or emotionally abused by the perpetrator.
- In an overview of American studies, in 32% to 53% of all families where women are being physically beaten by their partners, children are directly subjected to violence and abuse by the abuser.

From *Mothers and Children: Understanding the Links between Women Battering and Child Abuse*, by JL Edison, paper presented at the Strategic Planning Workshop on Violence against Women, Washington DC, National Institute of Justice (1995).

---

little old me

I see me, walking across the yard, long flowing dress 'too big',
High heels that I twist my ankle on again and again,
I carry Mum's old handbag, oh I can smell the age of it, two old coins at the bottom.
The 'kids' are waiting for their 'mother' to come home,
I carry my ten fags (empty box) and matches also,
Stones are used to pay for food so I count my 'change',
I start to prepare dinner.

---

you don't own me

I am tired of looking over my shoulder wondering if you are there. Wondering when are you going to show up at my door unannounced. So listen, I am sick of you thinking you can come whenever it suits and upsetting my family. So fuck off and leave my children and me alone. And by the way, you don't own me.

Difficulties in Leaving

People often wonder why it is so difficult for women to put a stop to a situation where their partners are abusing them. Women who have left violent relationships often ask themselves later how they could have stayed in the relationship for so long.

There are many reasons:
- Eighty-eight per cent (88%) of women who continued to live with violent partners claimed they did so because they had nowhere else to go. (*Making the Links* a research report for Women's Aid by Kelleher & Assoc with M. O'Connor (1995).
- The abuser usually tries to keep control of everything in relation to the household such as money, transport and outside contacts. As a result, women have access to very few resources and literally may not be able to make phone calls, or travel to a refuge, or keep useful information handy.
- Despite the fact that she is the victim of abuse, it is very often the woman who has to leave the family home as a result of domestic violence from her partner. He may refuse to go in the first place, or he may come back causing trouble from time to time. In order to put a stop to the violence, she may have to consider leaving her home, at least temporarily, to save the life of herself and her children.
- Women who have been belittled and battered for years generally have a very low sense of self-worth and find it extremely hard to have the confidence to take such a major step as seeking a barring order or going to a refuge.
- Women still often find that they have to persuade the service provider of the truth of their situation in relation to domestic violence. This does not encourage effective action by the woman. It should by now be possible for professionals to make an accurate reading of the realities of any domestic situation within a relatively short space of time.
- Developed over years of experience, women have a real fear of their abusing partners, and of what they might do in response to such an action. Will he re-appear? He might break into the house or come to the refuge. Will he kill me? What story might he give to the service provider? Will he demand to see the children? Fear has a paralysing effect, freezing women in the situation and preventing them from seeing solutions to their problems.
- Due to the silence around domestic violence, many women feel that they are the only ones living in such a situation. They are made to

- feel isolated and often carry a sense of shame and guilt for what is happening to them. This makes it very difficult to tell anyone about what is happening, let alone seeking help to make changes.
- Women often give priority to the needs of their children who usually want to maintain contact with their father. They worry about the consequences of moving them from their school and friends.
- Very often, women are unaware of the services that are available and that can give useful support such as the refuges, Citizen's Advice, M.A.B.S. or Women's Aid.
- Despite the abuse, it is still not easy to disentangle from a deep intimate relationship with someone who has fathered your children and to whom you have made a lifelong commitment. Conflicting feelings towards the partner commonly last for a long time, together with a desperate hope that things will change for the better. Time and again he'll return, declaring that he is sorry and seeking another chance. Given all the circumstances described here, it can be incredibly hard to say no in this situation.
- There is a stigma attached to domestic violence. Those on the receiving end often feel shame, guilt and confusion about what is going on – shame on behalf of their partners, guilt and confusion about their own role in the abuse. As a result, they often take a long time to tell their friends or family about it, not to mention the support services.

---

victim or survivor?

Fourteen years out of my marriage I believe I am a Survivor not a Victim any longer. Nobody knows what it is like to have been a victim of domestic violence unless they have lived in that situation. Now that I am free from all the pain and scars that go with domestic violence, I can speak out about my own personal experience. What help was there for me, what services were available when I wanted them?

---

the good life

I have had a good life and I have been safe for the last fifteen years. I can talk about it now. I know when I go home I am going into a secure environment. It is not the end of the world to be by yourself although the loneliness is hard. Eventually I met someone good. There are good men out there. I had to start all over again and find accommodation and get my life back. I was in a cold musty flat. I got on with it. I kept working and tried to sort out my lonely life and it was very lonely. I have since remarried and I am happy. I survived.

> Goodbye to being raped and being sexually abused. It can't hurt me anymore.
> Goodbye to my past life with that bastard.
> Goodbye to being in debt. I know now the red letters won't be coming in the door.
> Goodbye to fear. I don't have to be a frightened person anymore.
> Goodbye to rage.
> Goodbye to anger.
> Goodbye to him forever trying to hurt me.
> Goodbye to being afraid he would kill me.
> Goodbye to the mood swings.
> Goodbye to being a doormat.
> Goodbye to his family. I won't have to see them anymore.
> Goodbye to being controlled, no man can tell me what to do.
> Goodbye to my past. I am moving on with my life.

References

Bergman, R.K. *Wife Rape: Understanding the Response of Survivors and Service Providers* Thousand Oaks, CA: Sage, 1996.

Cork Domestic Violence Project. *The Effectiveness of Intervention Programmes With Violent Men.* Vol. 1 (June 1998).

Declaration on the Elimination of Violence Against Women United Nations. New York. 23 Feb. 1994. Resolution Number A/Res/48/104.

Hughes, C.A. *Mothers Surviving Child Sexual Abuse* London: Routledge, 1992.

National Network of Women's Refuges and Support Services. *Social Service or Social Change: Issues and Challenges for Women's Domestic Violence Services in Ireland* Nov. 2003.

Russell, Diane. *Rape in Marriage* New York: Macmilan, 1982.

Copies of *Living to Tell the Tale* are available for €8.00, plus postage, from Domestic Violence Response, The Courtyard, Main Street, Oughterard, Co. Galway, Ireland. Tel: + 353 91 866740.

Toni Johnson-Woods

Lurid Lasses of Australian Pulp Fiction 1950-1960

In *Who Framed Roger Rabbit* (1988), Disney reproduced one of the most memorable female cartoon characters, Jessica Rabbit. Clad in figure-hugging lurex, the husky-voiced redhead shimmies her way through the movie. Jessica is culturally immediately recognisable as a contemporary animation of the 1930s Verga/Petty pinup girl. But, like the pinup, Jessica is more than an object of male (heterosexual?) fantasy; she is a complex site – she might well be described as a *femme fatale*[1] – but, in reality, she is a wife desperately trying to help her milquetoast husband, Roger. She, thus, embodies both the fully sexualised female and also the idealised faithful, loving partner. This paper explores the visual representation of sexualised females, on covers of 1950s crime fiction;[2] specifically, it categorises four types of female representations and considers how these representations were informed by art, culture and book economics. Generally, pulp cover artwork offers an opportunity to investigate the role of covers in the broader culture context of female representation, however this is outside the scope of this paper and is worthy of a separate study.[3]

Representations of nude women have been investigated in relation to 'fine art' or pornography; some have considered the role of sexualised women in advertisements, but little has been done about one of the most iconic imagery of female 'beauty' – that of the pinup – a situation that still exists despite the recent publication of several books on the topic of book covers,[4] an increased interest in pulp fiction art,[5] and works focusing on females in pulp art.[6] Most books celebrate the artwork, but provide little critical commentary. As the covers marry art (in that they are painted[7]) with sexual posing, cultural avenues of pinup and burlesque[8] need to be considered. A handful of books celebrate the pinup, but, again, such publications tend to be limited to bio-coffee table books that celebrate artists (Armstrong, Elvgren, Petty, Varga), rather than critiquing the art itself. In 2001, the University of Kansas exhibited their collection of Alberto Varga/s[9] work, accompanied by a handful of critical essays on the pinup girl. Maureen Honey compares Vargas' languishing models to the muscular competence of Rockwell's Rosie the Riveter('The "Varga Girl" Goes to War'); Susie Bright finds "boyish" bottoms in 'Varga in Drag'; Maria Buszek feels the pinup icon is really a "creative convention with the potential to embody the plurality and contradictions of female sexuality", and Andrea Dworkin rejects his "lazy, fetishistic view of white women, pale women, usually blonde form" ('Vargas' Blonde Sambos'). Robert C Allen's *Horrible Prettiness: Burlesque and American Culture,*[10] offers more in positioning (ouch) the cultural role of transgressive/popular entertainment which exposed scantily clad women to a wider and increasingly respectable audience.

During the 1950s, a group of rambunctious publishing companies (Dell, Avon and Gold Medal) sought ways to effectively market their paperback originals (PBO), or pulp fiction.[11] They hired artists to create eye-popping covers that largely depended upon scantily clad women, 'cheesecake' poses and lurid colours. They had learned from their pulp forebears that a successful cover translates into sales. One month, *Amazing Stories* tried an abstract cover and sales plummeted 22% for that month ('Dime Novels'). Malcolm Cowley recounts a publisher boasting, "give me the right cover … and I could sell two hundred blank pages. I could sell *Finnegans Wake* on Skid Road as a book of Irish jokes.'[12] The success of the covers outlives the fiction and, today, they are merchandised on mouse pads, fridge magnets and business card holders.[13] Thus, the covers are part art, part pinup, part advertisement and, ultimately, surviving cultural icons.

So, what is the relationship between the female in artwork on PBOs, the artistic nude, the glamour fashion model, the pinup girl, and the burlesque artist? Well, the ***artistic nude*** is consumed as fine art, within the confines of sanctioned bourgeois museums; ***glamour fashion models*** (Charles Dana Gibson[14] and then Coles Philips[15]) came to present middle class American females with artistic renditions of female 'beauty.' The ***pinup girl*** retains the trappings of the glamour art associated with magazines, which is hardly surprising as the art of Petty and Vargas in the 1920s first appeared in glossy *Esquire*. Pinup/glamour art crossed commercial boundaries, and we find Coles Philips's women smoothing Holeproof stockings, Elvgren's models sipping Coca Cola and Petty girls climbing on Rigid Tools. The burlesque artist, most often visually represented in photographs, descends from the actresses on *carte de visite* of the 19th century. ***Burlesque*** posters of the nineteenth century provide female imagery of the most active kind. Unlike her passive glamour sisters, the burlesque artists rode horses, danced on table-tops, bowled, and swam. Unfortunately, in the later publicity photographs, the burlesque artists have adopted the passive posing of pinups. Gone is her energy and control, replaced by an invitation to the male gaze and her 'awarishness.' She has lost her transgressive threat of action/domination/ control and become as passive as her glamour cousins.

 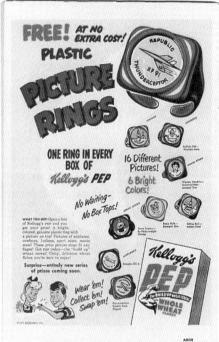

Plate 1

Birth of a Lively Lass

To date, most pulp art critics have enacted a simple binary to categorise the covers by dividing covers into good girl art (GGA) and bad girl art (BGA). But, like all binaries, this one fails to reflect the complexity of the female images.

GGA is drawn in the pinup tradition and the 'girl,' though sporting prominent breasts, is generally wholesome, happy and inviting:

> Humor, adventure, sci-fi and more have all featured good girl art. ... The scene might be risque for the time of publication. Prominent breasts (known as 'headlights') were the rule. Good girls were usually athletic, smart women who might fall into precarious positions.[16]

Though their costumes are skin tight and their voluptuous bodies sexually inviting (see Plate 1), the 'girls' are little more than sexy glamour models. GGA is most associated with teen and romance comics, and, in the 1990s, with fempower comics.[17] The journal title change from *Good Girl Art Quarterly* to *Good Girl Comics* encapsulates this. The 'good girl' is child-like and comics are her domain. For reasons unknown, good girl and bad girls often occupy the same visual space. The GG covers at 'Vintage Paperbacks and Designs' demonstrate this.[18] The first two covers, *Cracker Girl* and *Farm Girl* are typical GGA; however, the women (!) on *Girls Out of Hell* and

Gutter Star are clearly not 'good girls.' Even the titles give them away. Covers are intrinsically tied, not to the art, but to the semantics of the covers, which includes title, message and, probably, myth.

BGA is less easily defined, and many quote Dave Van Domelen's BGA Index rating system as a guide.[19] Van Domelen has attempted to quantity BGA by 'the degree of offence' BGA gives, and his systematic index is quite amusing but, again, the woman is more than the art. Yes, she has the prominent breasts of the good girl, but it is her lack of invitation, her aggressive (or 'abberant') sexuality, and her dangerous attitude that make her 'bad.' She embodies the transgressive female of the burlesque show. Some claim the bad girl didn't appear until the comics of the 1990s,[20] but I, an others, have found aspects of her from much earlier period.[21] Almost always, the bad girls are paired with 'criminal' activity, which accounts for her appearance on crime rather romance fiction covers.

The Study

The cover girls in this study did not fall into one or the other group; they deploy a little from both schools. Of the c.200 covers examined, four 'types' of female representation transpired, and I have labelled them to reflect their cultural heritage: Demure Damsels, Dangerous Dames, Passionate Pals, and Hootchie Kootchie Mamas. The Demure Damsels and Passionate Pals fall into the GGA category and demonstrate a domesticity and compliance associated with fashion/glamour and more bourgeois models of femininity. The Dangerous Dames and Hootchie Kootchie Mammas come from the BGA, and are differentiated by their clothing and accessories, hair colour and style, pose, gaze and presence/absences of male figures.

The **Demure Damsel** (*One Live Blonde*) is closest to the genteel Gibson girl—without the bourgeois/consumer display of fashion glamour. She wears 'street' clothes that cover her body; respectable skirts, blouses and hats in pastel colours. She may have a watch, but little else in the way of jewellery. Her hair is usually brown, but it might be blonde, though not the vibrant colours of her other pulp sisters. A male protagonist protects her; usually she is on the ground or in a dangerous situation. But no matter how threatening the situation, her legs remain covered. Because she does not court sexual desire, she fails to meet the male gaze; she looks down or away and, often, her face is obscured. Because size does matter, she is smaller than the male,[22] and, literally, stands in his shadow. Artistically, she is often blurred and rarely achieves the clarity of the other cover females; it's as if the artists didn't know how to draw a traditional female outside a domestic environment. Thus, the 'damsel in distress' embodies a traditional representation of the acquiescent female who has strayed from her home and needs rescuing. Her male protector acts as her knight errant. The Demure Damsel graced the covers of the earliest pulps and was superseded by the Passionate Pal.

The **Passionate Pal** is an early male Playmate (*The Blonde, So Lovely She Lies, Hi-Fi Fidelity*). Her clothing accentuates her voluptuous figure—skin tight, plunging necklines, sheer lingerie, and swimsuits. Her breasts are her prominent physical feature and are highlighted through judicious application of white paint; similarly, her mouth, eyes and hair receive close artistic treatment. Her hair colour, whether blonde, redhead or brunette, is vibrant compared to the background; unlike more independent misses, her hair is long and luxurious. She adopts classic 'cheesecake'[23] poses (*The Blonde*) and, sometimes, a semi-humorous pose suggests playfulness (*So Lively She Lies*). This playfulness is furthered by her style of dress, which is best described as inappropriate and, sometimes, ridiculous costumes— abbreviated pirate gear, off the shoulder peasant dresses, slinky evening gown in an office. Goffman postulates that such playfulness invites the reader not to take the female seriously. Further, it gestures to a theatricality linked with actresses and, vaguely, the burlesque. She can be posed with finger to mouth, adopting a breathless little-girl-lost look; if posed on bended knee, she is subordinate to the male. She dominates the cover and her very isolation suggests a fantasy and, thus, she is more akin to the calendar girl. However, unlike the calendar girl, her large size and foregrounding, in relation to the male figure, gesture to her power. Of all the cover girls, the Passionate Pal is the best known, she is the one most associated with PBOs. She is more glamorous than the Demure Damsel, but her childlike wonder and blatant sexuality makes her fabulous, but potentially accessible, unlike her threatening sister, the Dangerous Dame. This accessibility gestures to a male rather than a female readership (unlike the Demure Dame).

The **Dangerous Dame** (*Duchess Double-X*) presents a physical danger to the male character. She is bad to the bone. Her face is hard and she glares at the reader, daring them to respond. Her clothing might be revealing, but it is not about sexuality, it merely labels her as a woman who comes from 'that' kind of life — a gangster moll, a nightclub owner — she is glamorous and has attitude. Her aberrant appropriation of high culture clothing, evening dress and opera gloves,[24] gestures to burlesque artists and, thus, positions her as antithetical to the glamour girl. Indeed, she appears more an avaricious black widow or a succubus; she looks more like Madam Lash than a Duchess. She wears diamonds and other expensive jewellery because she is high maintenance; she is potentially a gold digger[25] or more likely someone who makes her own way in the world. She does not pose in supine positions, but stands as a man's equal and often confronts him. Her most important accessories are her cigarette and her smoking gun – a gun that is poised to shoot the male protagonist. Her smouldering look differentiates her from her pulp sisters, since the look challenges rather than invites — as Linton notes, directness of gaze is equated with "hard."[26] The Dangerous Dame is visually threatening, she is not contained or controlled like the Passionate Pal or Demure Dame. Her transgressive stare reeks of power and potential — the *ubberfemm* offers impertinence and an inversion of traditional femininity.

The **Hoochie Koochie Mama**[27] (*Hard Racket, Come in Sinner, Dagger of Flesh*) is a sexually ripe woman. She too adopts evening clothes, but they are tighter and accentuate her hips, belly and breasts. She is one of the few women to show her legs. Often, she stands with her hands on her hips, pelvis thrust forward. Thus, the focus is more intimate — her vagina rather than her breasts. She is bold and hard but not 'dangerous' in a physical sense; her danger is the threat of the sexually uncontrolled female. She faces the onlooker, but her eyes tend to slide to the men on the cover; she, thus, fleeting refers the onlooker to them as if in warning. But she refuses to engage with them. Her body and her head are held high "stereotypically a mark of unashamedness, superiority and disdain."[28] Hers is the most powerful female representation. What are they scared of? The males can deal with pointed guns, there is the possibility they can physically disarm the Dangerous Dame, but the fully sexualised female scares them. She is the rarest of images, and informs bad girl art.

As a group, the covers demonstrate similar features as those Goffman notes in his analysis of gender roles in advertisements. The women adopt prostrate poses, they are often lower than the males — sometimes they lie on their backs and sometimes on their stomachs. Of course, this not only indicates subservience but, particularly for women, it is a conventional expression of sexual availability. Her pose often reflects those adopted by strippers and burlesque dancers — typical 'cheesecake' poses, hands behind head (to emphasise breasts), legs outstretched (to emphasise pelvis), the inviting glance over the shoulder ('Grande Odilesque'). Size indicates importance, and while males, historically, have generally been larger in advertisements, on the pulp cover the female is the bigger figure and, therefore, more important. The female who caresses herself indicates not a self-love, but appreciation of her body as a precious thing and something to be fondled. The models do not smile, they might hold their mouths slightly opened, but smiling in any pinup pose, male or female, adds too much humour to an essentially sexual contract between viewer and viewed.

The four broad categories reflect different cultural heritages and influences. The Demure Damsels have their historical roots in courtly love, the male romance, and the boy's adventure story where women have little, if any, social agency. The Dangerous Dames and the Hootchie Kootchie Mamas reflect the sexual agency of the 1920s and the 1930s flapper and vamp — whose rejection of marriage and domesticity were reflected in their gyrations, partying, short hair, and rolled down stockings. The infantilised playmate pet, the most common representation of the 1950s, comes from the pinup girl who adorned the nose of airplanes in World War II, the images of George Petty and Albert Varga/s.

In 1940, Vargas replaced Petty as *Esquire*'s illustrator. His new interpretation of the pinup caused considerable debate and highlighted the anxieties of pinups (still relevant today). The Petty girls were sexualised versions of the girl next door, whereas the hyper-sexualised Varga female intimidated men. Petty advocates felt that the Varga/s woman "is good ... and shapely ... but she is ... far more hardened and callous ... she ... is not as likely to be taken out in public" (Dec. 1940 *Esquire*). Thus, she is sexualised Other. On the other hand, Varga/s supporters celebrated the women's confident sexuality, a sexuality which they felt mirrored the attitudes of contemporary women. The different views reflect, of course, a wider debate about the role of women, and highlights the changing attitude to women who had left the house during the war effort and had actively occupied male public spaces. When soldiers returned from the war, new stereotypes had to be deployed to assuage their fears, not only about female employment, but also about female power. During this period, popular culture reinscribed the ideal female as naïve, but explicitly sexual, that is to say woman were infantilised, becoming the passionate playmate.[29] This is most evident in magazines such as *Esquire* and *Playboy* which, alongside the pinups, filled their pages with jokes and cartoons of aging bosses with shapely but unskilled secretaries perched on their knees, as well as other variations, such as the fat 'oriental' potentate bored by his harem of sexually attractive 'wives.' As these women became inconsequential playthings and lost their power because they were disposable and/or incapable, men regained their control.

The mimicry depicted in the poses cries parergon, since they are derivative of a larger corpora of body display. They can lay claim to glamour, fashion, burlesque and pinup modes of address — aimed at a knowing audience. Not purely male, for there is no evidence that the consumption of the cover was limited to men. Indeed, the covers present fashions, hairstyles and dress, which may have offered potentiality for the female consumer. The wholesale labelling of pulp cover girls as 'good girl art' immobilises the power of the bad girl image and refutes the image's cultural context, and it is noticeably applied by males who claim "not to like BGA."[30] The bad girls offer a selection, albeit a smallish one, of women who actively occupied men's spaces, both figuratively and literally. She does not, like the Petty girl, drape herself across furniture chatting on the phone; she does not offer a fantasy to the private voyeur. Her glamour tends to be that of the night and the public space. She is seen in urban streets, in offices, gambling dens, night-clubs actively participating in a public world and rejecting the private space of the home.

It is a mistake to dismiss the cover designs as 'incidental', both culturally and industrially. Publishers deliberately created a visual metonymy in their covers, which became branded to their literary product. When Carter Brown was taken up by American publishers Signet, the editorial team's first priority was a marketing strategy that focused on the covers. They hired one of America's most sought after pulp artists, Bayre Phillips to execute the covers. In late 1959, Phillips was replaced by the equally famous Robert McGinnis. Both artists were given detailed instructions to adopt different cover treatments for the three detectives:

> *Al Wheeler*: long partly undressed girl, plain background and elongated two word title . . .
> *Mavis Seidlitz*: feature Mavis in a situation on the cover each time; she's a cross between Marilyn Monroe and Judy Holliday. Possibly give her a detailed atmosphere background and a longer title . . .
> *Danny Boyd*: women could wear the maximum [Wheeler minimum] ie high fashion in gowns, jewellery, matador pants—or any other garment from Vogue and Harpers that also looks sexy. Maximum can also be strapless and not curve concealing. [31]

The different cover treatments visually replicate the 'types' of textual females; Mavis is a private investigator and is given a busy background because she's a working woman. On the other hand, Al Wheeler's women are his playthings and, thus, their body display is important; Danny Boyd is a New York private eye and requires more sophisticated women.

The McGinnis covers demonstrate the trend away from sensational covers; his style mimics high fashion: his women are thinner and less voluptuous and the emphasis is on the clothing, not the bodies. The three variations of *The Blonde* show how the same illustrations were reinterpreted by different artists; indeed, the difference between the Australian covers and the overseas covers is a fascinating study in itself.

A cover is more than the illustration. Cover design blends fonts, colours, text size and layout in an effort to produce a visual semiotics. While the covers declared a male protagonist/author Carter Brown, Larry Kent, the 'heroes' were dwarfed to a fully fleshed female (*Hi Fi Fadeout*), relegated to the background (*The Hard Racket*) or absent (*The Blonde, Duchess Double-X*). Semantically powerful words – 'stripper', 'tramp', 'blonde', 'redhead', 'baby', 'cutie', 'dame' and 'sweetheart' – offered potential insight into the narrative. Sometimes, however, the covers were misleading. Because of strict deadlines, artists illustrated from titles rather from the written text; for instance, *Hard Racket* is not about the 'hard' life of prostitution, but about the 'racket', the mafia. No doubt many readers were disappointed when the women on the cover rarely provided the thrills they promised

Do pulp covers celebrate or exploit the female figure? Recently, feminists, art historians and cultural critics have re-examined, re-fashioned and even reclaimed the pinup (Maria Buszek, Joanne Meyerowitz, Linda Nochlin, Annie Sprinkle). While sides might never agree, the 'pinup' or 'cover girl' is not as homogenised an image as one might think. The lovechild of *Esquire* illustrators and the burlesque artist, the chanteuse and the vamp, the cover girls of the 1950s are not merely idealised representations of females. They also offered visual resistance and images of power and control. As Jessica Rabbit crooned, 'I'm not bad I'm just drawn that way.'

Notes

1. http://www.who2.com/jessicarabbit.html
   www.petcaretips.net/jessica-rabbit.html
   www.rainbo.net/jessica_shop.html
   www.thrillingdetective.com/eyes/valiant.html
2. Covers are from two Sydney publishing houses and adorned two similar and competing detective series—Carter Brown and Larry Kent. Both were penned by local authors and illustrated by local artists. Crime fiction was chosen because of the perceived intended, male, reader. The images are restricted to those pre-1960. Post-1960 covers replaced pinup cheesecake with a glamour model look.
3. Some of the most culturally complex covers adorn romance, horror, war and sports pulp paperbacks.
4. Steven Heller and Seymour Chwast, *Jackets Required* (1995); Alan Powers, *Front Cover: Great Book Jacket and Cover Designs* (2001); Richard Lupoff, *The Great American Paperback: An Illustrated Tribute to the Legends of the Book* (2001); Jennifer McKnight-Trontz, *The Look of Love: The Art of the Romance Novel* (2002); Stephane Duperray and Raphaele Vidaling, *Front Page: Covers of the Twentieth Century* (2003).
5. David Earle's thesis on modernism and pulp book covers, Robert Lesser, *Pulp Art* and various Collector's Press and Adventure House publications.
6. Douglas Ellis, *Uncovered the Hidden Art of Girlie Pulp*, Jaye Zimet, *Strange Sisters: The Art of Lesbian Pulp Fiction 1949-1969*.
7. Of course, the question as to whether or not they are 'fine' art is not the point of this paper. They are handcrafted paintings, if one prefers.

8   Burlesque's principal legacy as a cultural form was its establishment of patterns of gender representation that changed the role of the woman on the American stage and influenced her role on the screen. The female body not covered by accepted forms of costume forcefully, if playfully, called attention to the entire question of the 'place' of woman in American society.

9   Varga changed his name from Vargas. For details of the exhibition, see, Alberto Vargas: The *Esquire* Pinups. http://www.ku.edu/~sma/vargas.htm

10   Robert G Allen, *Horrible Prettiness: Burlesque and American Culture* Chapel Hill: University of North Carolina Press, 1991), 258-259.

11   Originally 'pulp fiction' referred to all-fiction magazines printed on cheap wood-pulp paper (for example *Black Mask*). Over the years, 'pulp' has become shorthand for mass-produced fiction that is formulaic rather than literary. Australian pulps are slim (usually fewer than one hundred pages), stapled publications around 18-20cms in size; they are more accurately called digests.

12   Malcolm Cowley, *The Literary Situation* (New York: Viking, 1954), 120.

13   http://www.luridfridge.com/, http://www.cafepress.com/pulpart http://classichardware.com

14   Gibson drew dewy-eyed females as representations of American womanhood in the late nineteenth and early twentieth centuries:
see http://www.gibson-girls.com/

15   Phillips became famous for his fade-away beauties:
www.bpib.com/illustrat/phillips.htm

16   http://www.samuelsdesign.com/comics/agoodgirl_romance.html

17   http://rkscroy1.tripod.com/goodgirlcoversc.htm

18   http://www.vintagepbks.com/ggadigestcovers.html

19   Dave Van Domelen's attempt to quantify the degree of offence given by BGA, as presented to general audiences in solicitation material, such as Diamond's *Previews* magazine. Any depiction of the female form in a solicitation is fair game for assigning a BGA Index, but the threshold that must be passed in order to be truly considered BGA has not yet been determined, although 5 seems like a lower bound. Every depiction starts at 0 points, then adds points based on the Format, Pose, Body Type, Clothes Type and Clothes Coverage of the female shown.

20   http://home.comcast.net/~brons/Comics/Women2.html

21   http://www.samuelsdesign.com/comics/agoodgirl_romance.html

22   Goffman, 79.

23   Webster defines cheesecake as "photography displaying especially female comeliness and shapeliness."

24   Websites devoted to opera gloves attest to its powerful fetishisation.

25   The gold digger is particular potent during this period; the Varga/s Esquire illustration depicting a female chatting on the phone and its mercenary verse. Hardened the girl let door image of George Petty.

26   Allen 140.

27   Term first used in 1893 when Little Egypt introduced the 'hootchie-kooch' at the Chicago World's Fair (History of Burlesque).

28   Goffman 40.

29   Most obviously embodied in the 'Playmate' and 'Pet' of the Month/Year pinups.

30   http://home.comcast.net/~brons/Comics/BGA.html

31   Letter to Stanley Horwitz to Victor Weybright, 24 Nov 1958. New American Library Archives.

A Body Narrative

He broke my mouth.
My little-girl mouth that wasn't finished growing.
Stunted in time and moment – always in this moment.

Must wash my teeth.
Remove the taste of memory – of rancid memory.
No entry, no exit signs – must protect. Must not break again.

I did not break.
I was broken – a little piece of me broken.
Always broken. Always unclean.

Touched. Damaged goods. Not my fault.
My fault. My silence. No words.
Lips silent, scared; silent and blamed.

Scarred – no sign though.
Secret held. Secret festered.
"My tummy is sore"

My nose gets cold sores.
The festered secret exposed here.
Not on my lips.

HE He hE he is not pictured.
Don't need to picture him.
His legacy – in my alphabet.
No picture is needed.
Always re-membered.

"Time moves", my lips re-mind.
Dis-member.
Discard and Re-form.

This is a journey through and from my body. A snapshot made up of disjointed pieces connected and pulled together in and by my body. My body that is still learning to truly plough her/my own furrow. It is a story of my body, my female body in this patriarchal overlay called 'real life.' A life where my body contends with expectations of how female meaning feminine should be, should perform and express it-self. I deliberately use the word 'it-self' because this is what femininity is – an entity, an expectation and a limitation that my female is measured against. It is the 'complementary' to its opposite masculinity in this reality. Hence, the feminine is less powerful, and less important than the normative privilege that is masculine.

Femininity is an it-cellf, an it-sellf[1] that is imposed on my female self, my Self. An imposition that I have struggled against and with, performed, been almost drowned by, and have attempted to redefine.

My body story in this moment is a focus on my lips. My lips do not exist disembodied from my entirety, nor do I wish they did. They are part and all of me at the same time. I choose my lips for reasons of pain and sorrow. Marked in a way that is common to my body yet singular also to my lips: the intrusion of the male gaze.

I was born with female lips.

In fact, or maybe it's fiction or fairytale? anyway, from the very start I had female lips. From the moment my mother's egg fused with my father's sperm I was spelt XX. It's a letters thing you know. Like having certain letters after your name means you can vote in the Seanad elections, XX confers a particular meaning onto my lips. 'XX'! Pronounced FEMALE! XX marks the spot, marks my lips out as female with the expectation of feminine. Available-kissable lips! The most valuable thing I can do with my female lips is to kiss a prince (or male frog)!

What it boils down to is XX means my lips are not only female, but somehow feminine and should only want to kiss male lips. Be they prince or frog my happy-ever-after is guaranteed with one kiss in once-upon-a-time empty promise bedtime stories.

Contrary to *The Concise English Dictionary*, my lips are not only my glorious "fleshy parts enclosing the opening of [my] mouth, or the edge or margin of [my] orifice, chasm, etc."[2] They are also my site of betrayal and devastation – a living reminder of just what XX truly marks them out for. Men! The XY of the species! XX is a false promise that I can be a separate subject. In the XY privileged Patriarchal Zoo[3] I am an exhibit[ion] with a dual role: a subject for the male gaze, and an object of it. (A) Subject to the expectation and imposition of femininity for the pleasure and gain of masculinity.

Let the circus begin! Let the show begin! The show must go on!

When I drag up in femininity, my lipstick corset constricts my breathing and alters my contours. Its leeching nature softens my edges. Fantastically bold colours and pastel-astic colours alike seek to erase (my colour) me. Seek to deny my menstrual red. Of course, not only are there lipstick products to buy so that my lips can say 'Hello boys – can you see me? Can you see the potential pleasure (for you) that lies here? I have dressed up my lips for you to notice.' There are products I need to buy to ensure I remove all trace of this feminine garnish (once I am on my own of course – out of the sight of the virile carnivore). These chemicals not only are removers of lipstick. They bleach me, seeking to create me without my consent, to blonde me into achieving the ultimate femininity. That ultimate crowning glory of blonde-hood!

How I don't look!

This is what it has always come down to. How I don't measure up, am just not feminine enough. Slim, compact lips that reflect my slim, petite body. On the one hand I am perfect – I do not take up much physical space. Given my body size and preference for hot water and healthy eating it is assumed I do not need much food, much taking care of, much money spent on me.

> Standing joke by male colleagues – 'You'd be a cheap date. Sure all I'd have to do is give you hot water and you'd be fine.'

Yet, I am too slim. There is no subtle roundness in my lips, no tantalising temptation of sexy voluptuousness. I do not fulfil this, but I fulfil the demand of confusion. The internalisation of being almost there but not quite there – never quite being 'right.'

And, so, the options open to me. Admit to failure? Resist? Try to fulfil?

Well, as a little girl I tried to ignore it. To pretend that it did not matter, that I wanted to be a tomboy because being a girl was sissy and silly anyway. No skirts or dresses for me. No thanks! Tatty cords and trees please and just bring on those boys who think they are stronger than me and I'll show them what's what!

But then, my tomboy lips were still marked 'girly.' I had not reckoned on this. When he imposed woman on them, marked them woman for all to see (but no one saw) all I could do was close them. I could not be a tomboy anymore. Amnesia! That's it. It never happened. What comes next? Puberty. Okay! Discomfort, silence. Better than 'that'! Better than what? Yes, I was good at amnesia.

> Running away only to run back again – no hiding place.

Have you ever seen lips run? Run as they seek to swallow an escaped thought or word or emotion? Run from pain, the taste that is too much for the tongue and that the lips are cursed with protecting, with blocking the entrance? I tried to run from mine, tried amnesia. It worked you know. For a long time it was successful. But then my lips re-membered. And no matter how I tried to amnese again, my lips were there, on-site to re-mind. Comfort-eating, crying, anger, affirmations, breathing exercises – no matter what I could not escape my own lips of pain.

Re-Minded.

Not until I learned to kiss myself better, to smile at my reflection in my lips and to give back what was never mine – that which was imposed. Now my lips do not need to run. A glorified jog in the park where breathing is pleasure and green is the colour of life – new growth and comfort.

My lips are green. When I grow up I want to be a tree.

> "she is importantly a body designed to please or to excite" [4]

I became good at compliance too! I made sure to sit with my lips together, never to spread them, to keep them mannerly. To make sure I fitted in, stayed hidden, could not be seen or targeted. Nice words, please, thank you, no fried food or biscuits for me, thank you.

Learned that my lips are about pleasing and smiling, being grateful for the crumbs, indeed eager for them. This is how femininity decrees my lips should be, should look. I am supposed to frame 'yes.' My (bee's) waxed smooth and supple lips are supposed to reflect the availability of my body. A coy, shy smile. An inviting smile that says I'm available but I need to be taught by you, a man. I need to learn from you how to part my lips so they can suck and simper, swell and moan. 'Yes!' is part of my mark as feminine. No wonder 'No' cannot be heard!

Failure.

Self-regulation. Denial. I did not look 'just so' QED I was not entitled to wear certain types of clothes, especially anything pretty. An endless list of deprivations. A form of resistance that denied my body, denied my lips- pleasure. Focus instead on the words and the intelligence that passed through (and from) my lips. No need to worry about non-beauty, non-femininity. My mind and thoughts are superior to that – they can be beautiful regardless of my body. The sacred intellectual.

Failure.

Self-improvement. Beauty (image) investment. Collagen perhaps? Stay thin, remove the wrinkles (not allowed to wear signs of age and aging) and perhaps get a little bit of that essential curve – fat-free, of course? But what about the ridicule? The moral judgements filed against me for caring too much? The vicious circle of repeat visits, repeat treatments, more treatments? Can I do this? Another form of resistance that centres me as the problem.

Failure.

Resistance!

A resistance that fits me, fits me as sexy, gorgeous, myself – not an it-cellf. Not a resistance that accepts the normative feminition.

'Why' questions! They took a long time to form. No more despair coated in nerd-ship or corduroy trousers. 'Why' demands rattled my bony lips. 'Why is femininity only spelt one way?' 'Why can't I define it for myself?' 'Who says I'm not feminine?' 'Why do I have to deny and limit myself because of dictates that are imposed?' 'I mean, I no longer believe that the

Pope is infallible or that the Bible is the word of God. Why should I limit myself because of femininity?'

Body building.

Originally to ensure strong muscles: so that my lips would not bite off more than they could chew. So that I could say 'No' and get away with my body intact. Aesthetic pleasure and enjoyment of my big, strong, defined muscles soon followed. In one fell swoop of many repetitions and increasing weights I got fat-free curves **and** subverted the notion of femininity. But it became an addiction, a way of running too until I met a bus. So I gave up my addiction to muscular, fat-free, flat-chested beauty. Ghosts of muscular definition remain though depending on how I flex my lips, most evident when I say 'No.' I am returned to my 'natural' thinness. I am predisposed to being a thin body but with diet (not quite dieting) and exercise I assist how nature and genetics have randomly built me.

Body building led to further 'whys' and explorations of a more cerebral nature. 'What does it mean for me to be a woman, a person in a female body?' 'A person in a female body in a male world?'

Quiet Revolutions

I learned to kiss my own lips, began to enjoy my thinness, to revel in my bony-being. I learned to say 'NO', to say it loudly and most importantly to say it to those who mark me. I learned to demand and expect pleasure – my pleasure. Learned to locate it first and then share it when my lips were safe.

My lips began to smile more. More secret smiles. Smiles just for me as I enjoy my secret, private political subversion. I am feminine according to my body. As defined and shaped by my lips. As spoken by my lips. I will walk out, will speak out – no more isolation in silence. I am not picking up my pieces for someone else anymore. You must pick up the pieces. If you cannot hold me in my thin hugeness then you cannot hold me.

Martina Boyle

Notes
1. Femininity is multi-faceted. It is a "cellf" in the sense of Foucault's panopticon, and a "sellf" in its consumer, consumption demands of its bearer.

2   Arthur J Hayward. and John J. Sparkes, *The Concise English Dictionary: The Concise One Volume Reference Book of The English Language* (London, New Orchard, Fourth Edition, Twelfth Impression, 1990).

3   In a zoo, animal species are contained in cages/areas. They are on show to entertain humans and to fulfil our fascination with the exotic. Their biological peculiarities are spelt out for us on information plaques. Indeed, their position in cages sets them up as somehow dangerous to us and, according to our evolutionary theories, inferior to the ultimate species, i.e. human. In a zoo, ideas of biology, cages and keepers, exposure and audience collide. In the Patriarchal Zoo the female of the human species is contained and on show for the entertainment of the human male. She is viewed and defined according to the norm of the male viewer. In patriarchal systems and structures the female is less than the male and this is justified through the (ab)use of biology.

4   Sandra Bartky, 'Foucault, Femininity and the Modernization of Patriarchal Power' in Rose Weitz, ed. *The Politics of Women's Bodies* (Oxford: Oxford UP, 1998), 117.

References

Smyth, Ailbhe. 'Loving the Bones Medi(t)ating My Bodies' in Janet Price and Margrit Shildrick, eds. *Vital Signs: Feminist Reconfigurations of the Bio/logical Body.* Edinburgh: Edinburgh UP, 1998, 18-29.

Ensler, Eve. *The Vagina Monologues*. London: Virago Press, 2001.

Nkweto Simmonds, Felly. 'My Body, Myself: How Does A Black Woman Do Sociology?' in Janet Price and Margrit Shildrick, eds. *Feminist Theory and the Body: A Reader*. Edinburgh: Edinburgh UP, 1999, 50-63.

Coles, Fen. 'Feminine Charms and Outrageous Arms' in Janet Price and Margrit Shildrick, eds. *Feminist Theory and the Body: A Reader*. Edinburgh: Edinburgh UP, 1999, 445-453.

Kelly, Liz. 'When Does the Speaking Profit Us? Reflections on the Challenges of Developing Feminist Perspectives on Abuse and Violence By Women' in Marianne Hester, Liz Kelly and Jill Radford, eds. *Women, Violence and Male Power*. Milton Keynes: Open UP, 1996, 34-49.

Shildrick, Margrit. 'Introduction' in Margrit Shildrick. *Leaky Bodies and Boundaries: Feminism, Postmodernism and (Bio)Ethics*. London: Routledge, 1997, 1-12.

Shildrick, Margrit. 'Conclusion' in Margrit Shildrick. *Leaky Bodies and Boundaries: Feminism, Postmodernism and (Bio)Ethics*. London: Routledge, 1997, 211-217.

Connell, R.W. 'Making Gendered People: Bodies, Identities, Sexualities' in Myra Marx Ferree, Judith Lorber and Beth B. Hess, eds. *The Gender Lens – Revisioning Gender*. London: Sage Publications, 1999, 449-471.

Chhachhi, Sheba. 'Raktpushp (Blood Flower)' in Janet Price and Margrit Shildrick, eds. *Vital Signs: Feminist Reconfigurations of the Bio/logical Body*. Edinburgh: Edinburgh UP, 1998, 102-131.

Bordo, Susan. 'Feminism, Foucault and The Politics of The Body' in Janet Price and Margrit Shildrick, eds. *Feminist Theory and the Body: A Reader*:. Edinburgh: Edinburgh UP, 1999, 246-257.

Minh-ha, Trinh T. 'Write Your Body and The Body In Theory' in Janet Price and Margrit Shildrick, eds. *Feminist Theory and the Body: A Reader*. Edinburgh: Edinburgh UP, 1999, 258-266.

In the Mountains

I struggle up the hill
after a night with my classmates
and sit in the kitchen
eating cheese and bread,
miserable in the dark.

At the weekend
we stay with the families.
My French is poor.
Isabel plays with her friends
at the village fair.

Her grandmother takes me in.
We bake apple pies
wordlessly.
She is brown, stick-thin
and constantly moving.

The family crowd the table
at dinner time.
They talk and talk.
She eats a mouthful of stew
and three slices of apple pie.

78A

Women on the bus to Ballyfermot
Greet each other Grand, Grand
Then lean their heads together
Very sad. Very sad.

Sheila Phelan

Sonja Tiernan

Tipping the Balance with Historical Fiction: *Tipping the Velvet* as a Lesbian Feminist Device

Caroline Gonda has suggested that theory, "need not emerge from, or remain bounded by, academic disciplines or institutions ... lesbian theory has often most fruitfully been worked out and exemplified in fiction and poetry."[1] Fiction is accessible to a wider audience than academic writing or theory is, and novels have the potential to convey the principles of lesbian feminism in a credible way. This paper shows how literature has been used in the past to portray a negative impression of lesbianism and how history has been distorted or destroyed to exclude lesbians from historical discourse. This analysis summarises how negative imagery has affected the lives of lesbians and been used to suppress the formation of a lesbian community. I analyse the novel, *Tipping the Velvet* by Sarah Waters, to reveal how historical fiction can rewrite lost history via the ideals of lesbian feminist theory. Fiction has the potential to reclaim lesbian culture and history, while addressing issues of (hetero)patriarchal injustice.

Histories of entire cultures have been excluded from mainstream historical discourse, while historical events have been manipulated or ignored from historical writings. People or groups who were left outside power structures were also left out of the history books, while the concerns of the powerful/dominant group consisting of white, heterosexual, males were represented. In this way the dominant group is historicised as the inventors, the discoverers, the artists, writers, and the people who mattered. Fleishman reminds us that, "history itself does not tell truths that are unambiguous or absolute; even the nature of historical fact is problematic."[2] Gay and lesbian culture has been manipulated or ignored by mainstream history, and this (mis)representation demonstrates that the significance of homosexuals needs to be quelled. Lack of historical data may be used to suggest that homosexuality is a modern 'phenomenon', which may prove problematic for homosexual identities. Lesbian history has further complications, and Waters notes that the fact that male homosexuality was illegal, "ironically guaranteed archival resource by if nothing else, homophobic legislation."[3] Castle refers to this as the "Queen Victoria Principle": "When asked by her ministers in 1885 whether the recent legislated Criminal Law Amendment Act outlawing homosexual acts between men should apply to women as well, she is supposed to have expressed disbelief that such acts between women were physically possible."[4] Without a wealth of official records from the Victorian era, Vicinus maintains that the "rediscovery of past lesbians has focussed either upon the lives of well-known writers, artists, and activists who have left extensive documentation."[5] The obvious problem with this research is that it only represents a small section of lesbians, arguably middle class and white women. Gowing acknowledges that "much of lesbian subcultural life took place in spaces and spheres that have been largely invisible to historians."[6] It is only in recent years that lesbian history has been recorded, and these studies have tended to be literary based, since the majority of lesbian historians come from a literary background: Lillian Faderman, Terry Castle, Bonnie Zimmerman, and Emma Donoghue. This is not surprising, given that, as Castle says, "literature is the mirror of what is known."[7]

To examine this rich source of fiction, I have classified the representation of lesbians in literature into three categories: apparitional, heterosexualised, and evil. My first category, 'apparitional', is a term coined by Castle, who maintains that, "to try to write the literary history of the lesbian is to confront from the start, something ghostly: an impalpability, a misting over, an evaporation, or a 'whiting out' of possibility."[8] In this context, the lesbian character appears in literature as a haunting force, almost invisible. There are many examples of past literary works in which the lesbian becomes a phantom. Daniel Defoe's *The Apparition of Mrs Veal* (1706), details a loving encounter between two characters, Mrs Veal and Mrs Bargrave. After intimate exchanges, the two women attempt to kiss, but this never materialises because it transpires that Mrs Veal is a ghost. Castle believes that the ghost is "a crucial metaphor for the history of lesbian literary representation since the early eighteenth century."[9]

My second category, which I term heterosexualisation, relates to the denial by heterosexist critics, that past authors were writing about sapphic love, and were, in fact, heterosexual. Even Sappho underwent a heterosexualising process from past male historians. Greene testifies that, "Addison claims in *Spectator* no. 223 that the *Hymn to Venus* was in fact written on occasion of Sappho's unrequited passion for Phaon, in an attempt to get Aphrodite to intervene and force the young man to return Sappho's advances."[10] Faderman maintains that historians and literary critics have "gone to great pains to deny lesbian existence."[11] Many biographers strive to establish authors as heterosexual, assuming that this automatically establishes their literature as heterosexual.[12] Such has been the case with Emily Dickinson, since some literary critics claim that Dickinson was in love with a man. An example of this (mis)representation is the *Norton Anthology: Literature by Women*, edited by two feminist scholars, Sandra Gilbert and Susan Gubar, who make reference to biographers' assumptions that Dickinson had an unrequited love for Reverend Charles Wadsworth. They state, "for years, biographers of Dickinson assumed that sometime in the early 1860s she had fallen hopelessly in love with a man whose identity has never been established … supposed to be the Reverend Charles Wadsworth." [13] The implication is that Dickinson was driven to create wonderful poetry in a bid to deal with her emotions for a man. Gilbert and Gubar do question whether it was, in fact, Wadsworth who was her muse, but they assume that the muse was male. This highlights how some feminist scholarship adheres to heterosexual presumption. Gilbert and Gubar neglect to mention the letters from Dickinson to other women, including her sister-in-law, Susan Huntington Dickinson, which clearly show intense emotional relationships between Emily and Susan. [14] Although not directly stated, it is evident from Dickinson's language that she is, indeed, referring to female same-sex love:

> Her breast is fit for pearls,
> But I was not a 'Diver' –
> Her brow is fit for thrones
> But I have not a crest.
> Her heart is fit for *home* –
> I – a Sparrow – build there
> Sweet of twigs and twine
> My perennial nest. [15]

In their edition of Dickinson's poetry and letters, Hart and Smith researched the original manuscripts to discover that the above poem was written in pencil. The name 'Sue' was vigilantly erased from the manuscript of this poem, probably by Dickinson's original editor, Mabel Loomis Todd. Todd published *Letters* (1894), a compilation of Dickinson's work and placed the poem in a section among letters to Samuel Bowles. "By falsely attributing the poem, Loomis Todd accomplished two objectives: she disguised a love poem to Susan, and she made Emily's correspondence to Bowles (with whom she is said to have been in love) appear more inclusive of his wife." [16] Past readings of Emily Dickinson are a prime example of the kind of distortion and denial that female same-sex literature has undergone. A more recent reading of Dickinson's poetry proposes that she used coded language to convey clitoral imagery and, thus, identified a sapphic sexuality. Bennett notes that the terms, "jewels, gems, pearls, peas, berries, nuts, buds, crumbs, and beads abound in Dickinson's poetry."[17]

Many lesbian authors used the cloak of assumed heterosexuality to cover their sapphic tendencies in coded language in order to avoid censoring or banning of their writing. Faderman devotes a section to this style of writing in her anthology, referring to it as, "In the Closet: The Literature of Lesbian Encoding."[18] She includes Charlotte Mew, Gertrude Stein, Amy Lowell, Katherine Mansfield, and Virginia Woolf. There are many writers who, for various reasons, camouflaged their writing; some simply did not use gendered terms or descriptors at all, as a deliberate strategy to cloak their sapphic intent. Others used words to play on meanings, for example Gertrude Stein used 'Miss Furr and Miss Skeene' to play on the term gay.

But, coded language or censored books does not mean that lesbianism did not exist in literature, and so my third category includes an array of literature from male writers who were both appalled and titillated by the expression of female same-sex love. Prior to the twentieth century, female sexuality was often defined in literature by heterosexist authors; the fact that men were considered to be the great writers, meant that male heterosexual definitions of lesbians achieved credibility. During the nineteenth century, readers witnessed the lesbian as evil, monstrous, and vampiric. Faderman explains, "The very exoticism of the lesbian could render her evil and monstrous, and thus a subject for sensationalistic literature that was often overlaid with moralism."[19] Literature in this genre can be seen from the sixteenth century onwards, such as Brantôme's *Lives of Fair and Gallant Ladies,* or eighteenth century examples, such as William King's *The Toast*. With the onset of the sexologists of the nineteenth century, there was a huge increase in this moralistic anti-lesbian literature, such as Sheridan Le Fanu's *Carmilla* or Balzac's *The Girl with the Golden Eyes*. There are many examples of nineteenth century literature that presented the lesbian character as evil, most famously, perhaps, Charles Baudelaire's *Les Fleurs du Mal*, originally entitled *Les Lesbiennes*, whose poems are a description of two anguished female lovers as sick spectres roaming forever in a tormented hell.

The lesbian image was distorted or suppressed in this male-dominated literature; therefore, when the lesbian feminist movement became politicised in the late 1960s, there was an attempt to redress this injustice. Lesbian feminist publishing houses were established and a new breed of self-identified lesbian writers penned novels that, as Faderman notes, "presented sex between women as mutually fulfilling, guilt-free, constructive, and a cause for celebration."[20] Prose such as Judy Grahn's *Edward the Dyke* (1971) and Rita Mae Brown's novel *Rubyfruit Jungle* (1973), used comedy to mock patriarchy and homophobia.

Lesbian feminists recognised homophobia as a prejudiced system of beliefs in the 1970s, when the term homophobia was coined. A youth education leaflet produced by 'Talking Point' informs us that the term is used, "to describe the fear of loving or being intimate/sexual with someone of the same sex and the hatred of those feelings in others." [21] Homophobic behaviour can range from name calling in the street to loss of life. In-between these actions there is a reality for lesbians that their civil liberty, educational and career prospects are negatively affected because of homophobia. Pharr notes that, "Heterosexism creates the climate for homophobia with its assumption that the world is and must be heterosexual and its display of power and privilege as the norm."[22] Lesbian feminist literature fought against heterosexism and homophobia by portraying them in novels as unjust and ultimately laughable beliefs. Out of this portrayal grew what Faderman terms "post-lesbian-feminist literature" in the 1980s and 1990s.[23] In this genre of writing, novels and poetry depict female same-sex passion, and authors such as Jewelle Gomez and Katherine Forrest re-appropriate the lesbian vampire image as a queer icon of transgressive sexuality. In addition, writers such as Jeanette Winterson and Rebecca Brown, put a post-modern twist to novels. This genre of fiction plays with the constructs of gender, and offers an alternative to the rigid binary of male/female and homo/hetero.

More recently, authors such as Emma Donoghue and Sarah Waters have used historical fiction to develop a homosexual consciousness. Indeed, historical fiction is a powerful medium through which lesbian history can be rewritten:

> We might compare the historical novelist to the restorer of a damaged tapestry, who weaves in whole scenes or figures to fill the empty places which a more austere museum curator might leave bare. But if the insertion is made on the basis of sympathy, experience, and aesthetic propriety, it can lend revived expressiveness and coherence to the tapestry.[24]

This is evident in Waters' novel, *Tipping the Velvet*, which was published in 1998 by Virago Press. Waters was interested in this genre of novels after researching the subject of lesbian and gay historiography for a PhD thesis entitled 'Wolfskins and Togas: Lesbian and Gay Historical Fictions 1870 to the Present.'[25] This novel includes the lesbian sexual outlaw, a character presented in post-modern literature, while redressing the injustice of suppressed and distorted lesbian history. *Tipping the Velvet* won the

Lambada Literary Award for fiction, and has also been adapted as a mini-series by the BBC. It appears that the novel has captured the imagination of lesbian and heterosexual readers throughout Europe and America. It is evident that the novel deploys lesbian feminist theory to reinstate a different historical perspective.

Tipping the Velvet is set in England from 1888 to 1895, and follows the story of an oyster-girl, who becomes a male impersonator, then a rent boy, a mistress to a rich sapphic and, finally, an out lesbian suffragist. In this way, Waters portrays a number of different lesbian identities. Before even opening the pages of this novel, there are clues about what is held beneath the cover: the title of the book, *Tipping the Velvet*, is a Victorian euphemism for cunnilingus. Waters does not share this information with the reader until near the conclusion, when the slang term is used in relation to lesbian sexuality. When, Nancy asks, "'Tipped the velvet: what does that mean?' Florence parted her lips and showed me the tip of her tongue; and glanced, very quickly, at my lap" (416).[26] The explanation is clearly given in relation to a female same-sex act; it is explained in relation to two women, in a lesbian environment.

The use of such imagery is particularly poignant to lesbian readers who, for decades, have read between the lines of novels, or decoded literature, looking for signals to establish their own form of sapphic texts. Allison Hennegan addresses this process by describing how, unable to access lesbian literature in the early 1960s, she read 'mainstream' books, adapting themes, plots and characters, to suit her own end. Hennegan describes how this "created my own 'popular fiction', developed my own cherished canon."[27] Waters plays on the process of reading a novel from a lesbian perspective by including many 'in' jokes. The introduction of the main character in *Tipping the Velvet* as 'Nancy Astley' establishes this tongue-in-cheek humour. The name is a play on homosexual terminology, a 'Nancy' or 'Nancy Boy' is a term applied to an effeminate gay man while, in pronunciation, the 't' in Astley is silent making the surname sound like 'Assley', a further pun on male homosexuality. When Nancy becomes a male impersonator, she chooses the stage name Nancy King, which is a link to the term 'drag king.' This is the term applied to contemporary male impersonators, and is the opposite of 'drag queen.' Waters follows this line of humour throughout the novel, using the term 'queer' to its best effect. According to *The Oxford English Dictionary*, this term was in common use after 1700, during the time *Tipping the Velvet* is set, as: "Not in normal condition; out of sorts; giddy, faint, or ill: to feel or look queer. Also slang for drunk."[28] The term was used frequently in literature of the era, the dictionary offers the example of Dickens's Dombay, "I am so very queer that I must ask you for a glass of wine and a morsel of cake."[29] Writing historical fiction, Waters has an excuse to use the term as it would have been applied in the 1800s, but with the contemporary definition in mind. The fact that queer described something not in 'normal' condition, led to the term being applied as a derogatory slang phrase for homosexuality. However, the 1990s saw the birth of a new, radical political group, which reappropriated the term 'queer' as an act of defiance.[30]

Waters uses queer with all of these definitions in mind. The first reference to queer in the novel is in relation to Nancy falling in love with Kitty. Nancy thinks to herself, "how queer it is! – And yet, how very ordinary: *I am in love with you*'" (33). This line encompasses all of Waters' intentions; it describes how female same-sex love is queer in the Victorian context, that it is not a 'normal condition', it is also queer in the contemporary context in that it fucks with (hetero)gender performance. Queer attempts to transform the (hetero) patriarchal structure, to break down unequal binaries of male/female, hetero/homo. After Nancy and Kitty establish a relationship, Nancy sums up queer theory: "The world, to me, seemed utterly transformed since Kitty Butler had stepped into it. It had been ordinary before she came; now it was full of queer electric spaces" (38). This is the goal of queer, to transform the 'ordinary' world of heterosexism, and replace it with a utopian structure regarding gender and sexuality. Smyth attests that, "queer promises a refusal to apologise or assimilate into invisibility. It provides a way of asserting desires that shatter gender identities and sexualities."[31]

The first introduction to the character of Nancy identifies her as a typical working class girl; she is not exceptional, except that Nancy had "a rather inconvenient passion" (5). The reader is told that this passion is for music halls, however, the "inconvenient passion" also equates to her lesbian desire. It is in the music halls that Nancy is introduced to a male impersonator called Kitty Butler, and ultimately discovers what is missing in her life. It is noteworthy that when Kitty first enters the novel she is wearing lavender gloves, since this colour is an international signifier of lesbianism.[32] However, lavender was not associated with the 'lesbian menace' until the 1970s, long after the time period in which the novel is set and, so, the reference can be read as an 'in' joke for the lesbian community, while also functioning as recognition that the lavender lesbian menace has always existed. Colour is often attributed to sexuality, in terms of the gay male, 'pink' is often used as a signifier. Or, in the case of Hitler's Nazi regime, a pink triangle was used to signify homosexuality.

The novel then follows a typical 'coming out' plot, which is a common story line for lesbian literature, especially for an author's first novel.[33]

Nancy slowly learns to recognise and name her lesbian tendencies; this realisation is closely followed by her awareness that society condemns female same-sex love. During a family meal, the discussion turns to Nancy's 'mash' on Kitty, and her Uncle Joe expresses disbelief. "'She's the gal what dresses up as a feller, ain't she?' He pulled a face. 'Pooh, Nancy, the real thing not good enough for you any more?'" (19). This statement promotes hetero-normative ideals that the only 'real' sexuality is heterosexuality and, therefore, lesbianism is deviant from the norm. Nancy's father further cements the view by informing the group, "I think there's a young chap in the orchestra pit what she's got her eye on" (19). This assertion shows that her father cannot even envisage, or refuses to recognise the idea that she may be in love with another woman; there must be a man involved. Hetero-normativity is the assumption that society and all relationships are heterosexual, as Monique Wittig states, "the straight mind cannot conceive of a culture, a society where heterosexuality would not order only all human relationships but also its very production of concepts."[34]

In her examination of 'Homophobia a Weapon of Sexism', Pharr describes how homophobic attitudes repress lesbianism, whereby a lesbian "is a threat to the nuclear family, to male dominance and control, to the very heart of sexism."[35] When Nancy brings Kitty home for tea, the reader is witness to the injustices of the (hetero) patriarchal society:

> To have to sit beside her at my father's table with that love within me, mute and restless as a gnawing worm. I would have to smile while Mother asked, Why didn't Kitty have a beau? And smile again when Davy held Rhonda's hand, or Tony pinched my sister's knee beneath the table – when all the while my darling would be at my side, untouchable. (44)

This excerpt signifies lesbianism as the 'love that dare not speak its name'. Nancy is literally 'mute' in relation to her love for Kitty. Nancy is aware that her sister can express her love for her boyfriend as can her brother, Davy, for his girlfriend; however, same-sex love is literally 'untouchable.' This passage identifies the injustice of hetero-normativity, which makes it acceptable for some individuals to express their love, while others are silenced. This scene is also a realisation for Nancy that her family will not understand her love for Kitty. In order to be with her, Nancy leaves her home in Whitstable and moves to London. This move is significant, as it represents her exchange of one culture for another, and she must also exchange the surety of heterosexual culture for the unfamiliar homosexual.

Nancy and Kitty live together in London, where they both continue careers as male impersonators on the stage. Their relationship grows into a 'romantic friendship', the reader is aware that no sexual contact has occurred between them.[36] However, we are given an insight into Nancy's fantasies about the relationship. She describes her feelings as 'passion' and 'hot desire':

> How Kitty would have blushed, to know the part she played in my fierce dreamings – to know how shamelessly I took my memories of her, and turned them to my own improper advantage! Each night at the Palace she kissed me farewell; in my dreams her lips stayed at my cheek – were hot, were tender – moved to my brow, my ear, my throat, my mouth. (40)

Lesbian feminist academics have attempted to establish a history of female same-sex love; however, without proof of sexual contact, many scholars within mainstream academia debate naming these women as lesbian. A passage such as the one above highlights how a woman may not have thought it possible to have a sexual dalliance with another woman. However, if her thoughts, feelings, emotions, and erotic attraction are woman-centred, does that make her a lesbian? Nancy and Kitty do eventually establish a sexual relationship, the novel then moves on to what Zimmerman has described as "the sexual initiation".[37] The scene after they first make love conveys why women thought it necessary to silence their lesbianism. Nancy confesses to Kitty that she desired her for a long time as a 'sweetheart', but was worried that if Kitty ever discovered her true feelings, she would be horrified. Nancy proclaims that she did not think it was possible for two women to be sweethearts, "well, I never heard of such a thing before" (107).

It is possible that a girl such as Nancy may not have heard of lesbianism before, during the Victorian era when *Tipping* was set; there was a refusal to acknowledge sapphic love. As late as 1920, a British Conservative MP attempted to include an Act of Gross Indecency by Females, which would outlaw lesbianism, but the House of Commons was horrified.[38] Lord Birkenhead expressed his concern: "You are going to tell the whole world there is such an offence, to bring it to the notice of women who have never heard of it, never dreamed of it. I think is a very great mischief".[39] Refusing to name lesbianism, even in the form of a homophobic law, partly ensured that many women did not think of such love as possible. Women who did act on lesbian desire were aware that they should never be found out, that they should continue to keep it silent. We discover in this scene that Kitty did know such things were possible, and she admits to having had sexual encounters with women before. However, she is afraid of what will happen to both the women if their relationship is discovered, she appeals to Nancy to keep silent, "You won't let on, will you, to anyone? You will be careful – won't you?" (108). The two women continue to exist in this way, closeted and hidden.

When Nancy returns from the family visit, she discovers Kitty and Walter together in bed. The two women had a friendship and working relationship with Walter, their agent. Kitty explains her decision to marry Walter, she asks Nancy, "Can you not see, how this is for the best? With Walter as my husband, who would think, who would say" (172). In other words, this is to be a marriage of convenience for Kitty, she could have the dignity of a heterosexual marriage, and no one would suspect she was a tom.[40] This scene addresses the reality for many lesbians throughout history, compulsory heterosexuality meant that a woman's goal in life should be to find a man and get married.[41] Nancy leaves her home, her job, and the life she has established with Kitty in London. She flees with only a few belongings, her male costumes from the theatre, and a little money, and moves into a room in a lodging house. During this time, she realises that she has never walked the streets of London alone before. Nancy is shocked to discover that it is not safe for a woman in London; to combat this problem she decides that she will act and dress as a boy. On the surface this action may not appear to comply with the goal of lesbian feminist literature, which is to challenge patriarchy and heteronormativity. Rather than challenging these structures, Nancy may be read as assimilating, because she takes on the role of the dominant group, masculinity.

However, throughout history there is evidence to suggest that some lesbians did live and act as men, in order to avail of opportunities not available to their female sex, such as marrying a woman.[42] Indeed, Waters probably based Nancy's action to extend her male impersonation from the stage to the street, on the life of a real male impersonator of that era – one of the first recorded – Annie Hindle, who was on London stages from the early 1860s, and her manager brought her to New York in 1867.[43] Hindle played to mainly female audiences, and had close relationships with her female dressers. In 1886 she and her then dresser, Annie Ryan, got married in a hotel room in Michigan. Hindle wore a dress suit and went by the name Charles, and aptly her best man was a female impersonator called Gilbert Sarony.[44] It was not Hindle's intention to pass as a man throughout her life; she simply used her male persona to achieve what she wanted at a given time. After the wedding, the newly married couple retired to a cottage in Jersey City and they both lived out their lives dressed as women. Their marriage did not go unnoticed, and indeed it caused much public controversy, and when questioned regarding the ceremony the minister made a statement:

> I know all the circumstances. The groom gave me her - I mean his - name as Charles Hindle and he assured me that he was a man. The bride is a sensible girl, and she was of age. I had no other course to pursue. I believe they love each other and that they will be happy. (*Stranger than Fiction.* 1891.)[45]

Sarah Waters is not the first lesbian writer to reclaim the image of the Victorian male impersonators. Irish writer Emma Donoghue penned a play – *Ladies and Gentlemen* – based on Annie Hindle's life story. *Ladies and Gentlemen* is a memory play in which a vaudeville male impersonator relives her two marriages, one to a man and one to a woman.[46] Feminist historian Jean Howard further addresses female to male cross dressing in her study of the Elizabethan era. Howard maintains that this act was potentially threatening to the patriarchal structure; she concludes that "female cross-dressing in any context had the *potential* to raise fears about women wearing the breeches and undermining the hierarchical social order."[47]

Waters uses Nancy's new persona to uncover further injustices of the (hetero)patriarchal structure. The unique situation of cross-dressing is used to address other forms of oppression; Nancy dresses and passes as a young soldier, but it is arguable whether she gains any patriarchal power. While out for a walk, dressed as a soldier, a man approaches her, he assumes she is male, and he propositions her for sex. When she denies any knowledge of his intentions, he asks, "Don't you, now. And I thought all you guardsmen fellows knew the game all right" (197). From this we learn that many young soldiers rent themselves out to men for sex, thus identifying a further oppression – that of class structure, affirming that woman is not the only victim of sexual oppression. In addition, after Nancy is paid for giving the man oral sex, he kisses her on the cheek, and when she flinches he says, "You don't like that, you soldier-boys, do you?" (199). This is a chilling reminder that male homosexuality is also repressed.[48] The man is most certainly a male homosexual, although he may not name himself as such and his sexuality is 'othered', his sexual liaisons are restricted to back alleys. These scenes do not trivialise prostitution, or idealise it, rather, they identify further injustices of the (hetero)patriarchal system.

During Nancy's life on the street as a rent boy, she encounters Diana Lethaby. Waters play on Diana's second name, 'Lethaby' is suggestive of 'leather' and bondage. Diana's character oozes sexuality in the novel; she picks Nancy up from the streets one night and brings her home with her. Diana is a rich upper class sapphic; she does not need to closet her sexuality in the same way as Kitty, her class and money secure her a certain amount of protection. When Nancy asks what would happen if she were to 'out' Diana to the public, Diana states, "I have no fear of sensation: on the contrary, I court it! I seek out sensation" (249). This section of the novel further highlights oppression in relation to class. Diana's social position protects her to some extent from imprisonment for her deviant sexuality. Similarly, she is not dependent on work and, therefore, she has no job to lose. Diana abuses her power over working class lesbians. She takes Nancy in to live with her, but under unequal terms, she controls her: "You should eat from my table, and ride in my brougham, and wear the clothes I will pick out for you – and remove them, too, when I should ask it" (248).

The injustice of class oppression is further dealt with in the story of Diana's maid, Zena. Zena explains how she was sent to a reformatory at the age of seventeen for having a sexual relationship with another maid, Agnes. This section identifies the fact that although there were no laws specifically naming lesbianism, same-sex female relations were seen as perverted and punished. Zena is punished by incarceration in a reformatory and is released into Diana's charge to work as a servant. Castle maintains that the governing powers ignored sapphic relations due to "morbid paranoia", which resulted in what she terms as "juridical phantasm".[49] Therefore, lesbianism did not receive the advantages of being legally recognised, however, sapphic acts, when detected, did not go unpunished.[50]

Diana subjects Zena to horrific humiliation, expressing the erotic nature of Diana's power play. During a party scene, she calls Zena, in front of her guests, and proceeds to degrade her verbally, while implying they will also degrade her sexually: "We thought …That you must have frigged yourself so long and hard, you frigged yourself a cock. We think you must have a cock, Blake, in your drawers. We want you to lift your skirt, and let us see it!" (314). Diana tells Zena that she has just read a book by a doctor, which she received as a birthday present and, in it, Diana attests, "the doctor says you have a cock" (314). This reference is almost certainly to the literature of sexual inversion, which was circulated during the time *Tipping* is set. Waters uses the novel to portray the impact that this sexological writing had on homosexual identity during the Victorian era. Diana's book has a Latin title, is written by a male doctor, and is a recent publication. We can assume, therefore, that the book was *Psychopathia Sexualis* by Richard von Krafft-Ebing, first published in 1889.

The late nineteenth century witnessed the birth of the sexologist – medical men who sought to define and label sexuality in scientific terms. Faderman notes that, "It was this perception of a woman's masculinity that most often identified her as a sexual invert in the writings of the sexologists ... The sexologists examined head size, foot size, genital size, anything for telltale signs of the masculinity that betrays inversion."[51] The sexologist's notions were taken seriously at the time, and defined how lesbians were viewed well into the twentieth century. However, Diana's character shows how ludicrous these notions actually were. The sexologist's research attempted to 'other' lesbians from the category of woman, and inferred that these inverts were actually men trapped in women's bodies. The fact that Waters includes *Psychopathia Sexualis* in *Tipping*, is what Castle refers to as, "intertextual references."[52] This form of referencing is a common occurrence in lesbian literature; Castle uses the example of Stephen Gordon in the *Well of Loneliness* reading a book by the sexologist, Krafft-Ebing, and the characters in *The Children's Hour* reading Gautier's *Mademoiselle de Maupin*. Waters uses further intertextual reference by showing Diana's character having read the sexologists, while Nancy has read Oscar Wilde's *Dorian Gray*.

The same party scene is perhaps Waters' most beautiful display of how a novel can rewrite lesbian history. Diana's party enables the reader to witness reclamation of wonderful homosexual imagery: the party is fancy dress, and the characters attend dressed as lesbian icons. Evelyn arrives as Marie Antoinette, five women arrive dressed as Sappho, the lesbian poet, six women dress as the Ladies of Llangollen. Nancy tells us, in a tone of horror, that she "had not even heard of the Ladies from Llangollen before I met Diana" (307). Indeed, many readers of *Tipping the Velvet* may also be unaware of the Ladies of Llangollen, but its inclusion may spur them into investigating this lesbian past.[53] Another woman comes to the party dressed as Queen Christina of Sweden, who Castle states was a "notoriously lesbian queen".[54] Nancy, who dresses as Antinous, also bought Diana a bust of the Roman page for her birthday. Nancy had recently read about the life of Antinous and was fascinated. Her choice of costume and present is symbolic since, in her thesis, Waters informs us that Antinous, "figured at the turn of the century as a particular sensitive register of homosexual desire and cultural anxiety".[55] The party scene concludes part two of the novel, after Nancy defends Zena and both are punished by Diana for insubordination. The two women, as if in retaliation at their oppression, have sex in Diana's bed. Diana and her party guests witness this, and the pair are subsequently thrown out of the house.

This leads into the third and final part of the novel, and it is in this section that Zimmerman's goal of a feminist coming-out novel is realised. Nancy eventually recognises that rejecting heterosexuality, while 'coming-out' and accepting her lesbian sexuality will give her power over her own destiny. Nancy goes in search of Florence, a character introduced in an earlier part of the novel. Now in her hour of need, Nancy decides to seek Florence out, and it is pertinent to note that Nancy "thought her almost tommish" (354). Therefore, she was almost certainly seeking the company of other lesbians. However, when Nancy arrives at Florence's house, we witness heterosexism in action once again. Florence lives with her brother, and together they are bringing up a baby whose mother died after childbirth. Nancy assumes that this must be Florence's husband and child and, as a result, she lies about her own situation, telling Florence, "I've been living in the house of a gent … I let him make me … a pack of promises … He said he would marry me!" (354). This scene animates the invisibility of lesbianism, Florence and Nancy are both lesbians, however, Nancy pretends to be heterosexual in case Florence is offended and refuses to help her. Similarly Florence neglects to tell Nancy about her sexuality, or her past relationship with the mother of the baby she is bringing up: "'Cyril ain't mine,' she said quickly, 'though I call him mine. His mother used to lodge with us, and we took him on when she – left us'" (357).

In this final section of the novel, Waters addresses feminist politics of the late nineteenth century. Suffragettes first emerged in the Victorian era; these women challenged the patriarchal pattern of society in order to bring about a shift in gender norms. With the introduction of Florence, Waters ensures that she includes as much detail about this first wave of feminism. Florence and her friends all fit the category of early feminists by working towards gender equality. Florence herself works at a girls' home, and she volunteers for the Women's Co-operative Guild, a body formed in 1883, which was instrumental in urging a law to be passed regarding divorce by mutual consent. The Guild also advocated the introduction of a minimum wage in 1912. Florence's friends "all worked for charities or in homes" with minority groups such as "cripples, or immigrants, or orphaned girls" (376). Florence and her brother are politically aware and active as socialists and members of the labour movement. Eleanor Marx is mentioned as a heroine of the cause, and Florence makes a speech to Nancy that highlights the changes these women brought about:[56]

> Things are changing. There are unions everywhere – and women's unions, as well as men's. Women do things today their mothers would have laughed at to think of seeing their daughters doing, twenty years ago; soon they will even have the vote! If people like me don't work, it's because they look at the world,

at all the injustice and the muck … But the muck has new things growing out of it – wonderful things! – new habits of working, new kinds of people, new ways of being alive and in love … (391)

Symbolically, after Florence mentions "new ways of being in love", she reads to Nancy from Walt Whitman's *Leaves of Grass*, which represents same-sex love, and a book that created quite a stir when it was first publicly available in 1881. Nancy informs us that Diana also has a copy of this poetry, in which Whitman wrote profusely of his love for men. The New England Society for the Suppression of Vice maintained that Whtiman's poetry was unacceptable for public reading, and they threatened to sue his publisher.[57]

Eventually, Florence confides to Nancy that she had loved a woman called Lilian, who died giving birth to the child she and her brother now raise. Once Florence and Nancy have declared their sexuality to each other, they both begin to act more like their 'natural' selves. Nancy is empowered, she feels "more of a tom than ever" (403). Nancy begins to wear clothes, which suit her identity, rather than her gender. She buys trousers, a shirt, and lace-up boots, in male outfitters, and she gets her hair cut short. Nancy describes this transformation as almost spiritual: "It was not like she was cutting hair, it was as if I had a pair of wings beneath my shoulder blades, that the flesh had all grown over, and she was slicing free" (405). Nancy and Florence eventually set up an alternative family life. They live as a couple, together with Florence's brother Ralph, and they raise Lilian's baby. Florence brings Nancy to a lesbian bar where she introduces her to more lesbians and a lighter side of sapphic life. Water's attention to detail is evident in this scene; the lesbian bar is called 'The Boy in the Boat': Faderman informs us that this term is a euphemism for the clitoris.[58] Florence is horrified at the stories of Nancy's past life, mainly regarding her closeted relationship with Kitty: "To think she kept you cramped and guilty for so long, when you might have been off, having your bit of fun as a real gay tom" (343).

Tipping the Velvet reclaims lesbian history that has been ignored, which is an important aspect in the formation of a positive lesbian identity. This novel shows that lesbians have always existed; it expresses the views of women who may have existed in a previous lesbian community. In *Tipping*, Waters examines unjust systems, such as homophobia, heterosexism, patriarchy, and class oppression, and she also portrays past lesbian identities, such as cross-dressers, Romantic Friendships, and suffragette sapphics in a believable manner. Waters has, therefore, given a voice to lesbians who were previously powerless and neglected. Fiction is, thus, shown to be a powerful device in redressing injustices, as Zimmerman notes:

Fiction is a particularly useful medium through which to shape a new lesbian consciousness, for fiction, of all literary forms, makes the most complex and detailed use of historical events and social discourse. By incorporating many interacting voices and points of view, novelists give the appearance of reality to a variety of imaginary worlds. Novels can show us as we were, as we are, and as we would like to be. This is a potent combination for a group whose very existence has been either suppressed or distorted. [59]

Notes

1. Caroline Gonda, 'Lesbian Theory.' *Contemporary Feminist Theories*. Stevi Jackson and Jackie Jones, eds. (Edinburgh: Edinburgh UP, 1998), 113-31.
2. Avrom Fleishman, *The English Historical Novel: Walter Scott to Virginia Woolf* (Baltimore: John Hopkins, 1971), 4.
3. Sarah Waters, 'Wolfskins and Togas: Lesbian and Gay Historical Fictions 1870 to the Present.' Diss. Queen Mary University. Classmark ZTH3194, 58.
4. Terry Castle, *The Apparitional Lesbian: Female Homosexuality and Modern Culture* (New York: Columbia UP, 1993), 66.
5. Martha Vicinus, 'They Wonder to Which Sex I Belong' in *Lesbian Subjects: A Feminist Studies Reader*. Martha Vicinus, ed. (Bloomington: Indiana UP, 1996), 236.
6. Laura Gowing, 'History' in *Lesbian and Gay Studies: A Critical Introduction*. Andy Medhurst and Sally R Munt, eds. (London: Cassell, 1997), *61*.
7. Castle, 9.
8. Castle, 28.
9. Castle, 30.
10. Greene, 186.
11. Lillian Faderman, *Chloe Plus Olivia: An Anthology of Lesbian Literature from the Seventeenth Century to the Present* (New York: Penguin, 1994), 441.
12. This is what Eve Sedgwick terms 'presumptive heterosexuality' and Monique Wittig terms 'the straight mind'.
13. Sandra Gilbert and Susan Gubar, *The Norton Anthology of Literature by Women: The Traditions in English*. 2nd ed. (New York: Norton, 1996), 857.
14. There is strong evidence to suggest that Dickinson was in love with Sue Gilbert, who eventually became Emily's sister-in-law. See Ellen Louise Hart and Martha Nell Smith, *Open Me Carefully: Emily Dickinson's Intimate Letters to Susan Huntington Dickinson* (Ashfield: Paris Press, 1998).
15. As cited in Faderman, 1994, 56.
16. Hart and Smith, 91.
17. Paul Bennett, 'The Pea That Duty Locks: Lesbian and Feminist Heterosexual Readings of Emily Dickinson's Poetry' in *Lesbian Text and Contexts: Radical Revisions*. Karla Jay and Joanne Glasgow, eds. (New York: New York UP, 1990), 40-65. As cited in Faderman, 1994, 45.
18. Faderman, 1994.
19. Faderman, 1994, 295.
20. Faderman, 1994, 549. Lesbian feminist publishing houses such as Naiad Press, Diana Press, and Daughters.
21. Val Lunn, 'Tackling Homophobia.' *Talking Point*. 141 (March, 1993).

22. Suzanne Pharr, *Homophobia: A Weapon of Sexism* (London: Chardon Press, 1988), 246.
23. This is the title of a section in Faderman's *Chloe plus Olivia* (1994).
24. Fleishman, 7.
25. Waters, 'Wolfskins and Togas.'
26. Sarah Waters, *Tipping the Velvet* (London: Virago Press, 1998). All future in-text references to *Tipping the Velvet* are to this edition.
27. Alison Hennegan, 'On Becoming a Lesbian Reader' in *Sweet Dreams: Sexuality, Gender and Popular Fiction.* Susannah Radstone, ed. (London: Lawrence, 1988), 169.
28. *The Oxford English Dictionary* Vol. VIII POY-RY. A corrected re-issue of *A New English Dictionary on Historical Principles* (Oxford: Clarendon Press). (1933. Reprint 1978, 42).
29. *Ibid.*
30. Smyth summarises the birth of queer politics and how the term queer was re-appropriated. "In April 1990 a group met in New York to discuss the frequent bashings of gays and lesbians in the East Village. Queer Nation was born with the slogan, 'Queers bash back' and stencils were drawn on the pavements: 'My beloved was queerbashed here. Queers fight back..." Cherry Smyth, *Lesbians Talk Queer Nations* (London: Scarlet Press, 1992), 17.
31. Smyth, 60.
32. According to Joni Crone, "Lavender has been adopted as an international lesbian colour after Betty Friedman had dubbed lesbians 'the lavender menace' in the early 1970s."
33. Other first novels that address 'coming of age' issues include, Jeanette Wintersons's *Oranges Are Not the Only Fruit* (London: Pandora, 1985); Emma Donoghue's *Stirfry* (London: Hamilton, 1994); and Rita Mae Brown's *Rubyfruit Jungle* (Plainfield: Daughters, 1973).
34. Monique Wittig, *The Straight Mind and Other Essays.* Louise Turcotte, ed. (Boston: Beacon Press, 1992), 28.
35. Pharr, 247.
36. Romantic friendship was a term coined in the eighteenth century to describe a close emotional bond between two women, which was generally believed to be platonic.
37. Bonnie Zimmerman, *The Safe Sea of Women: Lesbian Fiction 1969-1988* (Boston: Beacon Press, 1990), 35.
38. MP Frederick Maquister proposed to include a bill outlawing lesbianism. He thought that "female morals were declining and that lesbianism threatened the birth rate.", Diana Souhami, *The Trials of Radclyffe Hall* (London: Virago Press, 1999), 112.
39. As cited by Souhami, 112.
40. 'Tom' was a Victorian slang term for lesbian.
41. A famous example of a lesbian who kept up the conformity of a heterosexual marriage is Vita Sackville-West who married Harold Nicholson. Vita and Harold indulged in homosexual relationships after they were married.
42. For a critique of this, see Sheila Jeffreys *Unpacking Queer Politics* (Cambridge: Polity Press, 2003).

43. Through London Music Hall Mashers, such as Hindle, male impersonation was introduced to the U.S. This form of entertainment appeared on English stages first.
44. Hindle's decision to call herself Charles may relate to a song she made popular, 'Have you seen my Nellie?' The second verse of this includes a line, 'They call me dear Charlie, and they vow they love me true.' Boston: Oliver Ditson, 1869; Sheet music in the Harvard Theatre Collection. Cited in Laurence Senelick, *The Changing Room: Sex, Drag and the Theatre* (New York: Routledge, 2000), 304.
45. Reference in Senelick, 329.
46. *Ladies and Gentlemen* (Dublin: New Island Press, 1998). Premiered by Glasshouse Productions at Dublin's Project Arts Centre on the 18th April 1996. It premiered in the U.S at Outward Spiral Theatre Minneapolis on the 14th April 2000.
47. Jean Howard, 'Cross-dressing, the Theatre, and Gender Struggle in Early Modern England' in *Crossing the Stage: Controversies on Cross-Dressing*. Lesley Ferris, ed. (London: Routledge, 1993), 29.
48. For a detailed discussion of this, see Randolph Trumbach, *Love, Sex, Intimacy and Friendship Between Men 1550-1800*. Katherine O'Donnell and Michael O'Rourke, eds. (New York: Palgrave Macmillan, 2003), 99-128.
49. Castle, 6.
50. Louis Crompton details in *The Myth of Lesbian Immunity* that women were sentenced to death for what were termed 'crimes against nature'. Catharina Linck was hanged and then burnt in 1721 for dressing as a man and having 'sodomitical' relations with another woman. Cited in Castle, 240.
51. Faderman, 138.
52. Castle, 63.
53. "Marie Antoinette was accused of bringing the vice of 'tribadism' with her from Austria into France" (Castle 129.) Many rumours circulated around France during the queen's reign that she indulged in lesbian practices. She was suspected of having a sexually intimate relationship with the Princess Lamballe. The Ladies of Llangollen were Lady Elanor Butler and the Honourable Sarah Ponsonby. Faderman describes them as "one of the great 'success stories' of eighteenth-century romantic friendship … They resisted their families' attempts to marry them off, commit them to a convent, and imprison them until they relented, and starve them into submission" (1994), 32.
54. Castle, 2.
55. Waters, 1995, 75.
56. Eleanor Marx is the daughter of Karl Marx; she was noted for her high intelligence and was instrumental in helping her father complete a lot of his political work. In her own right Eleanor wrote several books and articles, she was also involved in the Women's Trade Union from 1886.
57. Walt Whitman self-published *Leaves of Grass* in 1855, however, it was not a commercial success. Several other literary figures were impressed with his poetry and a publisher took on this collection in 1881.
58. Faderman, 1991, 64.
59. Zimmerman, 2.

Runt

Mem calls me the runt; she says, 'Oh what a piggy pong', when I'm in the kitchen. Grandaddy says, 'Will you ever stop', to Mem, but she just slints her eyes at me and cuts her throat with one finger. Grandaddy has long teeth that are brown and rough like tree bark, they stick out when he opens his mouth; his cap smells as greasy as his head. Mem calls him the blackguard – even though she's his daughter – but she says it with a twisty smile.

Grandaddy and Mem own me now; I live in the back room with a picture of Elvis and the brown statue of Saint Anthony. The walls are cold and sweaty, and the window is tangled with ivy, so it's always dark. All my clothes are in a trunk and my books and toys are on the floor. My job is to help Grandaddy in the shed and keep out from under Mem's feet. That's important; she doesn't want the likes of me trailing muck through her nice clean house.

The shed is full of things: two black bicycles, a bench covered in tin boxes full of nails and bolts, a fishing net, a motorbike engine, a box of onions, a nudie lady calendar, a smell like old grass, a can of petrol, and mice, mice, mice. We're building shelves for my room, but first we have to kill the mice, every last fecker of them. They're scruffy: they chew the onions and leave dots of poo all over the bench and floor.

'Why don't we make a big trap with a box and a stick, then we can catch them all at the one time?' I say.

'Hmmm, we'll see. Mice are clever little bastards; maybe we'll just set a few small traps.'

'With cheese?'

'A bit of cheese and a bit of bread rolled together. They love that.' He smiles at me. 'Or maybe we should just let Big Tom in?'

Big Tom is Mem's cat and no way does she want him chawing mice; their blood might get on his fur and make him dirty. If she saw him with a mouse she would probably blame me. I shake my head.

Grandaddy and me go in the car to town for the traps: eight for mice and two big silver ones for rats, just to be on the safe side. We stop at the Ball Alley for a pint on the way home; the woman working there calls me a poor craythur and her eyes go all swimmy. She gives me orange and crisps and kisses my head with her lipstick mouth; I hope it's not on my hair. The woman goes back behind the bar and wipes glasses and lights a cigarette; I watch the smoke jetting out of her nose while she talks to Grandaddy and the other men. I sit at a table near the door, by myself. She comes over to me and points out the window, to the trees across the road.

'Can you see the upside-down tree, loveen?' She winks at Grandaddy. I look over at the trees on the other side of the road. They all look right-side-up to me. 'See that one', she says, kneeling beside me and pointing with her skinny finger. ''The roots are where the branches should be. Do you see it?'

I nod, to let her know that I can see the upside-down tree too, because she sees it and she seems happy about it; then she lets out a huge laugh and ruffles my hair.

'The craythur', she says again.

'Come on, boyo', Grandaddy says, lugging his pint, 'time to go'.

Mem is sitting at the table when we get home; her eyes are googly and her nose is red. She has a letter in her hand.

'Bad news?' Mem nods. Tears spill over her eyes onto her cheeks; a line of snot dribbles down her lip. Grandaddy taps her on the shoulder. 'It'll be alright'.

'It won't be alright!' Mem screeches, jumping up. 'I'm bad enough without this'. She balls the letter up and holds it in front of Grandaddy's face. 'Who'll want me now?'

'Now, Mem, now, sweetheart'.

Mem's whole body shakes and she cries and cries, loud like a baby. She plunks back down onto the chair and says, 'What the fuck are you looking at?' to me.

I go into my room and lie on the bed; I can hear muttery talking from the kitchen. Elvis sneers at me with his blubbery lip, so I stick out my tongue at him; I'd love to smack him. I pull a book from the floor and read a bit of it but it's too pukey, so I drop it back on the pile. They're not talking anymore.

'Come on, so', Grandaddy is standing in the doorway. We walk to the shed; he hands me a greasy paper bag. 'Get cracking'.

I squash bits of cheese around pieces of bread to make small smelly clumps. Grandaddy pushes them into each trap, one at a time, then bends back the hinge and clips it in place.

'Now', he says, when they're all done, and we lay the traps carefully around the shed.

'Why is Mem so upset?'

His long teeth catch his upper lip and bite it; he sighs.

'She's not well'.

'How do you mean? She looks OK'.

'She was at the hospital for some tests and the results are not good'.

'Oh. Like my Mammy'.

'A bit like that. Mem has to have an operation. Here'. He lays his hand across his chest. I look at him and giggle. Grandaddy's hand comes out of nowhere and lands hard on my ear. 'You little bastard', he says, 'this is no laughing matter'.

My fingers fly to the side of my head; my ear is flaming. I start to whimper and Grandaddy puts out his hand.

'You're a bastard' I scream, pushing him away. I run from the shed, back up to the house.

Mem has her blue suit on; her hair is washed and tidy. She is sitting on the side of my bed; I'm dressed, even my runners are still on my feet. Mem is holding the two bits of the statue of Saint Anthony and looking at me. He's broken right across the middle.

'What happened to this?' I put on a puss and eye her. 'The face on you'. Mem wiggles the two bits of the statue and grins. 'It doesn't matter, anyway, it's a horrible old yoke'. She drops Saint Anthony onto the floor; his head breaks off and we both laugh.

'Well, Runty, I've to go to the hospital to get my boob hacked off'.

'I'm sorry, Mem'.

'Ah well, you and me both, kiddo'. She gets up. 'Be a good boy and keep an eye on the old blackguard for me while I'm away, won't you? Make sure him and your Daddy don't drink all the bottles of stout in the press'. I nod and Mem leans forward and kisses my cheek. Her mouth is soft. 'I want flowers when you visit me in the hospital. Decent ones'. She shoves away tears with her hand and sniffs. 'The shed is full of dead bloody mice. I want them all gone by the time I get back and don't let my Tom anywhere near them'.

'Are you right?' Grandaddy is wearing a suit too. 'Come on, you. Up out of that 'til we get this one off to the hospital and out of our sight at last'.

'Oh shut up', Mem says, and the three of you walk together out to the car.

*

We all knew Kate was on the way out; everyone except for Daddy. He kept saying, 'Sure she looks grand; she's fine'. But I could tell she was a goner. Her hair was falling off her head in clumps, like horsehair from a tom mattress, and she wasn't able to get out of the bed to mind the child. Barney was less than useless, as usual. He pissed himself into a comer in Hartigan's and didn't come out of it. Even when she died.

And of course we all knew who'd have to take in the little runt when she popped: me and Daddy. There was no question. I, for one, didn't mind but I knew Daddy was too old to be listening to the goings-on of a child, day in, day out: all that running and leaping and carrying-on. Anyway, within days of the funeral the boy's trunk was packed and he was standing in my kitchen when I got back from the shops, a ferrety little thing with sad eyes. I didn't know what to do with him.

'I'm warning you: don't get in my way', I said. He stared at me. 'I'm not soft like your Mammy was'. He kept on staring, like a sheep. 'Go on so, go outside and play'. He turned and went out. I called after him: 'Wipe your feet before you come back in here, or your Grandaddy will kill you'.

It was that night, in the bath, that I found the lump. I was soaping myself, enjoying the comforting heat of the water, when my fingers just landed on it. I pulled my hand away, lay back and scrunched up my eyes. I felt hot and cold. Slowly, I slid my hand up and felt again: it was hard and solid, like a walnut growing under my skin. I couldn't believe it. First Kate and now me; I wasn't even able to cry.

I didn't tell Daddy at first; the old blackguard would've dropped dead on me. I called to Rita's house the next morning, to see if she could tell me what to do next; she was gone to work. I walked down the village and stuck my head into the snug at Hartigan's, hoping she'd have nipped in for a quick one to set her right for the day. All I found was Barney, swaying over his pint like a side of beef in a butcher's shop.

'Mem, Mem, my darling, step in', he said, patting the stool beside him. I didn't go in right away; I held the door in my hand. 'Come in, girl, you're letting out the heat'.

I thunked down beside him. He asked after his little son and ordered a drink for me. I let the heat of the whiskey warm my neck and next thing I knew I was sniffing and bawling, telling Barney about the lump and asking him what the hell was I going to do? I babbled on and on, said I couldn't go and die on the child, just after he'd lost his mother – he needed me. Barney clucked and patted my hand. He gave me his hanky; it was grey with snot but I used it anyway.

'And what about Daddy?' I wailed. 'Poor, poor Daddy, losing his daughters like flies'.

Barney took me in his arms and pushed my head against the heat of his chest.

'Now, now, Mem', he crooned, 'you're going to be fine. It's all going to be grand. I'm here for you, darling, I'm here'. He held me for a long time, petting my hair and kissing my ear while I sobbed and hiccuped. Then he told me what to do.

*

Mem is liverish - she was always that way: even as a baby she found it hard to smile. Life doesn't like to go her way, she says. But, the more you keep on with that kind of talk, the less likely it is that things will turn out good. The eels in the river know that.

She was fit to be tied when the young fella was left to us.

'What do I want with a little brat running all over the place?' she roared.

She went on like a mad thing over it: plucked at her hair, effed and blinded, threw things around; even Big Tom got a belt of her sweeping brush that day, and he's used to mollycoddling. She was upset over Kate dying, I suppose, and over Barney collapsing under his loss; it all got mixed up together.

I was glad to take the little fella in; I'm fond of children and Kate's boy was always my favourite grandchild. He's so wee: a scrawny pucker of a thing. We couldn't leave him with Barney – he just got pissed and stayed that way, once he realised Kate wasn't going to get better. The child didn't even cry when his mother died; too stunned, I suppose. I found him below in the house, starving, so I brought him home to stay with us, sooner rather than later.

It wasn't long after he came to us that Mem found out she was sick herself. I was gutted when she told me. One daughter dying on you is bad enough, but the idea of losing another was too much. We decided not to tell the little fella, at least until we knew what was happening ourselves. Mem was brave; as angry and mad about the whole thing as all-get-out, but very brave. She found things for me and the young lad to do, to keep us busy: building shelves, laying traps for the mice, that sort of thing.

I told him about Mem's condition eventually. She was upset when the results from the hospital were bad and he twigged that something was up. Sure, he'd been through it all before. Anyway, didn't the little bugger laugh when I said it – nerves probably – but, God forgive me, I gave him a clip on the ear. He went wild, but we were friends again in no time. It was a hard spell for all of us.

Of course, he's like a new child now. He has Mem wrapped around his little finger – when he can manage to get her attention off Barney. The pair of them spend the days cooing at each other, like love's young dream. It'd make a weaker stomach sick. Myself and the little fella laugh at them.

Her hair fell out after the operation, but she liked wearing the wig. They'd only a blondie one left in the hairdresser's, but Mem said she always thought of herself as a Marilyn Monroe type and snapped it up. She was some sight in that wig, it has to be said: walking down the back lane in her apron and wellies, picking blackberries with the child, her wig-hair sparkling like a halo. Her own hair is growing back now – wispish and thin – but please God, it'll be back again in all its glory for the wedding. They say a door doesn't close but another one opens. It's been true for us.

Nuala Ní Chonchúir

Eva Rus

From *New York Radical Feminists* to *Rivolta Femminile*: Italian Feminists Rethink the Practice of Consciousness Raising, 1970-1974

In the larger context of other well-known national feminisms, the Italian 'subject' is more or less 'unknown.' Italy has always been characterised by a substantial interest in foreign cultural production, and this has been indeed confirmed by the wide circulation of foreign books and journals, as well as by a habit of quick translation of most controversial foreign texts. The influence of American, French, and British feminist thought, interacting with the enduring weight of a rich cultural heritage, can be seen at work in the reformulation of a specifically distinctive 'Italian' form of feminism. Hence, for instance, the practice of consciousness-raising groups was originally 'imported' from the USA, but the name given to this practice in Italy, '*autocoscienza*' (self-awareness), indicates its distinctively Italian character.

In this paper I will consider the practice of small group discussion – consciousness-raising (C-R) – as inspired by second wave US feminism in one northern Italian feminist group from Milan in the period between 1970 and 1974, well-known in Italy as the period of experimentation and learning of 'historical' feminism, when the basic features of the new feminist politics were established and put into practice by a few hundred women in collectives in different parts of the country. During this period, in fact, all currents in the Italian movement saw the process of personal change as a key to liberation and, thus, posed the practice of *autocoscienza* and separatism as the shared instruments for a process of individual, collective and social transformation.

1968 was a crucial year for the new feminist movement on both sides of the Atlantic. In an atmosphere of political assassinations, urban riots, and anti-war demonstrations, the First National Women's Liberation Conference took place late in November in Chicago. At the conference, Katie Sarachild outlined the original programme for 'Radical Feminist Consciousness-Raising' and stressed the importance of its rootedness in the work of women who all considered themselves radicals, in other words, those who were interested in getting to the root of problems in society.[1] In the attempt to break free from any traditional 'male' approach to politics, the practice of C-R rapidly became the new instrument for second wave US feminism. The liberal and socialist positions of earlier feminist groups were thus rejected in the light of a new search for a more radical answer that could, therefore, reach the roots of women's subordination, then identified with the field of sexuality and reproduction, in which biological and physiological differences were being transformed into separate roles based on gender.

C-R groups in the US began as non-hierarchical structures created specifically for the purpose of altering the participants' perceptions and conceptions of themselves and society at large, developing self-esteem, and valuing the importance of group solidarity. The concepts of participatory democracy, equality, liberty, and community, largely valued by the younger branch of the American feminist movement, emphasised that everyone should participate in the decisions that affected their lives, and that everyone's contribution was equally valid. The values led very easily to the idea that all hierarchy was bad because it gave some people power over others and did not allow everyone's talents to develop, so a conscious lack of formal structure, an emphasis on participation by everyone, sharing of tasks, and the exclusion of men rapidly became the main characters of groups in which C-R was practised.

The writing that came from the consciousness-raising meetings of New York Radical Women entered the canon of feminist theory and became part of the most influential work for the new feminist movement in the US and abroad. *The Dialectic of Sex* by Shulamith Firestone, *Sexual Politics* by Kate Millett, the essays 'The Myth of the Vaginal Orgasm' by Anne Koedt, 'The Politics of Housework' by Pat Mainardi, and 'The Personal is Political' by Carol Hanisch, all published in 1970, were quickly translated into Italian. Small groups of women sharing personal experiences, problems, and feelings soon realised that what was thought to be individual was, in fact, common, and that personal problems could have a social cause and a political solution.

Between January and March 1970 every leading publication and network in the US did a major story on the new feminist movement, provided information of its existence and, to some extent, legitimated it – notably Kate Millett's picture on *Time*'s cover 'established' her as *the* first feminist spokeswoman after Friedan, and subjected her to very severe criticism from the movement.[2] At the same time, the new feminist movement was spreading throughout Italian society with unprecedented strength and radicalism, involving women from different social backgrounds, both middle class intellectuals as well as working class activists. It started in the large cities of the North and the centre of Italy, where the politics of 1968 had originated and been most influential, and gradually spread to all regions with differing rates of development. At the root of this movement were several structural transformations of Italian society, including a general increase of women's access to higher education that, since the 1960s, rose much more steadily than men's; a rapid and stable decline of the fertility rate marking mostly the industrial North and the urban areas; and increasing participation of women in the labour market.

It is important to remember that at the end of the nineteenth century and at the beginning of the twentieth, a strong emancipationist movement had spread in Italy. At the time, Ada Negri, the celebrated Milanese 'social' poet of *Fatalità* (1892) and *Tempeste* (1895), the extraordinary prose writer of the autobiographical *Stella Mattutina* (1921), and *Erba Sul Sagrato* (1939), as well as one of the founders of the National Women's Union (*Unione Femminile Nazionale*) in Milan in 1899, was the first Italian writer to emerge from the working class. The Italian emancipationist movement began again after WWII with UDI (Union of Italian Women), a group created to fight for better conditions for women, which tried to appeal to all women regardless of their socio-political affiliation, but which was in fact made up of left-wing women. For some years, this was a source of incomprehension and suspicion in the feminist movement, which stressed its autonomy from all formally constituted parties as establishments of male authority. In the new feminism of the 1970s, many of the women involved came out of the experience of 1968, with its strong anti-authoritarian bias, and were or had been members of extra-parliamentary groups[3] that criticised the traditional left.[4] In Milan, the anti-authoritarian movement above all, with its focus on personal and collective liberation through heightened self-knowledge, provided the intellectual source that gave Milanese feminism its particular character.[5] In effect, and especially in the early 1970s, the city of Milan played a key part in Italian cultural change, as the city operated as a window on continental Europe serving as a point of attraction for foreign ideas – in other words, as the most cosmopolitan city in Italy. Although Milan did not feature the artistic treasures of Florence or Palermo, the ancient university tradition of cities like Bologna or Padua, the brilliant architecture of Rome or Venice, it was the source of new ideas, of Italian interpretation of foreign concepts, ideologies, and intellectual trends, and because of this it has played a leading role in the re-emerging Italian women's movement.

Significantly enough, in Italy, and specifically in Milan, the new movement stressed the importance of the positive evaluation of women's *difference* with an emphasis on the politics of the self and issues of identity, instead of orienting towards issues of equality and emancipation, which were perceived as too centred on 'male' principles of competition and hierarchy and, hence, as ideological attempts to subject women even further.[6] Actually, issues of equality and emancipation in the 1970s were at the core of the crucial question of 'dual loyalty' – the simultaneous participation/involvement in the feminist movement and the activities of an organised party or political group. In Milan, the choice between the pursuit of 'external activities' (propaganda, confrontation with public institutions, political parties), or an exclusive focus on 'internal activities' (C-R, *autocoscienza*)[7] easily resolved in favour of an internal focus, first of all because Milan lacked a strong *workerist* political tradition,[8] and, secondly, because of the cosmopolitan nature of the city and its openness to foreign influences. However, even the most leftist groups seemed unable to understand the new consciousness women were developing in the *autocoscienza* groups, and were hostile to women's determination to gain a full autonomy of expression, as well as to any separatist activity.[9]

In 1970, the Italian feminist movement was constituted by independent units connected in a web of communication, through which both people and information were exchanged. At the time, two main currents were emerging – *groups of thought*, and *groups of social practice*. Groups of thought tended to privilege the practice of *autocoscienza* as a mode of political action and theoretical construction. Groups of social practice, despite often using the *autocoscienza* approach, set the need to generate actual change in the public sphere as their main goal. The collectives *Rivolta Femminile* (Female Revolt) and *Anabasi* belonged to the former current, and their fundamental concern, whilst acknowledging the formative influence of the major Anglo-American theoretical texts, was to develop a feminist practice. At the time, Milan was a pole of attraction for many women in search of better educational or employment opportunities, as well as of a more open and tolerant social context. Precisely because of this, experimental lifestyles could be worked out in Milan much more than anywhere else in Italy at the time, with the exception of Rome.[10]

The collective, *Rivolta Femminile,* formed in Milan around 1970, and consisted of a small collective composed of intellectuals rather than political activists, critical of the thought and political activity of the Left, whose aim was to establish a new feminist theory and practice drawing heavily on the example of the contemporary American movement. Their research was for self-awareness: it questioned the whole cultural tradition and analysed personal experience. In 1970, the *Manifesto of Rivolta Femminile*[11] was issued in Rome and Milan together, with *Sputiamo su Hegel* (Let's Spit on Hegel), a work by Italian radical feminist, Carla Lonzi. The *Manifesto* claimed the need for women to turn away from mainstream politics and male culture in order to start anew as authentic feminine subjects – in the words of Lonzi, theirs was the way of *authenticity*, the unforeseen way of discovery, and of personal expression. *Rivolta* has never been interested in political propaganda and its groups never directly participated in the specific struggles carried on by most Italian feminists; however, their writings have been deeply influential, in particular those by Lonzi.

Autocoscienza was first introduced into Italian feminism by Lonzi in the context of a theoretical speculation around the autonomous production of interpretive categories of reality. Associated with *Rivolta* since its foundation, Lonzi offered an invaluable theoretical contribution to the movement, particularly with the writings *Sputiamo su Hegel* (1970) and *La Donna Clitoridea e la Donna Vaginale* (1971).[12] Lonzi was against any formal equality between men and women, and for an affirmation of a dual subjectivity which admitted the partiality of both male and female positions.[13] Claiming that principles of equality hid the real foundation for the oppression of women, Lonzi criticised Hegel, Marx and Freud as guilty of legitimising patriarchal structures, which she also identified in the functions of the nuclear family, the vaginal model of sexual pleasure, and motherhood. Lonzi's ideas, inspired by Carol Hanisch's famous essay on the *personal* and the *political*, clearly met with those of the renowned 1970 essay by Anne Koedt on the myth of vaginal orgasm, but they went even further in the theorisation of the actual existence of the two conditions of 'vaginal woman' and 'clitoral woman.' Despite urging the 'vaginal woman' to raise her consciousness and become 'clitoral' – i.e. 'liberated' from patriarchal oppression – Lonzi was not against heterosexual pleasure; however, she thought this ought to be renegotiated according to the desires of women's pleasure.[14]

Autocoscienza, according to Lonzi, meant independent, small groups of women, meeting to discuss various issues on the basis of personal experience, but, unlike the English expression 'consciousness-raising', the term *autocoscienza* stressed the self-determined and self directed quality of the *process* of achieving a new consciousness/awareness.[15] The process itself was deeply introspective and could not be properly studied unless through direct individual experience. *Autocoscienza* refused any cultural mediation in order to assume the intrinsic value of women's lives, thus establishing a link between theory and practice and even further between the practice and its context.[16] In other words, the source that Lonzi had called *authenticity* became the guide towards a mutual exchange of personal experiences through a lifelong process of analysis leading to awareness.

In 1970-71, *Rivolta*'s publishing house, *Scritti di Rivolta Femminile* (still operating today), started to publish and distribute the writings of the women involved in the group, including the whole body of Lonzi's work, individual accounts of personal *autocoscienza* experiences, and collective reports on the development of the group. None of the writings proposed for publication by the women of *Rivolta* has ever been rejected because the written personal accounts are considered by *Rivolta*'s publishing house as a very important step towards the raising of personal awareness – the value of each text has been located, not in the written book-'object' but, rather, in the writing woman-'subject.' An important feature has marked the works published by *Rivolta* in comparison with works published by other feminist groups, that of the inclusion of the name of the author.[17] The identification of a work with its specific author has, in effect, been often seen by other groups as an expression of narcissism and in contradiction with the principle of a collective participation and sharing. By contrast, *Rivolta* considers the stress on the individual as a necessary acceptance of responsibility toward the content of the writing itself on the part of the author, as well as a symbol that would mark a woman's way out from silence.

The period 1970-74 witnessed an extraordinary quantity of writing, mainly in the form of journals and documents. One of the most remarkable publications was the periodical *Sottosopra* (Upside Down), published in Milan on the initiative of the Demau collective, among others, which was open to various different feminist groups.[18] The periodical was conceived according to the small-group principles and, consequently, no selection process was applied to the texts submitted. Virtually every woman or group could have a text published. Most of the work published in the first two issues of *Sottosopra*[19] did not aim to establish a theoretical or political perspective but was, rather, in the form of written commentary on the new practical experiences of the women's collectives, and was often in the form of diaries and autobiographical notes. Nevertheless, by 1974, the editors' choice to operate a mere collection of many different or, at times, very similar experiences, instead of a selection, achieved the effect of generating confusion and repetitiveness, and the editorial strategy had to be changed.[20]

The prevailing political form of Italian feminism between 1971-74 was, and remains, the small *autocoscienza* group, and among the discussion topics since 1971, under the influence of Lonzi's work, is the analysis of sexuality above all, of lesbianism, and relationships among other women. It must be said, moreover, that Italian feminists have generally shared the idea of a 'political homosexuality', so that separatism has not implied a refusal of relationships with men but, rather, the existence of separate spaces of theoretical production and political action. From 1971, *Rivolta* decided to concentrate exclusively on *autocoscienza*. It divided into small sub-groups, and its participants were explicitly asked to assert their agreement with the project – those who privileged a more theoretical work, those who preferred traditional political approaches, and those who acknowledged only a limited value to *autocoscienza* could no longer identify with the group.

From 1974 the focus of attention of *autocoscienza* slowly and markedly shifted from the mechanics of oppression to an investigation of the relationship between/among women. The first large collective group meetings, started in 1973, had actually triggered a profound general change of perspective. The change started after a few encounters with a French group called *Psychanalyse et Politique*. The debates arising in the groups as a result of these encounters were focused on the proposal of going past and then expanding *autocoscienza*, in order to face issues of sexuality and relationships among women through the psychoanalytical approach later called 'practice of the unconscious', which sought to overcome traditional, hierarchical psychoanalytical techniques and institutions, and turn psychoanalysis into a collective feminist experience.

Since the early 1970s, the foundation on a theory of the **practices** – among which the practice of *autocoscienza* – has become the distinctive feature of Italian feminism. So, an approach based on the practice of *autocoscienza* first, and then on the other subsequent practices of the unconscious, of the symbolic, of entrustment and so forth, has gradually marked the preference for an approach established on the interaction with the real-life contexts in which the practices were actually being pursued.

Although it has not become widely diffused, the practice of the unconscious was widely discussed and indirectly influenced later theoretical developments.[21] It gave an outline of the changing direction in the practice of *autocoscienza* around the mid-1970s and, eventually, opened the new stage of Milanese feminism as the early feminists found themselves with a growing number of followers. By the mid-1970s Milanese feminists had, in fact, perceived an increasing sense of crisis due to the national role they had come to play. As new women who had not played a part in the 'historic' phase of feminism began to become active through their involvement in the broad national campaigns around the divorce and abortion legislations, even in Milan, the non-institutional feminists began to feel a pull of attraction to groups of a more structured, conventionally political nature, and feminists' energies went into specific, highly concrete, professional projects, such as the Milan Women's Bookshop (1975), or as the Milanese Centre for Historical Studies on the Italian Women's Liberation Movement (1979). In the 1976 issue of *Sottosopra*, entitled 'Some Documents on the Political Practice', a woman from a Milanese collective[22] accounted that:

> 'the personal is political' has been effective as long as the personal has meant oppression, privatization, loneliness ... now we realize that our personal has changed and it's no longer immediately political ... for us women the separation between personal and political is dangerous because it leads us to a detachment from sexuality, from relationships among women ... however we still want to maintain the link with the political.[23]

In general, as the intense concentration on *autocoscienza* began to loosen, those feminists who did not withdraw altogether from collective activity were increasingly drawn into external activities and, despite the marked anti-institutional, anti-organisational origins of Milanese feminism, externally focused feminist activities had gained importance and legitimacy, even in Milan.[24]

To conclude, the pioneering value of the practice of *autocoscienza*, and of its emphasis on the positive evaluation of women's difference for what concerns the general central role of political **practices** rooted in small-group contexts, has been central to an Italian feminist philosophy. The expression 'to start from the self' in the contextual relation to other women, characterises *autocoscienza* in the function of exchange of self-narratives and contributes to the creation of a symbolic order originating from the desires, practices, and words of women. In *autocoscienza*, women talk about their own experience, and their specific self informs the very practice that generates the theory. The theory lacks the detachment that traditional philosophy requires, and is confirmed instead as a **contextual** and **relational** language. The contextual/relational aspect establishes the theory of sexual difference as hegemonic in the Italian feminist scene.

Italian feminism has not concentrated on a theory of the subject, it has rather speculated on a relational theory intended to create a symbolic female order in which the overall signification is derived by the mutual relationships among women according to the *autocoscienza* model of practice. Within that practice, in fact, the self is open to relating and is linked to a context. If it is true that, according to post-structuralist Jacques Derrida, the power of the patriarchal symbolical code is marked by its capacity to re-produce, the subversion of this iterative mechanism could be represented by the sudden occurrence of uniqueness. In fact, the relational self of Italian *autocoscienza* finds refuge in the space of a unique narrative freedom that derives its uniqueness from the very individuality of the selves involved in the practice. Therefore, the seminal importance of the impact of C-R in the early 1970s Italian feminist socio-historical context is testified today by Italian feminists' limited attention to postmodernism, and by the radical originality that characterises this movement as a result of the gradual elaboration of the C-R practice within a tradition of anti-authoritarian politics.

Notes

1. Consciousness-raising evolved independently of, but is similar to, the Chinese revolutionary practice of 'speaking bitterness.' Kathie Sarachild, 'Consciousness-Raising: A Radical Weapon' in *Feminist Revolution* (New York: Random House, 1978), 144-150; William Hinton, *Fanshen* (New York: Vintage Books, 1966). See also Nancy McWilliams, 'Contemporary Feminism, Consciousness-Raising, and Changing Views of the Political' in *Women in Politics*, ed. Jane S. Jaquette (New York: Wiley, 1974), 157-70; and Gerlach and Hine, *Movements of Social Transformation*, 135-36.
2. Jo Freeman, *The Politics of Women's Liberation: A Case Study of an Emerging Social Movement and Its Relation to the Policy Process* (New York and London: Longman, 1975), 120.
3. For example, Lotta Continua, Potere Operaio, etc.
4. Paola Bono and Sandra Kemp, *Italian Feminist Thought: A Reader* (Oxford: Basil Blackwell, 1991), 10.
5. Judith Adler Hellman, *Journeys Among Women: Feminism in Five Italian Cities* (Oxford: Polity Press, 1987), 84-5.
6. Carla Lonzi, *Sputiamo su Hegel*, in Bono and Kemp, 41.
7. Mary Fainsod Katzenstein, 'Comparing the Feminist Movements of the United States and Western Europe: An Overview' in Mary Fainsod Katzenstein and Carol McClurg Mueller, eds. *The Women's Movements of the United States and Western Europe* (Philadelphia: Temple University Press, 1987), 121.
8. For example, in Turin instead were established women's clinics, *consultori*, out of a feminist demand for free and accessible contraception, abortion, and general gynecological treatment, to push down the barriers between women and medical authorities (the struggle to win legislation establishing *consultori pubblici* to provide, free of charge, services in popular neighbourhoods reached its approval as a law in 1975).
9. *Italian Feminist Thought: A Reader*, 11.
10. *Journeys Among Women*, 86-7.
11. Written by Carla Accardi, Elvira Banotti, and Carla Lonzi.
12. Transl. *The Clitoral Woman and the Vaginal Woman*.
13. In *Sputiamo su Hegel* Lonzi maintained equality as a juridical principle, difference as an existential principle.
14. By the end of 1972, though, Lonzi left *Rivolta* urged by the excessive influence that her role had acquired with respect to the other women in the group, influence which clearly contradicted her own anti-leadership beliefs as well as hindering her potential personal development within the practice of *autocoscienza*. The absence of Lonzi from *Rivolta* did not eventually dismember the group, which continued its small-group practice until after 1974, but then limited its activity to that of its own publishing house when the group perceived the need to pursue individually what had been started as a group. In fact, by 1974, the repetitiveness of discussion topics, and the growing of personal anxieties that heightened as the small groups developed a 'pressure to conform to collective identity' had been generating a sense of uncertainty and predictability, which

finally invalidated any attempt to self-improvement at a personal as well as collective stage.
15 *Italian Feminist Thought: A Reader*, 9.
16 *Italian Feminist Thought: A Reader*, 11.
17 Carla Lonzi was co-editor of *Rivolta's* publishing house until her death in 1982.
18 Including *Lotta Femminista* (Feminist Conflict), a Marxist-feminist group that advocated wages for housewives.
19 1973 and 1974 issues entitled 'Experiences of Feminist Groups in Italy.'
20 In the meantime, even *Anabasi* had started to work on two periodicals called *Donna è Bello* (Woman is Beautiful) and *Al Femminile* (Feminine Approach), but they were both issued only once in 1972. In any event, the main concerns of the group until its dissolution in 1975 were related to a strong emphasis on 'togetherness' and community which even involved collective living at some point, the exchange of experiences and the practice of consciousness-raising, the creation of an intense atmosphere of affection oriented to the quality of communication. After five years of practice, the group eventually perceived that a different perspective, centred on the body and the irrational, was generally prevailing on a practice that, to this point, had been centred instead on the raising of conscious, matter-of-fact awareness.
21 For example, in Milan, the problem of violence was often discussed as an essentially masculine characteristic that women may also possess, while in other cities, where the tradition of psychoanalytic debate was less rooted, an issue like 'violence' was apprehended in the form of denunciations of male violence against women.
22 The collective was *Col di Lana,* founded in 1976, and constituted by twelve small sub-groups.
23 'Appunti del Gruppo numero 4', in *Sottosopra* (1976): 7-8, translation mine. Earlier in 1972, Anne Koedt, with reference to the movement's split on the issue of sexual preference, had stated: "The original genius of the phrase 'the personal is political' was that it opened up the area of women's private lives to political analysis. Before that, the isolation of women from each other had been accomplished by labelling a woman's experience 'personal'.... However, opening up women's experience to political analysis has also resulted in a misuse of the phrase. While it is true that there are political implications in everything a woman *qua* woman experiences, it is not therefore true that a woman's life is the political property of the women's movement." Anne Koedt 'Lesbianism and Feminism.' *Women: A Journal of Liberation* 3, no. 1 (1972): 33.
24 *Journeys Among Women*, 92-4. The US movement's change of direction towards nationally organised groups had already taken place in 1971.

Feminine Past/Times

At Coffs Harbour my mother would sieve the wet sand
with her fossicker's eyes. She would scallop the edge of the waves
with bare cracked feet, her shoulders poised, head tipped
forward, right arm swinging lightly but at the ready to reach
down and salvage. She would sometimes stop, kick with
her toe, meditate for a moment. Move on.

My daughter sifts the tidemark of long decades for scraps –
salt-laced remnants, weed-embroidered silk, watery grey
and white portraits with those pellucid, unrippling eyes, as though made of
milky glass. Cuttings from newspapers, soft as flannelette
wrap the past like a drowned infant who never learned to talk.

I search the lapping ether for words layered as agates, or sharp
as mussel sherds – words caught like old dried outs sighs on every
dry-as-parchment tussock, or pressed between scuffed
chamois-shark-skinned kelp as tender as inner thigh.

Day after day we three walk the tidemark,
sometimes finding only a line of cuneiform characters
left behind by the feet of gulls.

Philomena van Rijswijk

Reviews

Ora Prilleltensky, *Motherhood and Disability: Children and Choices*. Palgrave Macmillan, 2004.

In this publication, Ora Prilleltensky explores the possibilities and problematics of mothering from the perspectives of women with physical disabilities, including in her research both those who have, or wish to have, children and those who choose to remain childless. By focussing on the intersection between motherhood and disability by way of women's lived experience, the author unravels the complex strands of objective and subjective factors which variously impact on their self esteem, their personal, social and sexual identity, and their relationships – with parents, family, peers and professionals.

The research was first undertaken and written as a doctoral thesis, and this framework remains visible in the transition to publication; thus the first chapter discusses the various theoretical models that have influenced the thinking of the author. But, as she charts the shift from biological to socio-political explanations of disability, references to Prilleltensky's own experience as a disabled girl, woman and mother, provide the human and personal element which is often missing from such work. Her small asides and the examples she provides of empowering or disabling practices, images and attitudes considerably enrich what might otherwise be a rather dry 'academic' discussion. The importance of individual agency is, of course, particularly highlighted by this approach, the main emphasis of which is to point to the intersectionality of experience inherent within the new paradigm in definitions of disability, which "espouses the belief that biological, environmental, social, cultural, and behavioural factors interact and often serve as the precursor to disability" (26).

In chapters 2 and 3, the multiple components of identity are further teased out by focussing on sexuality, reproductive choice and motherhood in the context of disability and women's lived experience. Here, both the external and internal barriers to the quest for love and intimacy are explored. The former include practical problems around gaining information on pregnancy and childbirth, or indeed on preventing pregnancy – difficulties arising from the assumptions and expectations of family, peers and the social and medical services, frequently reinforced by lack of access to financial and other benefits and resources. While women more generally are familiar with the pressure of societal expectations, that young women with physical disabilities are perceived as asexual, passive and sexually inactive, can severely limit or undermine their opportunities for personal fulfilment. Prilleltensky points out that in a society which, even in the twenty-first century, equates woman with mother, and despite feminism's long struggle to win for women the right to control their own fertility, women with disabilities (along with other minority groups) have been omitted from the theoretical discourse. As she goes on to demonstrate, for those whose status is often defined as 'non-parent' and who are likely to be subjected to the close scrutiny of 'authority', issues of choice around reproduction and childcare practice are often complicated by errors of omission and commission. She also cites, however, examples of humour, courage and empowerment, of family, friends and professionals engaging in positive and enabling discourses and practices, so that "stories of joy and fulfilment are at times laced and intertwined with frank explication of barriers, frustrations and even worries". Such stories encourage us to move beyond traditional ideological strictures, to stretch "the boundaries of what we consider an appropriate parent-child relationship and speak to the diversity of acceptable parenting practices, family constellations, and home environments" (79).

Chapter 4 outlines the research methodology, which embraces several key feminist approaches. It is qualitative, reflective, acknowledges the voice and situation of the researcher, and the researcher-researched relationship. The methods used were focus groups and in-depth interviews, with the author clearly acknowledging the limitations of her sample, which was made up almost entirely of middle-class, well-educated white women, with visible physical disabilities. While this narrowness undoubtedly limits the scope of the exercise, it does provide a model that can be adapted for other projects. The following chapters discuss the research findings under the headings of 'Growing Up as a Girl with a Disability', 'To Have or Have Not: Motherhood, Disability and Choice' and 'A Ramp to Mothering', reflecting, in other words, the focus of the earlier literature reviews. Balancing images of passivity and oppression with impressive accounts of resistance and survival, the overall impression gained from the stories told is of a passionate desire to make independent choices about whether or not to become mothers. But while there is an argument that in this they are more similar to than different from non-disabled women, Prilleltensky herself suggests that the participants sometimes underestimate the barriers and impediments that restrict choice, and that real self-determination requires more equitable policies and increased resources. Similarly, while the diversity of experiences of parenting among those research participants who became mothers is clearly demonstrated, the risk posed by stressors such as poverty and lack of support are reported alongside loving relationships and positive communication in well-adjusted caring families.

The attractions of this book are numerous – written by a woman who is a feminist, an academic, a disability advocate and activist, who is herself disabled, it offers keen insights from personal experience in addition to a comprehensive discussion of the literature and an analysis of the life experiences of (an admittedly limited) group of women. An interesting addition to the literature on disability, and indeed to discourse on the construction of identity, it provides a theoretical and methodological model, which could be adapted to other groups. As such, it should be of value to policy makers, students, researchers and all interested in the means whereby we might pursue the goal of a truly inclusive society.

Tamsin Wilton, *Sexual (Dis)Orientation: Gender, Sex, Desire and Self-Fashioning.* Palgrave Macmillan, 2004

Tamsin Wilton has written extensively in the field of sexuality studies and gender studies, and in her most recent publication she turns her attention to an exploration of the processes "whereby individuals come to fashion sexual identities for themselves." Professor of Human Sexuality at the University of the West of England, a former 'straight' woman who is now lesbian, an ardent activist who embraces (queer) postmodern feminism, Wilton's work is thought-provoking and demonstrates real concern for the human experience at the centre of theoretical analysis. Her aim – "to challenge and disturb" – is met by consistently problematising and complicating the mainstream, particularly the standard polarisation of essentialist/social-constructionist perspectives; only a "consciously disorientated and unstable queer-feminist epistemology", she explains, is adequate to the task of understanding sexuality and the complex means by which our individual sexual identities take shape. Although this is a theoretically sophisticated work, Wilton engages with the reader directly, informing us in her introduction of what is absent from the 'conversation': bisexuality, transexuality, men and race are issues which are not addressed in this particular publication. The focus is primarily on lesbian identity and experience, and a thorough review of existing literature introduces a research project that gives voice to the thoughts and feelings of almost one hundred women on negotiating their sexualities.

With due regard given to the "historical moment, social and geopolitical place and cultural positioning", within which 'sex' is located, Wilton takes her reader through the feminist, queer and biomedical debates on eroticism, desire and pleasure which attempt to explain sexual orientation. Her analysis, involving the dismantling of accepted binaries and the decentring of privileged discourses, while retaining sensitivity to the continuing impact of the mainstream on individual experience, is a complex process. But I think this chapter would be particularly useful for postgraduate students grappling with the nature/nurture paradigm and working their way through the labyrinth of theoretical perspectives on sexuality and lesbianism. The methodological discussion is also both comprehensive and insightful, discussing the legitimacy of truth claims, personal motive, reflexivity, and issues surrounding the deconstruction of discourse, with the author locating her own experience in the domain of the study. The research design does not follow the orderly pattern usually prescribed by academia, but evolved in response to the changing needs of the project as it developed depth and complexity.

The first, pilot, stage consisted of a series of unstructured in-depth interviews with women who had made the transition from heterosexuality to a self-defined lesbian position. Wilton describes her sampling at this stage as "opportunistic"; having a tape-recorder constantly at hand to capture the experiences of those fitting the criteria and willing to participate. The resulting data is thus diverse, both geographically and in terms of experience. The majority of the project's participants, however, were self-defined lesbians recruited from an article in the British lesbian magazine, *Diva*, which included a description of the project and a questionnaire. This attracted 136 responses, with 86 women expressing interest in being interviewed – evidence, Wilton asserts, of women's desire and need to 'tell their stories'. To set against this core qualitative data, the author made use of material gathered at an earlier workshop where eleven self-declared heterosexuals had spoken about their views of lesbianism, thus providing a "snapshot of the non-lesbian mainstream view with which lesbians have to interact." At the final stage, twenty non-lesbian women were interviewed to give comparative experiences about various aspects of sexuality and identity formation. The research process outlined by Wilton placed particular emphasis on the strategies developed to ensure high ethical standards were maintained, and that the principles of sensitivity and transparency governed every stage of the work.

There is no doubt that this research generated a rich and diverse database of personal reflections and experiences about some of the most intimate and subjective aspects of life. However, there was little in the actual findings that I found surprising. What was clear from women's accounts of sex and the erotic was the complex and contradictory nature of sexual attraction: girls who had been tomboys were just as likely to be heterosexual as lesbian; negative or positive experiences of heterosexual sex were shared by those who remained with male partners and those who later embraced lesbianism. The power of normative gender discourses to constrain or shape women's choices did emerge as a potent force. Whether about dress or behaviour, and together with the social construction of bodies, emotions, motherhood and so forth, Wilton's work demonstrates yet again how dominant hetero-erotic norms impact on life experiences in ways that are complicated, subtle and nuanced. In her final chapter Wilton calls for a "new sociology of the erotic", drawing particular attention to the "trap of essentialist theories" and their power to impede women's self-choice.

This is a useful addition to the literature on lesbianism, sexuality and identity and, both for its review and critique of relevant theoretical perspectives, and the space given to women to articulate their reflections on their complicated sexual journeys, is worthy of a place on the shelves of departments of women/gender/sexuality studies.

Myrtle Hill
Centre for Women's Studies,
Queen's University Belfast

Ann Braithwaite, Susan Heald, Susanne Luhmann and Sharon Rosenberg. *Troubling Women's Studies: Pasts, Presents and Possibilities.* Toronto: Sumach Press, 2004, 264 pages, Notes & Bibliography. $28.95 Cdn/$24.95 US, paper, ISBN: 1-894549-36-8

The starting point for writing this book is the authors' uneasy attachment to the field of women's studies and the increasing instability of the very term 'women's studies.' Central for the four authors, all of them current and former full-time practitioners in Canadian Women's Studies, is the question of how to pass on the intellectual project of Women's Studies to future students and future academics.

In the first chapter, Susan Heald reflects on her experience of teaching students autobiographical practices, crucial for Women's Studies. Students learn to see themselves not as the 'unique' or 'autonomous' individual that liberal theory and its manifestations in western culture encourage them to be, but as social actors both constituted and constrained by broader social forces, which they need to analyse and try to understand (46). The difficulties of teaching autobiographical thinking and writing arise from the students' "voyeuristic desire to 'explore' (in order to possess) the Other, which is prevalent in dominant Western ways of knowing" (53). Exploring their own social status would mean (for the majority of students) analysing their belonging to the white middle-class heterosexual dominant group of society. Another problem, as Heald argues, is the (mis)use of empowerment. Mostly understood to imply the promotion of equality of opportunity and participation, empowerment has often been used as a means to foster individualism and self-assertion, rather than to analyse social power structures. What Heald calls for is the use of autobiographical practices to challenge the liberal humanist theory of the subject in the interest of a subject who is always/already in community (66). However, in an increasingly market-driven university, where students don't see themselves as part of a community of knowers and learners, but as individual clients of a service industry (71), autobiographical work seems more and more at odds with contemporary academe. Suspending, instead of reproducing, the theory of the liberal humanist subject in which students and universities are embedded and which permits the persistence of various forms of oppression is what Women's Studies needs to do, according to Heald (83).

Reflections on Women's Studies and the women's movement, as Ann Braithwaite argues in the second chapter of the volume, are characterised by the largely unquestioned connection made between 'the women's movement' (always referred to in the singular) and Women's Studies as an academic project. By yoking together these two separate sites, according to Braithwaite, the phrase 'the women's movement' comes to act as a magical sign which functions to condense, displace and reduce Women's Studies to an academic pursuit assumed to be linked with a certain construction of 'the women's movement' (105). Braithwaite argues that many authors writing about the inception of Women's Studies foster, for example, the assumption of race and class as always having been central to Women's Studies and feminism in a broader definition. This 'writing in', she believes, is actually working to 'write out' the difficult, complex, and challenging history of those issues in Women's Studies (107). 'Writing in' a particular set of issues, such as race, as always having been of central concern ironically leads to the fact that those challenges are then 'written out' as not relevant through their very inclusion (128). Hence, "inclusion can also work as a type of exclusion" (tokenism, political correctness) (131). Thus, mobilising the term 'the women's movement' risks obscuring the complexity and multiplicity of meaning and identity.

In the third chapter, Susanne Luhmann challenges the thinking of the past, present and the future as linked in a linear manner. For Women's Studies, considered as a counter project to the existing university and to mainstream knowledge production, and as potentially and eventually able to transform thought and thus produce social change, "losing its central narratives about its role, foundations, ambitions and aims constitutes a problem" (153). Luhmann asks why these fundamental doubts, anxieties and feelings of loss emerge at a point in time, when Canadian Women's Studies seems to be much more secure than ever before. Institutional integration, as Luhmann argues, can also lead to dilemmas and problems for the self-definition and understanding of the field. What happens if Women's Studies, as it matures, takes a different route from that once imagined by its founders? Although Women's Studies and feminism are closely linked in their emergence and appearance, they are not identical. For Luhmann, feminism is in some way a theory and Women's Studies a practice, that is, Women's Studies is the "site of the academic investigation of feminism" (158). This is not to suggest that Women's Studies is to be understood as the academic arm of the women's movement or of feminism. And, yet, the narrative of continuous identity of the two persists. The tendency in contemporary debates over the history of Women's Studies is to suggest that the field's history is a guarantee of the field's future. To imagine the past, present and future as linear, risks conservatism; this might hinder the further development of Women's Studies.

In the last essay, Sharon Rosenberg turns toward the question of how to pass on Women's Studies, which is caught in a paradox of the modern university: challenging disciplinary boundaries, on the one hand, and constituting a distinct area of study – a discipline – on the other (208). By looking at the feminist memorial response to the Montréal Massacre, when 14 women were shot dead at the École Polytechnique, University of Montréal by Marc Lépine[1], who blamed feminism for ruining his life, Rosenberg seeks to find instructions for the current troubles facing Women's Studies. For Rosenberg, the experience of loss is a site of learning (202) and remembering has also always had to do with loss. Drawing on the theories of Irit Rogoff (2002)[2] and Patti Lather (2000),[3] Rosenberg maintains that "looking away" and "getting lost" are necessary conceptual and methodological practices for passing on Women's Studies as a troubled and troubling intellectual project of the modern university (203). According to Rosenberg, the Montréal Massacre has been neglected by feminist scholarship, since it has mostly been dealt with in terms of violence against women. This conception has displaced the killer's own accusation, which was explicitly against feminists. In a similar mode, as Rosenberg argues, the category of 'women' in Women's Studies functions emblematically, that is, as a stand-in for all women (228), which holds the risk of excluding as much as it includes (231).

Troubling Women's Studies: Pasts, Presents and Possibilities is a very illuminating and useful source for anyone interested in what is at stake for Women's Studies in the modern university. Topics include autobiography as a feminist method for teaching and research, (feminist) memoirs of Women's Studies, the past, present and future of Women's Studies as an unquestioned linearity, and remembrance of Women's Studies as a troubled/troubling project. By addressing the current, rather apocalyptic, debate on the 'end' of Women's Studies, the authors insist that another Women's Studies is possible. The volume provides a vast bibliography and it would have been even more useful had it provided an index of both names and subjects.

Anna-Katherina Pelkner
Women's Studies Centre,
NUI, Galway.

Notes:
1. Marc Lépine had been rejected in early 1989 for a place at the Polytechique's engineering faculty.
2. Irit Rogoff, 'Looking Away: Participations in Visual Culture.' Paper presented at the 'Museums After Modernism: Strategies of Engagement Conference', Toronto, Ontario, 2002.
3. Patti Lather, 'Getting Lost: Feminist Efforts Toward a Double(d) Science.' Paper presented at 'JCT Bergamo Conference', Dayton, Ohio, 2000.

Fiona McHardy and Eireann Marshall (eds.), *Women's Influence on Classical Civilisation*, London/ New York: Routledge 2004, 196pages.

This is an edited collection of essays that originated from a conference entitled 'An Alien Influence' held at the University of Exeter in 1998. The editors attempted to unify the theme of the volume under the more general title of *Women's Influence on Classical Civilisation* in order to achieve greater cohesion. However, the essays focus on very specialised topics and, in most cases, they do not seem to have anything in common with each other. The lack of distinct sub-sections accentuates the problem, while the random placement of essays pertaining to Roman themes, close to the ones relevant to the Greek classical period, increases the confusion of the reader. Although the editors pay a substantial effort in the introduction in pointing out common themes, the most important unifying element seems to be the comprehensive bibliography and the index at the end of the book.

The theme of the book elaborates on a subject that became popular among scholars as late as the 1970s. The significant role of women in the political sphere of contemporary societies has been pointed out initially by famous anthropologists such as Rosaldo and Lamphere in the 1970s, and Dubisch in the 1980s.[1] Subsequently, ancient historians of the 1990s became increasingly interested in the power women held in the classical world and, thus, tried to reconstruct their place within the elaborate social structures of the Greek and Roman societies.[2] All of these scholars aimed at revising previous hypotheses according to which the role of women in the ancient world was passive and their impact in the public arena was limited.

The first essay of the volume, authored by G. McLauchlin, is entitled 'The Logistics of Gender in Classical Philosophy.' The author explores successfully the subject of female philosophers in antiquity, while she focuses specifically on the mathematician Pandrosion and the misogynistic attitudes she faced. In the second essay, J.P. Hallett revisits once more the subject of the active, nevertheless indirect, political influence of the mother of the Gracchi in an article called 'Matriot Games? Cornelia, Mother of the Gracchi, and the Forging of Family-oriented Political Values.' In the next chapter – on 'Politics of Inclusion/Exclusion in Attic Tragedy' – N.S. Rabinowitz explores the indirect influence of Athenian women on democratic policies and the way their potential participation in active political life is portrayed in ancient Greek tragedy. In the fourth essay, entitled 'Exemplary Housewife or Luxurious Slut: Cultural Representations of Women in the Roman Economy', S. Dixon attempts to prove that the economic enterprises of Roman women were not restricted to the private domain; instead, women participated in the production of cloth destined for the markets and in several other commercial activities. Later on in the book, M.L. Woodhull expands on the idea that ancient women had substantial economic power and focuses on their active role as architectural patrons in her essay on 'Matronly Patrons in the Early Roman Empire: The Case of Salvia Postuma.' The rest of the chapters emphasise the influence of ancient women on Greek and Roman culture. F. Mc Hardy in 'Women's Influence on Revenge in Ancient Greece', R. Langlands in 'A Woman's Influence on a Roman Text: Marcia and Seneca', E. Marshall in 'Women and the Transmission of Libyan Culture', M. Harlow in 'Galla

Placidia: Conduit or Culture', and J. Rowlandson in 'Gender and Cultural Identity in Roman Egypt', all explore case studies on the cultural roles of women throughout the Mediterranean in several different periods, asserting the impact of a woman's interference in the development of cultural identities.

All in all, *Women's Influence on Classical Civilisation* is a very ambitious book, because of the breadth of the subject-matter treated. However, despite the fact that most of the essays are well-written and timely, they seem to be only loosely connected to each other. Yet, I have no doubt that students and scholars alike will find it very interesting reading.

Notes:

1. M.Z. Rosaldo and L. Lamphere, eds. *Woman, Culture and Society.* Stanford: University of Stanford Press, 1974; J. Dubisch, ed. *Gender and Power in Rural Greece.* Princeton: Princeton University Press, 1986.
2. For example, S. Fischler, S., 'Social Stereotype and Historical Analysis: The Case of the Imperial Women at Rome' in L. Archer, S. Fischler and M. Wyke, eds. *Women in Ancient Societies.* Basingstoke: MacMillan, 115-133; K. Walters, 'Women and Power in Classical Athens' in M. DeForest, ed. *Woman's Power, Man's Game.* Wanconda: Bolcazy-Carducci, 1993, 194-214; P. van Minnen, 'Did Ancient Women Learn a Trade Outside the Home?' *Zeitschrift Fur Papyrologie und Epigraphik.* 123 (1998): 201-203.

Constantina Katsari
History Department
National University of Ireland, Galway

Notes on Contributors

Martina Boyle was born in Dublin at the start of what is known as the second wave women's movement. She works in the violence-against-women sector for the past couple of years and, in the challenging safety of WERRC, she is also studying part-time for her MA in Women's Studies.

Carole Ferrier is Associate Professor of English and Director of the Centre for Research on Women, Gender, Culture and Social Change in the School of English, Media Studies and Art History at The University of Queensland, Brisbane, Australia. Carole is President of the Australian Women's Studies Association, and was instrumental in establishing Women's Studies programmes in Australia.

Gabriele Griffin is an interdisciplinary scholar in the field of women's cultural production, whose work is located both in Gender Studies and in Cultural Studies. She co-ordinated an EU-funded research project on 'Women's Employment, Equal Opportunities, and Women's Studies', and has developed a regional network for postgraduate research methods training across the Humanities and Social Sciences.

Niamh Hehir is a PhD student with Women's Studies and the Department of Languages and Cultural Studies at The University of Limerick. The subject of her dissertation is a Kristevan reading of Medbh McGuckian's poetry.

Hanna Herzog is a Sociologist who teaches at Tel Aviv University. She is the former President of the (International) Association for Israel Studies, and is one of the founders of the Women and Gender Programme in Tel Aviv. Hanna is Editor of *Israeli Sociology - A Journal for the Study of Israeli Sociology*.

Myrtle Hill is Director of the Centre for Women's Studies at Queen's University, Belfast. A senior lecturer in social, religious and women's history, she has published widely in these areas.

Martina Hynan has an M.Phil in Women's Studies from Trinity College, Dublin, and a BA (Hons) in Visual Art from the University of Wales. Her areas of interest include feminist visual culture and post-colonial theory.

As a visual artist, her ambition is to develop a participatory art pedagogy, from a feminist perspective.

Toni Johnson-Woods teaches Media and Communication in the Contemporary Studies programme at the University of Queensland, Australia. She has an abiding interest in the popular, and studies the phenomenon, whether in nineteenth century serialised fiction (*Index to Fiction in Australian Periodicals*, 2001), reality TV (*Big Bother*, 2002), or pulp fiction (*Collector's Book of Australian Pulp Fiction Covers*, 2004). She has just completed a book on *South Park* (Continuum 2006).

Constantina Katsari lectures in the History Department of the National University of Ireland, Galway. She is the co-editor of *Patterns in the Economy of Roman Asia Minor* (Classical Press of Wales 2005), and co-author of *The Mint of Amorium and the Coin Finds, Amorium Reports V* (BAR International Series 2006, forthcoming). She has also published articles and reviews in refereed journals and edited collections on all aspects of the society, economy and ideology of the Roman Empire.

Agate Krauss is a Sociologist involved in promoting social issues in general, and women's equality in particular. Agate began her formal social activities as a researcher in the Knesset (the Israeli Parliament), working mostly for the Committee for the Advancement of the Status of Women. Since 2001, she has been the director of the Israel Women's Network, policy research centre. In the last year, Agate served as the Director of Education & Media in the Israel Aids Task Force.

Yvonne McKenna holds an IRCHSS Government of Ireland Post-doctoral Research Fellowship at the University of Limerick where she is conducting research on returned Irish women religious missionaries. In addition, she is involved in an oral history project researching Irish missionaries in India, also funded by the IRCHSS. She was awarded her PhD, an oral history study on the experiences of Irish women religious in England, from the University of Warwick in 2002. Yvonne is currently writing a book on Irish nuns to be published by Irish Academic Press.

Catherine M. Orr is Associate Professor and Chair of Women's and Gender Studies at Beloit College (Wisconsin). In addition to her interests in the disciplinarity of Women's Studies, she has published on third-wave feminism, academic activism, and US women's movements in a wide range of anthologies and journals. Catherine is currently co-editing an anthology titled, *Locating Women's Studies*.

Anna-Katharina Pelkner is a PhD student in Women's Studies at the National University of Ireland, Galway. She has studied in Berlin and Toronto, and completed her Masters degree in 1999 at Humboldt University, Berlin, as a social scientist in the field of women's research. Anna-Katharina's PhD dissertation is an examination of the relationship between Women's Studies and institutional structures.

Eva Rus is a second-year PhD candidate in American Studies at the University of Birmingham (UK) where she also collaborates as a co-editor for the online journal *49th Parallel*. Eva completed her undergraduate degree in Anglo-American Language and Literature with German language and Germanic Philology at the University of Padova, Italy. Her current research concerns the analysis of issues of subjectivity and identity as articulated in contemporary feminist autobiographical practice in both written text and the visual arts.

Christine St. Peter is Professor of Women's Studies at the University of Victoria, Canada. A former President of the Canadian Women's Studies Association/*L'association canadienne des études sur les femmes*, she has also worked extensively as an academic editor. She publishes in the areas of Irish and Canadian women's writing and women's health issues in Canada. Her book, *Changing Ireland: Strategies in Contemporary Women's Fiction*, was named one of the outstanding academic books of 2000 by *Choice* review magazine.

Sonja Tiernan is a Teaching and Research Scholar in the Women's Education, Research, and Resource Centre (WERRC) at UCD. She was the first graduate of the Certificate in Lesbian Studies and Queer Culture from WERRC, where she has since completed a Higher Diploma and an MA in Women's Studies. Sonja was co-convenor of The Dublin Queer Studies Group from 2002-2003, and co-organiser of the Lesbian Lives XII Conference for 2005. She is currently completing a PhD on the literature of Eva Gore-Booth (1870-1926).